THE QUINAULT INDIANS

By Ronald L. Olson

University of Washington Publications in Anthropology
Volume VI, Number 1

ADZE, CANOE, AND HOUSE TYPES OF THE NORTHWEST COAST

By Ronald L. Olson

University of Washington Publications in Anthropology
Volume II, Number 1

THE QUINAULT INDIANS

by

RONALD L. OLSON

UNIVERSITY OF WASHINGTON PRESS

Seattle and London

All rights reserved
Library of Congress Catalog Card Number 67-16032
Printed in the United States of America

The Quinault Indians was first published in 1936.
Reprinted, 1967

Adze, Canoe, and House Types of the Northwest Coast
was first published in 1927.
Reprinted, 1955, 1967

PREFACE

The material presented in this account of the Quinault was gathered during three visits of a month each in the spring of 1925 and the winters of 1925-26 and 1926-27. The visits were made under the auspices of the Department of Anthropology of the University of Washington.

In 1855 the Quinault ceded a part of their territory to the United States government, retaining, however, that portion which constitutes the present Quinault Indian reservation. Shortly after this a considerable number of the surviving members of neighboring tribes moved, or were transferred, to the reservation and were allotted timber lands there on the same basis as those of Quinault blood. By about 1890 all the Quinault had moved to the modern village of Taholah (named for Chief Tàxo'là, the grandfather of Billy Mason), the site of the native village of kwi'nail. This is now the only permanent village on the reservation and counts perhaps 400 residents, about half of whom are reckoned as Quinault.

The Quinault have been the subject of brief sketches or mentions by a number of authors (see B.A.E., Bull. 30), but except for the brief sketches in Curtis (*The North American Indian*, vol. 9) and that by Willoughby there have been no systematic descriptions of the culture. I have made no attempt to give full item references to these earlier works, since the descriptions there are so meager or vague that I have felt it necessary to amplify in almost every case.

The tribal culture has so completely broken down that scarcely anything remains of it but its memory in the minds of some of the oldest members of the tribe. Accordingly, my account can lay no claim to completeness. But for most features I have secured about the totality of information which can be salvaged at this late date. Exceptions are the materials relating to music and basketry. Much more information on these could have been acquired had time and equipment permitted.

My chief informants were Bob Pope, Billy Mason, Johnson Wakinas, Alice Jackson, and Sammy Hoh. All were thoroughly reliable, reasonably intelligent, and, being above 60 years of age (Pope was over 90), were familiar with the old life. Pope's knowledge was all that could be desired but he spoke no English. He was Farrand's main informant. Harry Shale (who was Farrand's interpreter) and Fred Pope acted as interpreters. Of these, Pope, Wakinas, and Hoh have since died. Informants of less importance included Julia Cole, Harry Shale, and Mrs. Otto Strom. In certain sections of my account I have referred to informants by name or initials.

Some miscellaneous information on neighboring tribes, which was secured from aliens resident on the reservation, will be presented in a separate paper.[1]

The sketches and diagrams illustrating various items of the culture are not all based upon actual specimens. Some are from descriptions, others from crude native representations, and others from photographs.

The phonetic scheme employed is the simpler system of the *Phonetic Transcription of Indian Languages* (Smithsonian Misc. Coll., 66, no. 6, 1916), except that long vowels are without diacritical marks.

---

[1] A nearly complete series of myths and legends was submitted as a part of my original manuscript, but unfortunately it has been found impossible to include it in the present publication. In part the myths duplicate Farrand's *Traditions of the Quinault Indians* (see Bibliography), but he failed to give verbatim renditions and omitted many tales, in particular the entire Xwoni Xwoni cycle.

CONTENTS

CONTENTS—Continued

CONTENTS—Continued

FIGURES

THE QUINAULT INDIANS

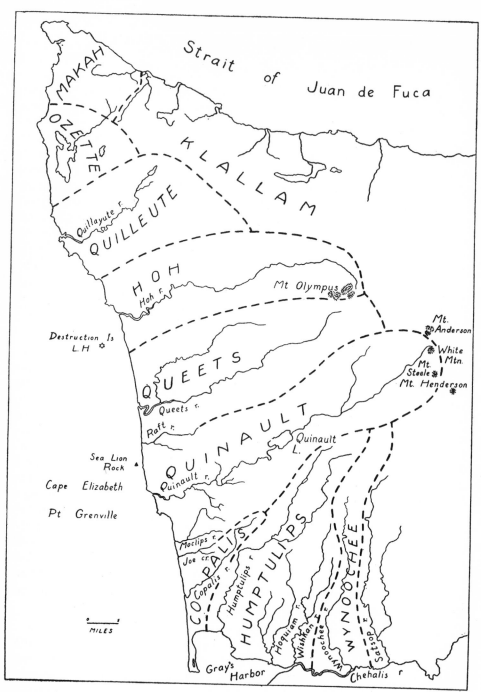

Map 1. The Quinault and their Neighbors.

(10)

THE COUNTRY AND THE PEOPLE

GENERAL CHARACTER OF THE CULTURE

"Quinault" is a corruption of kwi'naił, the name of the largest settlement situated at the present site of the village Taholah (map 2). The Quinault speak a Salish dialect, evidently identical with that spoken by their Queets neighbors just north. Their culture was not as advanced in the material sense as that of the Makah and Quilleute to the north, but neither was it as drab as that of the tribes to the south. Situated on the open coast of Washington just north of Grays Harbor, they were at the focal point of influences from several directions. Their cultural horizon extended from the Strait of Juan de Fuca on the north to the Columbia river on the south. The peoples of the southern part of the Puget Sound region were not wholly strangers, for the Quinault had intimate contacts with the several Chehalis tribes who occupied the territory between Grays Harbor and the southern extremity of Puget Sound. If we represent the region as a triangle having the coast from Cape Flattery to the mouth of the Columbia as its base and the southern extremity of Puget Sound as its apex, we have a reasonably accurate view of the limits of the area within which lived those peoples who exerted a direct influence upon the Quinault living at the middle point of the base.

Of peoples living outside this area the Quinault had some knowledge but it must have been of a hearsay nature. Probably none of them ever traveled, in pre-European days, outside the boundaries of the triangle, and it must have been a rare event when visitors from outside its limits came into Quinault country. But for the region within the triangle the Quinault were ethnographers in their own way. The differences and similarities in the cultures of their neighbors were things of common knowledge. At the northern extremity lived the clever Makah, descendants of a girl and her dog-husband, possessors of fine ocean canoes made by the Nootka or łokwi'làmatcu ("across the straits" people). The Makah were daring pursuers of the whale and were rich in whale oil and dentalium shells, which they were willing to barter for the famed dried Quinault salmon and for sea otter skins and dried elk meat. To the south lived the Copalis, noted for their dried razor clams. Farther down the coast lived the Chinook. Advantageous bargains could always be made with them, exchanging ocean-going canoes, shell-money, and sea otters for clams, lacamass, and wapato. In later years the mouth of the Columbia (Astoria) and Neah Bay at Cape Flattery were the rendezvous of white traders anxious to barter iron tools, bright cloth, trinkets, guns, and rum for furs.

Although this circle of cultural acquaintances was less wide than that, *e.g.*, of the Haida in the north or of the Chinook on the Columbia, yet within it were tribes of varying cultures. The Makah were but a Nootkan outpost possessing practically all the distinctive elements of Nootka culture. In Nootka-Makah culture were many elements easily recognizable as derived directly from specializations of the Haida-Tlingit-Tsimshian-Kwakiutl center. With the Quilleute, situated between Quinault and Makah, began the first sharp slope from the cultural peak of the center. This

(11)

slope continued in its rapid descent until the tribes of rather drab cultures to the south and east of the Quinault were reached. These tribes to the south and east were less Northwest Coast-like. In such features as the use of acorns, the early acquisition of horses and of cultural features connected with that animal, the extensive use of wapato and camas, and the manufacture of canoes of "shovel-nose" type, they showed the influence of Interior and even of Plains culture.

The location of the Quinault on the open coast had its influence on their life. It was down the open coast that the great culture-stream from the typical tribes of the north was flowing. The eastern margin of the area and the region about the inland waters of southern British Columbia and Puget Sound were eddies along the bank, feeling the influences of the current but not to as great an extent as the western margin. The reasons for this are difficult to determine. The open coast, harassed by storms for a considerable period of the year, lent itself but poorly to year-round intertribal communication. The Quinault often gave potlatches in mid-summer because their northern neighbors might find it impossible to negotiate the open water for days at a time in the winter season. This difficulty of travel was practically absent in the protected waters between Vancouver Island, the mainland opposite, and in the Puget Sound region. Yet it appears that such typical features as a definite sense of caste, emphasis on wealth, potlatches, secret societies, emphasis on elaborateness of objects made of wood, and the capture of whales traveled much farther down the open coast than in the region mentioned. It may be that something inherent in Salish temperament or culture acted as a barrier which, at the southern limit of Kwakiutl territory, slowed down those currents of culture which on the west coast of Vancouver Island flowed the length of Nootka territory and across the straits to the Makah. There is a greater qualitative difference between, *e.g.*, Chehalis and Makah cultures than between Makah and Kwakiutl.

The Quinault were the most southern people who engaged in the pursuit of whales and were near the southern margin of tsa'dják and klo'kwalle secret societies. They were on the northern margin of the range of certain southern elements. The gabled house of the south was not found north of the Queets (a small tribe just to the north whose language and culture were practically identical with Quinault). The Quinault were evidently the most northerly coastal tribe possessing horses in pre-European days. In their mythology Xwoni Xwoni and Misp are buffoon and hero transformer, while in Quilleute tales their place is taken by qwati. Quinault culture lacks much of that vigor and "drive" so prominent in Makah and less in evidence in Quilleute.

Elements of northern provenience were adopted in a more or less half-hearted manner. Only a handful of men ever took to whaling. Not more than three or four villages could boast the presence of a secret society chapter. The lack of a cove at the river mouth may have tended to inhibit whaling activities, but the never-failing year-round supply of salmon made life so easy and secure that only the most daring and ambitious men put forth the effort necessary to engage in whaling. Then, too, the majority of villages were situated along the river at considerable distances from the ocean. The difficulty of getting to and from the ocean, especially in large canoes, made whaling impracticable except for residents of towns quite near the river's mouth. Other features of northern culture there undoubtedly were, but they are hard to define.

In the veins of every Quinault flows some blood of other tribes. Marriages into tribes to the south were as frequent as marriages into northern groups. It is puzzling that such intermarriages did not result in bringing in more elements of the cultures of the north, especially since the northern groups were admittedly superior. The Quilleute were "smart people" while the Makah were virtually supermen. But ambition was hardly one of the vices of a Quinault, and ambition in a hundred ways was necessary if one wanted to secure the luxuries of life possessed by Quilleute or Makah acquaintances. But did not their own river have the most bountiful supply of the finest salmon on the coast? Could not an overwhelming supply of toothsome razor clams be had for the digging? What need, then, to bother oneself with the rigors of whale hunting, the tortures of the klo'kwalle society, or the labor of putting fancy carvings on tools, canoes, or houses? Nature had provided that all the necessities of life could be had with little effort, and with those necessities in their simple form the average Quinault was content.

TERRITORY

In theory the tribal territory embraced the whole region drained by the Quinault river, and in addition a district along the beach between a point near the mouth of Raft river and a spot near the present site of the village of Pacific Beach or the mouth of Joe creek. In practice not a foot of the tribal boundary was sharply determined. The southern boundary is said to have followed Joe creek to its source and thence along the height of land of the Quinault watershed to the summit of the Olympic mountains. The heights about the sources of the river were more or less common hunting territory for Quinault, Skokomish, Klallam, and Queets. The northern limit of Quinault country was roughly along the northern rim of the watershed to the source of the Raft river and down that stream to its mouth. But the feeling of ownership or of exclusive right to this territory was unheard of, and if expressed would no doubt have been considered a great joke. Anyone had the right to travel along the beach, to dig clams where he pleased, and to hunt where the game was most plentiful, just as anyone had the privilege of voyaging after whale or seal. Yet the rights of members of the Quinault tribe were slightly different from those of aliens. A whale which drifted ashore between Joe creek and Raft river belonged first of all to members of the tribe. An alien hunting in the Quinault watershed might be shot at, but largely because it offered a better opportunity than if he were close by his home village.

Except for two unimportant villages on the upper river and the village at the present site of Moclips (which served as a retreat for adolescent girls), all Quinault settlements were along the river between lake and ocean. The remainder of the tribal territory was of importance only as a source of game or shellfish. Salmon was the staff of life and nearly all were taken on the lower river. Villages a few miles apart were clustered along its course, the sites being chosen largely on the basis of feasibility of erecting a salmon weir. The village of kwi'nait at the mouth of the river was the largest and most important settlement. Visitors from other tribes, whether traveling by water or land, usually stopped there for an exchange of news or to trade. The upper villages were regarded as provincial, those far up the river as almost backward.

Topography. The heart of Quinault territory is the Quinault river. It has its rise in a number of branches flowing from the snowy peaks of the Olympic range. The two main forks unite to form the upper river at a point about eight miles above Quinault lake. Canoe navigation was difficult on the upper river and was possible for only a short distance above the fork. The territory above the lake is mountainous and rugged and served only as a summer hunting ground. The lake is a beautiful body of water some six miles long by two wide, which abounds in all manner of fish. In the meadows reaching back from its shores were grasses of various sorts, which were used in the manufacture of baskets. Deer, elk, and bear were numerous in the forests and in the open places of the higher peaks. The country about and above the lake was an ideal place to spend the summer gathering grasses, drying meat, and preparing berries for the winter food supply.

Below the lake the river continues its west-south-west course to the ocean. The valley is no longer narrow and rugged, however, and the course of the river is meandering. Short rapids occur every few hundred yards but none seriously hindered navigation beyond necessitating the substitution of the pole for the paddle. There are frequent branch creeks flowing in from either side but only a few of sufficient size to permit ascent by canoe for more than a few miles. The lower river furnished virtually all the salmon that were taken. Every branch creek and the lake as well as the whole riverbed itself served as spawning grounds, so that the number of fish reaching the upper river was relatively small. Their quality became lower the farther up the stream they went until by the time the lake or upper river was reached they were quite thin and therefore less desirable than those taken at the river mouth. This must have influenced the choice of village sites more than did the actual topography.

The character of the country along the beach changes markedly in Quinault territory. Between Point Grenville and Raft river the beach is narrow and sloping, seldom exceeding seventy-five yards in width at low tide. Precipitous cliffs or steep hills rise from high tide mark, making travel along the beach impossible at extreme high water. In the northern part of the coastal strip bold headlands jut out into the ocean. Point Grenville, three miles south of the river mouth, and Cape Elizabeth, six miles north of Grenville, are the most southerly of these. From Elizabeth northward these headlands occur with increasing frequency until in Quileute territory the coast becomes very rugged and broken. Short trails crossed all these points, enabling one to travel the length of the coast on land. South of Point Grenville the land fronting the beach becomes gradually lower and lower and the beaches wider and more gently sloping. No clams can be secured between Point Grenville and Raft river, but south of Grenville a quarter-mile width of almost level sand makes the taking of the molluscs at ordinarily low tides easy in all but the most stormy weather.

FLORA

The whole region with the exception of the higher levels of the mountains is covered with a luxuriant growth of vegetation. Douglas fir, spruce, hemlock, and red cedar make up the bulk of the almost impenetrable forest. Trees with a diameter of ten feet are not uncommon. Alder, yew, larch, soft maple, and vine maple are found here and there and yellow (Alaska) cedar is abundant in the mountains.

Everywhere there is a dense growth of underbrush composed, for the most part, of berry bushes. Evergreen huckleberries, as well as the blue and red varieties, grow profusely. Blackberries, salmonberries, thimbleberries and black raspberries are found in the less dense parts of the forest and along the streams. The open glades of the mountain ridges are the spots favored by blueberries of several kinds. The somber aspect of the forest is heightened by a thick carpet of mosses, and every tree has its garlands and festoons of "Grandfather's beard." This last is an important element in the food supply of deer and elk.

Meadows (prairies) are rather infrequent but there were a sufficient number along the creeks and on the margin of the lake to insure an adequate supply of camas to vary the meat diet. In the meadows and swamps were a variety of grasses, such as tule, cat-tail, and bear-grass, which were used in making baskets and mats.

ANIMAL LIFE

The mammals were those found over the greater part of the Northwest coast. Elk were especially abundant. It is claimed that mountain goat and mountain sheep were unknown. Seal and sea lion were easily secured along the coast. Sea otter were frequently taken at Grenville and constituted an important source of wealth. Fish abounded in the lake, river, creeks, and ocean but salmon were the only important source of food. Four species of this fish came up the river. The run of sockeye was especially noteworthy, for upon the catch of this variety depended the bulk of the year's food supply. Candlefish and smelt fairly filled the waters of the beach and the lower few miles of the river at certain seasons of the year. The greater portion of the animal food of the people, however, consisted of salmon and elk made delicious by the addition of whale, seal, or candle-fish oil.

THE NEIGHBORS OF THE QUINAULT

The Queets (ḳwi′tsᵘ, "people made of dirt," or xà′kwap, "close to the anus") occupied the whole watershed of the Queets river (map 1). They had a number of villages. One was located on the south bank near the river mouth, another on the north bank near the mouth of the Clearwater. In language and culture this tribe was almost identical with the Quinault.

The Hoh (ho′x̣), occupying the Hoh river basin, speak a Quilleute dialect, but were regarded as a distinct tribe. According to one informant there were but three villages. One was located at the river's mouth on the south bank, a second on the north shore one-half mile above the first, and the third on the south bank two miles above the mouth.

A small group of people lived on Jackson creek (Goodman creek?). It is claimed they were distinct from the Quilleute, though they spoke the same language. They occupied a single large village on the south bank at the mouth of the creek. A deep shellheap and a few houseposts are all that remain. The Quinault called them lo'-xels.

The next tribe to the north was the Quilleute, who, with the Hoh and people of Jackson creek, were the only Chimakuan-speaking peoples of the west coast of the Olympic Peninsula. The only other representative of this stock was the Chimakum tribe, which occupied a small district on the northeast corner of the peninsula.

The Ozette, who lived about the lake of that name and the adjacent coast, and the Suez (tsue's?), who lived along the Suez river, were Makah groups but probably regarded themselves as distinct tribes. The Makah of the Cape Flattery district have been described by Swan.[2] The Quinault called the west coast of Vancouver Island xlokwi'làmatcu ("across the straits").

The tribe nearest the Quinault on the south was called ǩope'ls (Copalis). They occupied the coast from the limits of Quinault territory to the entrance to Grays Harbor and a portion of North Bay within the harbor. In addition they seem to have claimed the valley of the Copalis river. The largest village was no"shał, now called Oyhut after the Chinook jargon name.

To the east of this tribe lived the xàmtu'lapc (Humptulips), who held the north shore of Grays Harbor from somewhere near the middle of North Bay eastward probably to Junction City. They had several villages on the Humptulips river and perhaps claimed the whole valley. They may have held the valley of the Hoquiam river as well, though the Hoquiam may have regarded themselves as a distinct group.

East again from this district lived the Wynoochee and Satsop tribes, living along the rivers of the same names. It seems probable, however, that these minor tribes to the south and east of the Quinault are but subdivisions of Lower Chehalis. The lack of interest in tribal units and the particularism of the village units (i.e., family groups) make it difficult to determine tribal affiliations with any exactness.

The tsàhe'ls (Chehalis) tribe seems to have occupied the district between the Chehalis river and the Willapa river. They had villages on the northern arms of Shoalwater bay[3] as well as along the southern shores of Grays Harbor.

Along the upper Willapa river an Athapascan tribe had villages. The Quinault called them the swila'umic. It is said that the tribe is now extinct.

A Salish group, called the àxwe'lapc, lived on the shores of Shoalwater bay near the mouth of the Willapa river.

A people called xwa'xwotcl by the Quinault occupied a part of the eastern shore of Shoalwater bay just south of the Willapa. The ǩlàpe'elks lived around the southeastern shores of Shoalwater bay. The long peninsula between the bay and sea, extending from the mouth of the bay nearly to Cape Disappointment, was the territory of the tsàdju'kkw. The Chinook lived to the south of them.

---

[2] Smithsonian Contributions, 16.
[3] One was called na'kànstca"ts.

Data on these tribes about Shoalwater bay are very indefinite. A scattering village or two is all that remains. Their numbers were few even as early as 1850 and my informants had only the scantiest knowledge of them. Swan's information gives very little enlightenment but is worth quoting. [4]

"The Indians of Shoalwater Bay had no distinct language of their own, but used Chinook or Chehalis promiscuously, with the exception of the tribe on the Whil'a-pah river, who spoke a language somewhat resembling the Cowlitz. There are two or three of the Whil'a-pah Indians still living at Shoalwater Bay, but the rest of the tribe is all extinct. The other names of the Shoalwater Bay Indians were the Necoman'chee or Nick'omin,[5] who resided on a river of that name flowing into the north side of the bay.

"The Que-lap'ton-lilt, whose village was at the mouth of the Whil'a-pah river, on the banks of a creek whose name they took, and where at present the house and claim of Captain Charles Stewart are.

"The Whar'hoots[6] village occupied the present site of the town of Bruceport, and the Quer'-quelin village at the mouth of the creek where my house was.

"The Palux Indians,[7] on the Copa'lux or Palux river, the Marhoo, the Nasal, and several other villages on the peninsula of little account.

"The relics of old lodges, canoes, heaps of shells, and other remains give evidence that at some period there must have been a large body of Indians around Shoalwater Bay."

VILLAGES

I did not have an opportunity to travel along the course of the river and the location of many of the villages on my map (see map 2) is therefore somewhat indefinite, being based on estimates of distances by my informants. The following is a list of the villages as remembered by Billy Mason:

1. no'omo'lapc (Moclips). A village at the mouth of the Moclips river. In some obscure way the word refers to menstrual blood. At the first occurrence of a girl's menses her parents took her to this place lest her presence on the Quinault river stop the run of salmon. She remained at this place for about a year.
2. łałe'lap, "on the bluff." A village of three or four houses on the north bank at the mouth of Quinault river.
3. me'tsugutsałàn, "middle of the point." A small village on the south bank of Quinault river at the mouth.
4. kwi'nail. The largest Quinault village and the tribal name. Situated at the present site of Taholah. Although this village was situated directly beside the preceding one, the two were counted as distinct, probably because persons of different lineages occupied them.
5. kwȧtai'tumixʷ, "burned place." A village on the south bank about 500 yards above the preceding.
6. djexwe'ls, "round rock." A village on the north bank about 400 yards above łałe'lap. A monster (skuku'm) lived in a near-by creek, so it was an unpopular place of residence.
7. no'słuk, "deepwaters" or tocȧno'lxk, "Raven's house." A large village located not far from the preceding one.
8. no'skałàn, "where the whale," or, in the Chinook jargon, Whale Ilihee. A village of five houses (1860) a few miles above kwi'nail, on the north bank of the river. Thunder once dropped a whale in the river at this place. The whale became a rock which can still be seen.
9. nosk̓łàko's, "water coming." A village of two or three houses on the south bank, perhaps a mile above the preceding.

---

[4] Northwest Coast, 211, 212.
[5] Probably one given me as the village of na'kȧmstcaʰts.
[6] Given me as xwa'xwotce.
[7] Evidently given me as k̓łȧpe'elks.

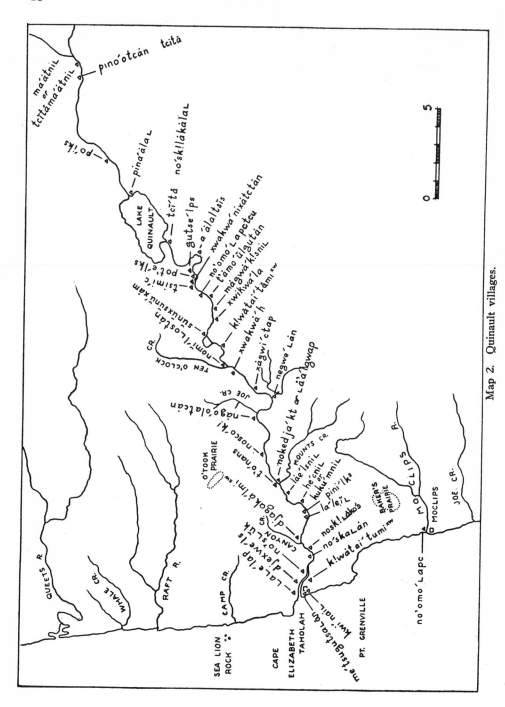

Map 2. Quinault villages.

10. djagakà'lmix^w, "sand drifting (with the current) place." A large village a half mile above the preceding one. There were houses on both sides of the river. It was remembered as the home of a famous woman shaman a number of generations back. The people of the village had an evil reputation as "outlaws" who were always seeking trouble.
11. la'lciɬ, "vine maple place." A large village perhaps a mile above the preceding.
12. pini'lks, "above the point." This village was directly adjacent to the preceding one. It was the home of the man (chief) who ranked above all others, one ɩe'sàmàts.
13. he'cniɬ, "place of the monster," or kuku'mniɬ, "place of the dead." A village of but two houses, on the south bank about 500 yards above pini'lks.
14. làe'lsniɬ, "sea lion bone place." This was a village of but one or two houses, located on the north bank a mile or less above he'cniɬ.
15. t'o'nans, "logs floating," was a small village less than a half mile above he'cniɬ.
16. nokedja'kt, "prairie," or là'a'lgwap, "gravel bar." This was one of the largest villages and was on the south bank a few hundred yards above t'o'nans. Trails led from here to the Queets river, to Humptulips, and probably to Baker's prairie.
17. nosco'k̓, "get up," a small village not far above the preceding.
18. nàgo'olatcàn, "island there," a village of four houses not far from nosco'k̓.
19. negwe'làn, "salmon river." The village at the mouth of Cook creek.
20. xàgwi'ctap, "hard grass." A village about one and one-half miles above Cook creek.
21. xwakwà'h, "clean hill," was a small village not far from the preceding.
22. nomi'lɩostàn, "shaking head," was a small village just above xwak̓wà'h. It was customary for all travelers to close the eyes and shake the head upon coming in sight of the place. "The old people joked that way."
23. sunuxsunu'xàm, "roaring creek." A village not far from the preceding.
24. xwikwa'la, "long stretch (of river)," was a village perhaps a half-mile above the preceding one.
25. màgwà'k̓sniɬ, "big nose place." This village was but 300 yards above xwikwa'la.
26. no'omo'lapctcu, "little no'omo'lapc." The village was not far above the preceding.
27. xwakwa'nixàtctàn, "threw fish entrails away," was a village four miles below the lake.
28. a'àlaltsis, "big place," was a village three miles below the lake. It was the home of hard-bitten fellows who recognized no chief or other authority.
29. tci'tà no'sk̓làkàlaɬ, "village of see the lake," was at the lake's outlet. It was reputedly peopled by "outlaws."
30. pina'àlaɬ, "upper lake," was a village where the upper river enters the lake. It was also peopled by "outlaws."
31. po'iks, "crooked nose." A village on the upper river above Finley creek. There were several small houses there where people camped during the salmon run.
32. pino'otcàn tci'tà, "pino'otcàn's village," was named for a man of that name. It was a favorite place for drying fish and meat.
33. ma'àtniɬ, "sharp point place," or tcitàma'àtniɬ, "to grind something place." This village was one mile below the fork of the upper river. In the only house lived an old bachelor outlaw famous in legends.

A shorter list of villages, given by Bob Pope, included the following not mentioned by Mason:

34. k̓wàtai'tàmix^w, "burned place," located three miles above xwak̓wà'h (21).
35. tsimi'c, a village two miles above màgwàk̓sniɬ (25).
36. pot'e'lks, "on the point," a mile above tsimi'c.
37. gutse'lps, "to cross the door," six miles below the lake.
38. t'àmo'ulgutàn, "stake there," just below no'omo'lapctcu.

PLACE NAMES

Like most primitive groups the Quinault had a great number of names as means of reference for particular spots or localities within their territory. These present nothing novel in the way of type or pattern. Most of them are descriptive of the place, or they refer to legendary events that occurred there, or they name an activity carried on. The following list is, naturally, far from complete but it includes those localities volunteered by Mason as of sufficient importance to merit noting:

1. ka'tsålx^w, "throat." The mouth of Joe creek. It is claimed that the creek is the old boundary between Quinault and Copalis territory.
2. no'ko'luktån, "come out to the beach." The place where the old boundary, according to the treaty of 1855 with the United States government, met the beach. A bunch of cedar bark tied to a pole marked the spot.
3. etlakwa'imi, "woman's cursing place." The mouth of Bob Wing creek.
4. no'sgwadjotsi, "moving creek." A creek a little way north of the preceding one.
5. loo'mscaɬ, "dig road creek." Baker's or Wreck creek. Along it went the trail up to Baker's prairie.
6. kwinaiɬ kla'kum, "Quinault prairie." Baker's prairie. A favorite rendezvous of Quinault, Queets, and Quilleute in the month of June, the time for digging camas.
7. noko'åltån, "drinking water." A little hidden spring or creek just south of Big Rocks creeks.
8. no''ånagwåels ka'ålos, "big rocks creeks." Twin creeks coming down near the big rocks.
9. no''ånagwåels, "big rocks." A group of rocks.
10. mo'xo'hxels, "water monster (?) rock." A "hunting spirit" lived here. People traveling by at night could often see lightning flash between the rock and the near-by cliffs.
11. no''xaliɬån, "leave canoe (creek)." Evidently the small creek just south of Point Grenville. When people went to Grenville to hunt sea otter they used to leave their canoes on the beach here. On stormy days the otter would swim around in the protection of the rocks and the hunters stood on shore waiting for a chance to shoot them.
12. kulo'kuo'lxk, "Squid's (?) house." The closer to the shore of two large rocks near the tip of Point Grenville.
13. lå'kålatih, "flat head." A rock close by the preceding. It is shaped like the deformed heads of the natives.
14. tsa'tcåmaɬ, "hole dug." Close to no''xaliɬån, where there are many rocks. It was here that Eagle dug for his dead son. (See the tale, Origin of Death.)
15. ci'pleu, "young elk." Near the preceding place. There is a group of rocks here.
16. ma'tsactsiolxk, "Shag's house." The tallest rock out in the water just south of the tip of Grenville.
17. t'otla'tsiolxk, "Rock Cod's house." Keyhole Rock.
18. a'tsak, "inside point." The south face of Point Grenville.
19. o'låmix^wci'tks, "soft sand point." The north side of Point Grenville.
20. o'låmix^u, "soft sand." The creek and the beach just north of Grenville.
21. tse'nåɬ, "clover roots." A place about one mile north of Grenville where such plants grew.
22. e'pxwa'ånotsi, "hidden mouth creek." The creek about one-fourth mile from the oyster rocks.
23. xeke'lap, "between woods and water" (?). The bluff just north of the oyster rocks.
24. tsoome'elakomoh (obsolete form), "———? marsh." A place on level ground a mile or less south of Taholah.
25. klåpa'lågwanaɬ, "rock oyster rocks." The soft claylike rocks one mile south of Taholah, visible at low tide.
26. pomosi'djiltcu, "cold water (coming from bluff)." The spring at the oyster rocks.
27. kwinai'ɬ qal, "Quinault river."
28. pole'pole', "bubbles." The gas well one mile north of the river mouth and some distance inland.

29. no'tsi'ltån, "landing place." A place where the surf is not bad, a half-mile north of the river. About 45 years ago a ship was wrecked on the reefs off Elizabeth. The Quinault built a great fire on the beach at this place to guide the boats so everyone was saved.

30. x̱kadja'hmin, "dress caught." A place in the rocks just south of Elizabeth. Once a woman caught her dress there.

31. nȧgwa'leps, "door." Cape Elizabeth. The point used to extend farther out. Through it was a tunnel (a "door") which served as a passage at low tide. The tunnel was about where the extreme end of the point now is. About fifty years ago a new passage was formed at the low place in the point. The small tunnel in the rock near Agate beach was formed a little over fifty years ago. The cape in ancient times extended out to the reefs.

32. ḍeleko'lxk, "north house." A flat-topped rock just north of Elizabeth. Its top was flat like the houses of the tribes of the north.

33. nukxe'leh. The place where the trail comes down to the beach. The word is in the old obscure language.

34. p'aclu'ḍt, "bluff slides." The word is in the "old language."

35. no'citcapac, "between creeks." A place between Lunch and Duck creeks.

36. no'sgwinuḵ, "camping place." Beside Camp creek.

37. no'sgwinuka'ȧloh, "camping place creek." Camp creek.

38. kȧpe'ls, "under rock." Just north of the preceding.

39. lo'xotsih nȧgwa'ȧlepi, "tunnels in rock bluff." The bluff just south of Raft river. Either this or the river itself was the limit of Quinault territory.

40. lo'xotsih, "tunnels in rock." Raft river.

41. lae'lsnil, "sea lion rock," or probably "sea lion place." Sea Lion Rock.

42. no'xlȧmȧtsi'x̌ʷtȧn, "place to tie when it is rough." A rock just north of the preceding one. It was a good shelter when rough water came while hunting sea lion.

43. djȧ'ḵmaxlȧn, "get caught there." A rock just west of the last named place. If one found a sea lion on a ledge of this rock it was impossible for the animal to escape.

44. ke'kwaluk, "leaves in the water." A spot on the river near the village of djexwe'ls where a small creek comes in. (See page 17.)

45. ḵo'olo'tsi, "fun bluff." The hill across from the village of ḵwatai'tumix̌ʷ (village No. 5).

46. ȧle'kxȧdjȧm, "slide." The sliding hill on the south bank just above no'skalȧn. It was a favorite playground for the children. In the flat just below was the village graveyard.

47. to'te'las, "sticks sticking out." A bluff and lagoon a half-mile above djagakȧlmix̌ʷ. The place was inhabited by a skuku'm. A long time ago some porpoises lived there. Until about one hundred years ago one could see all the way from this village up to la'lcil. The river bank was like a beach and was used for a shinny field. Now it is all grown over with trees and brush.

48. no'slȧts, "broken (bundle)." The hill across from pini'lks where the graveyard for the village was located.

49. so'lkcial, "trail." The trail to Baker's prairie leaving the river just above the graveyard.

50. ḵlȧmenu'mcial, ". . . dig (with adze) trail." A trail, perhaps 500 yards above the preceding one, which led to a favorite place for making canoes.

51. ma'knil, "dead place." The graveyard for he'cnil, situated about 500 yards above the preceding but on the opposite side.

52. gwaga'djolx̌ʷ, "frog's throat." A gravel bar on the north bank a few hundred yards above he'cnil.

53. kagwa'lap', "high bluff (lit., "above bluff"). A high hill on the north bank a half-mile above the "throat."

54. xwe'knil, "grass place." A spot across the river from lȧe'lsnil.

55. se'ktȧsic (obsolete form). It is the name of a creek a quarter-mile above xwe'knil.

56. gwȧxo'psiolxk, "Eagle's house." A place on the north bank 200 yards above se'ktȧsic.

57. xama'skal, "cold water." A spring across the river from the village of t'o'nans.

58. atsso'lak, "deep water," or ḵweloxo'litcȧn. A deep place in the river a few hundred yards above t'o'nans where the fish stay all summer.

59. nogwa'ǩtuh, "small bluff." A hill across from the village of nokedja'kt where the graveyard was located.
60. mådjo'stolotsi, "sandy bar." A bar near the lagoon not far above nokedja'kt.
61. la'els, "set there rocks." A group of rocks on the south bank not far above the bar.
62. djåla'ǩut, "river close to bluff." A place on the north bank up some distance from nosco'ǩ.
63. p'o'xwap'ȧm, "rump sticking out." A rock in the water not far above the village of nȧgo'-olatcȧn. One time a woman named x̣ȧlo'omic was bathing there. Xwoni Xwoni came by, saw her, ravished her and turned her into a rock which can still be seen. It is shaped like a woman.
64. negwe'lȧn, "salmon river." Cook creek. There was a village at its mouth.
65. djȧla'ǩȧt, "bluff." A hill about one mile above Cook creek.
66. peni'tstȧǩ, "camping ground." There used to be a jam at this place which made it necessary to pull canoes over the top of the logs.
67. xwaǩwȧ'h, "clean hill." The name for a hill (and a small village) on the north bank one and one-half miles from xȧgwi'ctap.
68. no'cd̟olȧk, "belly up." A rock on the north bank not far above the village of mȧgwȧǩsnil.
69. no'sǩlȧkȧlal, "see the lake." A spot on the river about one-fourth mile from the lake. One gets the first view of the lake from here.
70. tsa'ȧlal, "the lake." Quinault lake. Fish of every kind come up to the lake. There seem to have been no villages located on the lake.
71. aǩwecɛ'lȧlal, "west side of the lake." The corner of the lake where the road now goes over to Queets. In the old days a sea lion used to appear here. When it was going to be a bad day he would come to the surface and blow like a seal, wah! Then he would dive and not come up. A man once was making a crossbeam for a house on the bank at that place. He had finished hewing it and had painted the picture of his guardian spirit on it. When he slid it into the water it went under and never came up. Afterward some people found it on the beach north of Raft river. So people said there must be an underground tunnel from the lake to the ocean. That is how the sea lion could come up to the lake.
72. pina'ȧlal, "upper lake." The place where the upper river enters the lake.
73. tȧtlo'kwamil, "dragging board." A large creek (probably Finley) which flows into the upper river. Like all the creeks of the upper river it was a favorite spawning ground for blue-back salmon. A few silver salmon and some steelhead also spawned in these creeks.
74. suqwa'nil, "salmonberry place." Willaby creek, flowing into the lake from the south.
75. ta'ȧls. A creek flowing into the lake from the north.
76. nosǩokȧ'las, "fork of the river." The main fork of the upper river.
77. pala'l pala'l, "spouting water." A spot near a glacier high in the mountains at the head of the main source of the south fork. The water gushes out of a hole in spurts. There is a whale under the mountain who opens and closes the hole with his tail so that it does not boil out in a steady stream.

POPULATION

It is very difficult to estimate the size of the Quinault tribe for the period before the severe smallpox epidemics of the early part of the nineteenth century. Perhaps the safest reconstruction is on the basis of number and probable size of villages. My informants listed some 38 villages, but some were certainly village sites rather than villages. Probably not more than 20 villages were ever occupied at any one time. The average number of houses per village was perhaps four, with (as a guess) two families occupying each. Taking 80 as the total number of houses and 10 as the average size of a household, we get a figure of 800 for the entire tribe. If anything, I feel that this figure is too high rather than too low, but it represents an approximation which is probably within 200 of correct. The Quinault certainly outnumbered such groups as Queets, Hoh, Quilleute, and Ozette.

Johnson Wakinas had in his possession a yellowed paper which some Indian agent had given him. The following tabulation of tribal numbers, as of June 30, 1888, is taken from this:[8]

	Total	Males over 18	Females over 14	Children 6-16
Hoh.	64	20	32	13
Queets.	82	23	32	16
Quinaults.	95	29	36	15
Chepalis.	5	2	2	..
Oyhuts.	35	12	13	6
Humptulips.	18	8	7	2
Hoquiams.	14	6	6	2
Montesanos.	17	9	7	..
Satsops.	12	7	5	..
Georgetown.	102	34	39	17
	444	150	179	71

[8]These figures approximate those given by Willoughby for ca. 1885 (p. 267). The name "Chepalis" in the list probably means Copalis or Chehalis. (See p. 16).

ECONOMIC LIFE

The Quinault, after the winter season of partial idleness, began preparations for their most important economic activity, the taking of salmon. A few salmon of one kind or another are found in the river the year round, but not in sufficient numbers to provide an adequate supply. The great run of spring salmon begins in late March or April, reaches its height in May and dwindles on until late June or July. But for perhaps a month before the run began everyone was actively engaged in getting posts, boughs, in readiness for the actual construction of the weirs, which were the chief means employed in taking the fish. When the word was passed up the river that the fish were beginning to arrive in considerable numbers the work went forward with the greatest possible dispatch.

Men worked day and night to get the trap in readiness, for no one could predict whether or not it would be a good salmon year and it was imperative that the village trap secure its quota of the early run. During the time that the fish were running the men virtually lived at the weir. The fish were taken to the shore and given to the women, who dressed them and hung them over the continually burning fires in the houses.

The spring salmon run over, a variety of activities was open to the people of the village. A trip to the mountains for elk, bear and deer might be taken, or there was the expedition to the ocean beaches to the south for the gathering of clams. More slothful persons might elect to stay at the village and continue fishing for the straggling salmon, now of poor quality. For every family there was the year's supply of bark, grass, and roots to gather for the manufacture of baskets and clothing. Berries and edible roots formed a welcome variant in the diet and every good wife would secure a supply during the summer.

If an insufficient number of salmon had been taken in the spring most of the villagers would return for the coming of the black, silver, and dog salmon in August and September. By the end of the run the rainy season was beginning in earnest.

An adequate supply of dried fish and meat meant that for three or four months one could indulge in the luxury of comparative idleness. Gossiping, feasting, visiting relatives in neighboring villages or tribes were the high lights of this, the social season in years of plenty. Lean years might entail both hunting and fishing even during the season of rains and storms. With the coming of late February the time for looking to the ensuing run of spring salmon arrived and the cycle sketched here began again.

The activities of the year varied considerably among different groups. A hunter of the upper villages would spend much time in the mountains, leaving fishing, for the most part, to those less fortunate souls whose "powers," received at puberty, were not inclined to aid them in killing elk. The people of the lower villages would naturally look with favor on the trips to Copalis, where for a month or more they would dig and dry razor clams. Those enviable men whose "power" enabled them to hunt whales spent much of the year manufacturing the necessary equipment and, from perhaps May to August, cruising for the animals. There was no hard and fast rule for anyone to follow and an individual's yearly pursuits undoubtedly varied in emphasis from year to year. In such matters he was a law unto himself and his own inclinations must often have varied the annual round. But for the tribe as a whole the spring salmon run, the summer period which combined hunting and the gathering of vegetable foods and materials, the autumn season of salmon fishing, and the winter period of comparative idleness and heightened social life were the high points of activity.

The daily round. Almost the year around the day's activities began at daybreak. Fathers roused their sons and urged them to the morning plunge "before the water awakened." The older women arose early and fanned the embers into flame and began the preparation of the morning meal. The older men usually repaired to the platform in front of the village chief's house, there to speculate on the kind of weather likely to ensue, to gossip, and to decide what the day's activities should be. Those who intended to hunt in the near future went through the bathing ritual. Often they went from the meeting to the house of one who had fresh meat or fresh fish. Their womenfolk ate in their respective homes.

Breakfast over, the day's activities began in earnest. During the salmon run men manned the weir both day and night. At other times activities were more varied. Some men usually went hunting, others worked at canoes, at gathering wood (but not carrying it in), or at any one of a number of tasks about the house or village. Women spent the morning caring for the children, putting away disarranged odds and ends, inspecting the dried meat and fish to see that none was moldy, and so on. These tasks finished, they took up their basketry, picked berries, or gathered clams.

The evening meal was served about dusk.[9] During the day no food was taken except perhaps a nibble of dried fish or a few berries. The evening was spent in enjoying the comfort of the fire. Every evening the father or grandfather spent some time admonishing and advising the children, particularly the boys. Women usually wove baskets.

Winter was the lazy season. During the long winter evenings nearly all the males of the village (including even lads of six or seven) often assembled at the house of some old man who was counted a good raconteur. Until far into the night they listened to his yarns and legends until the younger lads had long since fallen asleep and the eyes of even the elders became heavy.

People arose rather late during the winter months. It was the time of the giving of feasts, of performances by shamans, and on most mornings everyone was content to lie abed until late to sleep off the fatigue of the previous night.

---

[9]There was considerable variety in the diet, especially in families where the womenfolk were active, but the chief "course" was almost invariably fish, roasted, boiled as a soup, or in some other style.

FOOD GATHERING

SALMON FISHING

Fish was the one dietary staple of the Quinault. Although a variety of species were relatively abundant in both salt and fresh waters, the salmon was the only one of great importance. Upon the capture of a sufficient supply of this fish depended the very sustenance of life. The run of salmon, past, present, or prospective, was the year-round subject of discussion among them, just as the wheat crop is the focal point of interest in a North Dakota farming community.

All five species of salmon spawn in the Quinault river. A few blueback (red, or sockeye; *O. nerka*) enter the river as early as December. They gradually increase in numbers until April, when they come in great numbers. By the end of June the peak of the run is over, though stragglers may continue to enter the river until late July or even August. The black salmon (tyee, Chinook, spring, or king; *O. tscha-wytscha*) come to the river to spawn in August, though a few may be taken as early as June. Silver salmon (coho or white; *O. kisutch*) and dog salmon (keta or chum; *O. keta*) appear in greatest numbers in September and continue to run until mid-November. A few humpbacks (pink; *O. gorbuscha*) run in late August and September but they are of slight importance. The steelhead trout (*Salmo gairdniri*), often classed as a salmon by fishermen, runs in the river from November to May. The steelhead does not come in as great numbers, however, as do the salmon, and could never have contributed greatly to the food supply. There is no month in the year in which salmon or steelhead trout may not be taken with varying success.

The blueback run was the most important, the number taken probably being as great as the combined number of the other three species.[10] In flavor and fatness they are justly regarded as greatly superior to the huge black salmon, the silvers, and dog salmon.[11] All these fish were prepared in much the same way and identical means were employed for their capture. Harpoon, dip nets, drift nets, weirs, and gaffs were used according to varying conditions.

Salmon weirs. By far the greater part of the supply of fish was taken by this means. It is said that every village from no'skatła'n to the fork of the upper river had its weir (ska'lip) stretching across the river[12] (fig. 1). Several of the larger vilages had two or even three weirs. The gathering of the materials for the building of the weir had been going on for some time before the fish began to arrive in great numbers. Straight poles, about four inches in diameter and varying from four to twelve feet in length, were sought out, trimmed, and pointed. These were for the posts and braces. Then great quantities of slender hemlock or vine maple sticks,

---

[10]Cobb states that records show that 355,007 sockeyes alone were taken in 1915 (p. 23).

[11]The following words relating to species of salmon were recorded: kà'mka'n, general term for fish; also the general word for food. The blueback is called sa'djo'las. After they have spawned they are called lo'h or swà'tna'k, "come back." Coho are called su'gwa'k, but the females are sometimes distinguished by the term la'ci. The black or Chinook are called sake'c, and if very large are called kwa'li'h. The latter word is said to be the same in the Chehalis tongue. The female blacks are called mukła'a'c. Dog salmon are termed sxai ("teeth") or kutła tsi ("striped"). Steelhead are called ske'okx, skai'àkc, or klo'dja'ltc ("small eggs"). Pope gave their name as xwà'-nnoł but it was said by others that this is the name only after they have spawned.

[12]There was no weir at the village of kwi'naił, where only harpoon and dip net were employed.

one-half inch in diameter and as long as the poles, were made ready, as well as limbs from young cedars to be used as cross-weaving in the slender sticks.

As the time for the run grew near stakes were driven about eight feet apart in a row across the river. The tops were allowed to project varying distances above the water. Then a brace stake was paired with each one of these. The brace was driven into the river bottom as deeply as the upright pole. Its lower end was several feet downstream from the upright pole but its upper end crossed the latter several feet above the water line. Then the two were firmly lashed together. A series of poles reaching from end to end of the weir was placed in the crotch formed by the upright and the bracing pole (fig. 1a). Two or three lines of poles were lashed to the upright stakes, below the water line. The wattle work sections rested against these (fig. 1b-d). Two poles lashed to the brace posts above the high water line served as a walk (fig. 1e). At intervals along the weir sets of two or four poles were driven into the bed of the river to serve as supports for platforms (fig. 1f). Horizontally-placed poles were lashed across these. Then planks were laid on these stringers so as to form a platform where fishermen stood. The height above the water level for these platforms varied according to the rise and fall of the river. At medium water they would be perhaps four feet above the water. They were sufficiently large to enable one or two men to lie at full length. Blankets and robes were frequently

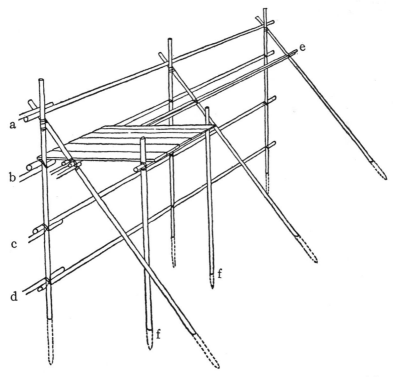

Fig. 1. Framework of weir. *a,* series of poles which rest in crotch of upright and bracing poles; *b-d,* lines of poles lashed to uprights below water line and against which wattle units rest; *e,* two poles which serve as "walk"; *f,* platform supports.

28

taken to them at night so that the men could rest comfortably in the intervals when no fish seemed to be running.[13]

In the meantime the women were busy weaving units of wattle work (fig. 2). This was simply cross weaving or twining slender cedar withes on a "warp" of hemlock or vine maple poles an inch or less in diameter. Each unit of wattle work was 12 "warps" wide and was wider at the bottom than at the top. The length varied according to the depth of the water, units being made for particular places in the weir. The lower ends of the poles were sharpened. The "warp" poles were placed about one and one-half inches apart. A series of units was made sufficient to reach from bank to bank.

All was now ready, and the fishermen awaited the coming of the salmon. However, the river must not be turbulent at the time, else the force of the current would not only prevent the placing of the wattle work sections but actually tear out those in mid-current. Freshets during the fishing season necessitated the removal of some of the middle sections for perhaps a day. When the salmon began to arrive in considerable numbers the men turned out in a body to insert the units of wattle. Expert divers removed the stones from the bottom, so that the sharpened ends of the wattle poles could be shoved into the sand. Divers worked under water, placing the lower ends of the wattle sections in the proper place and aiding in forcing the tips of the poles into the river bottom. When the unit was in its proper position they lashed the sides and top to the frame of the weir. All except the divers worked from canoes.

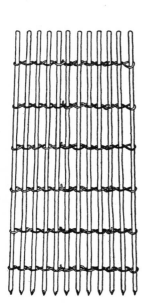

Fig. 2. Wattle work unit or section.

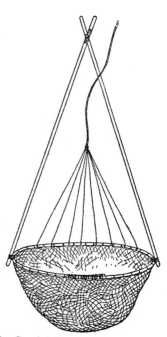

Fig. 3. Special dip net used at salmon weirs.

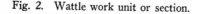

[13]One informant stated that there were invariably four such platforms at each weir. It is probable, however, that he was thinking of the weir at his home village. The number probably varied according to the size of the village or the width of the river.

The fish were taken in a special bag-like nettle fiber dip net, the mouth of which was secured to a frame (fig. 3). The mesh of the net was perhaps two inches—sufficiently small to prevent a small salmon from wriggling through. The frame was of yew, bent in an oval about seven by five feet. At either end a slender pole was lashed to extend above the frame, and helped when raising the net. The net and frame rested on the bottom. Eight signal strings of elk sinew, fine as grocer's twine, were tied at regular intervals on the (upstream) side of the frame. These converged to the surface of the water where they united to form the single strand held in the hand of the fisherman. A fish coming upstream, or searching along the weir, would come in contact with these strings. The tug on the string was the signal that a salmon was directly above the net. The lifting poles were seized and the net raised as rapidly as possible. Sometimes the fish succeeded in escaping, but usually the deep trap-like net assured his capture. Several fish were often taken in one lifting. Net and fish were laid on the platform and the struggling salmon quickly despatched with the ever-ready club. The fish were then thrown onto the platform, or into a canoe which was moored alongside. At intervals the canoe was paddled ashore and the fish given to the women who prepared them for drying.

No part of the weir would last for more than two years, and for the most part it must be built anew every season. The pilings would decay or be bent or torn out by the freshets of the rainy season. The brace poles were always removed at the end of the season, and, if vine maple, could be used a second time. Guide fences of wattle to force the fish to the places where the lifting nets rested seem to have been unknown. Torches were never used in night fishing at the weirs. Trout were occasionally taken while fishing for salmon.

It was said there were no rules requiring that the weirs of the lower villages be opened at times to allow the fish to proceed upstream where the people of the upper villages might take them. In this respect the people of the lower villages had an advantage.

Drift nets. At night, or during periods when the river water was muddy, salmon or trout might be taken in the drift net (kunt dja'n). These were made of nettle fiber in a long tapering shape (fig. 4). When in use the mouth of the net was spread to about four by ten feet. From the mouth the net tapered to the rounded point about ten feet distant. Two canoes with two persons in each were required to manipulate the contrivance. A man in the stern of each canoe handled his side of the net, while a man or woman in the bow paddled easily and splashed with the paddle and threw stones to frighten the fish into the net. At each lower corner of the mouth of the net a five-grooved sinker was tied. A pole tied to the sinker was held by the man in the stern enabling him to control the position of the net. He also held a cord tied to an upper corner to keep the net open.

The bows of the canoes were spread so as to guide the fish toward the net. The net could only be used as the canoes drifted downstream. Just enough more speed than that of the current was maintained to keep the net in position. The canoes came alongside each other when a fish was caught. One informant claimed that a second string was tied at the sinker and was held by the person in the bow. This

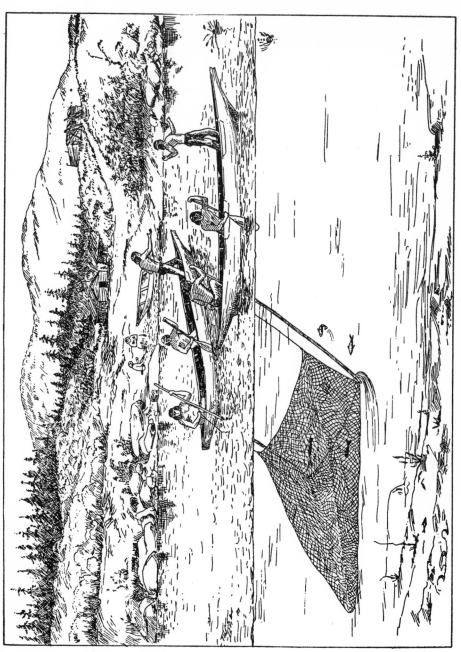

Fig. 4. Drift net used in salmon fishing. (After Willoughby.)

served as an aid in keeping the net in position. It is said that the sinkers were the five-grooved stones sometimes called "gambling stones."

Dip nets. Below the village of no'skałán no weirs were constructed, and the dip net was the chief means employed in taking the salmon. The Quinault still use this method, though set gill nets today catch most of the fish. The dip net is used only at the river mouth where the banks are free from brush and where the swift current of the river as it flows down the slope of the beach causes the salmon to swim near the banks. It cannot be employed at high tide because of the slackness of the current at that time. Times of freshet, when the water is muddy so that the fish cannot see the net, are especially favorable; but clear water does not seriously hamper the operations. The course and depth of the river at the mouth change with almost every tide, and have a great effect on the success of the fishermen.

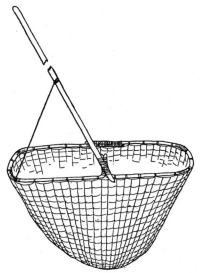

Fig. 5. Dip net used in taking salmon at river mouth.

The dip net is pocket-shaped, measuring about two and one-half feet from mouth to bottom (fig. 5). Ordinary gill net mesh is employed, but in pre-European days nettle fiber cord was used. The mouth of the net is tied to a frame (skàsi'h) at intervals of six or eight inches. The frame is made from two tapering yew wood (klama'k) poles. The butts of the frame poles are flattened for a foot or more and firmly lashed together for about four inches. They are then bent sharply in opposite directions so that each forms one-half of the frame; then each is further bent so as to come together at their tips and form a quadrangle. The poles chosen are very slender near their tips so that this part of the frame (the under part) shall be as inconspicuous as possible. The tips are slightly flattened and lashed together for a foot or less at the center of the under part of the frame. The entire frame is commonly about two by five feet, with rounded corners. A handle twelve to twenty feet long is lashed to the butts of the frame sticks which project six inches perpendicular to the plane of the frame. The handle is lashed not quite parallel, but in such a manner that one side of the frame forms an angle of fifty to sixty degrees with the handle. A stout cord is stretched from a corner of the upper part of the frame to a point perhaps five feet up the handle. Spruce is preferred for the handle and the pole is sometimes flattened to decrease the weight without lessening the strength for dragging the net.

When the tide is at the half, or lower, the fisherman carries his net to the water's edge, or ten feet or more out in the stream if the water is shallow, and drops it where the current is swift. The handle is held so that the outer end of the frame is farther downstream than the shore end and the net is slightly to the rear of the fisherman. The handle is held tightly and as the fisherman proceeds at a running walk pressure is exerted on it so that the net may move a little faster than the current and thereby be kept distended. The salmon, moving near shore to avoid the racing current of mid-stream is directly caught on its way up, or, glimpsing the fisherman or net, it darts away from the bank only to run into the open mouth of the net. The fish striking the net jars the handle sufficiently to warn the fisherman, who draws the net ashore as quickly as possible and unceremoniously strikes the fish a sharp blow on the head with a beach pebble. On a hot sunshiny day the fish are sometimes covered with sand to prevent their softening in the sun.

After dragging the net down the river as far as the depth is favorable, or to the point where breakers make further progress hazardous, the fisherman removes the net from the water, places it over his shoulder and returns upstream to the point where the rapid current begins. On days when few fish are ascending more time is spent idling about the beach than in actual manipulation of the net. The taking of a fish by more ambitious souls who persist despite infrequent captures is the signal for all the idlers to seize their nets and try their fortune again. Sometimes one may work the whole period of low tide without netting a fish. But on days when the fish are running freely several may be taken at one dip and hundreds by one person in a day. In 1924 one woman caught over two hundred dog salmon in a single afternoon.

Below high tide mark fishing is, and always has been, open to anyone. Lack of success on one bank often tempts the unlucky fisherman to try the other. But in order to do so he must change the tying of the handle (because it is not set at right angles to the frame) and paddle across the river, so it is usual to spend an entire low tide period on one side. During times of good run the more diligent men fish at every low tide, day or night. Night fishing is quite dangerous, however, because of inability to see just where the bank slopes sharply off to the deep current, and because it is not easy to tell just when a large wave from the roaring surf may sweep the fisherman off his feet and the current carry him out to sea. Accidents of this sort are quite common and few succeed in escaping from the pounding surf or the undertow.

On some days the river spreads out in a shallow broad fan on the beach at low tide. The fish ascending in this water about a foot deep may be seen from the shore. Their position is indicated by the points of the waves of their wake as they swim rapidly upstream. Another use is now made of the dip net. The fisherman stands on the shore or at a strategic point in the stream and watches the river downstream. When he sees a fish ascending he wades to a point near where the fish will pass, for they usually swim straight against the current. When the fish is abreast of him he drops the net just beyond and with a rapid pull usually succeeds in getting the fish in the toils of the net. He then either lifts the net clear of the water and carries the fish ashore, or, if already near the shore, he runs up the bank dragging net and fish after him. Several fish are often taken in a single dip in this way. It is said that the dip net was never used except at the mouth of the river.

Harpooning. Salmon were harpooned in the riffles at the river mouth where the dip net was used. Harpoons seem to have been used less frequently than the nets, perhaps because very shallow water was necessary for accurate determination of the position of the fish. When the water was very clear, however, the harpoon could be used anywhere along the river. Late in the season when the water was low the fish could be easily speared as they lay spawning on the gravelly bottom. Even where the water was too deep to permit harpooning from the bank or in the stream, the harpoon could be used from the canoe. But this last means was seldom employed because it was obviously inferior to the surer means of weir or net.

The harpoon was the type common over the whole Northwest coast (fig. 6). A handle of fir an inch in diameter and from ten to fifteen feet long terminating in two prongs of separate pieces three feet long tipped with detachable heads was the invariable form. The prongs were scarfed and lashed securely to the lower end of the main part of the handle. One of the prongs was always about four inches longer

Fig. 6. Salmon harpoon. (After Willoughby.) Inset: details of point.

than its mate. The heads were the usual type of the region. Two pieces of elk horn shaped to fit closely around a nail-like point of bone and firmly lashed together formed the body of the head. One end of a strand of elk hide was wrapped around the horn pieces inside the lashings. The lashings and upper part of the point were covered with a smooth coating of pitch so that the head would pierce through easily. The upper parts of the elk horn pieces diverged so as to form two barbs. The elk sinew came out at one side of the barbs at the upper part of the lashings. The inner sides of the barbs were hollowed out so that they would fit snugly over the carefully formed tip of the prong of the handle. The strings from each point met about three feet from the heads where they were tied to a thong or nettle cord about thirty feet long. This cord passed through a lashing near the lower end of the handle so that when disengaged from the heads the handle would not be lost. A loop at the end of the cord passed around the fisherman's left wrist. The extra feet of cord were held coiled in the left hand. The entire harpoon might be thrown at a distant fish but often the handle never left the hands of the fisherman. The head of the harpoon commonly passed entirely through the salmon.

Using the gaff. The Quinault practiced this unique method of taking salmon in pre-European times. In recent times the gaff is a very large hook socketed to a long handle. Swan has given a description of the method employed at Shoalwater bay which will serve as well for the Quinault method:

"We proceeded up the stream about a mile, where we commenced floating down with the ebb. The water was from ten to twenty feet deep, and the process of catching the salmon was as follows: The hooks . . . after being properly adjusted to the poles, which were about twenty feet long, are put over the side and held in a vertical position, keeping the hook just clear of the bottom. It is usual to have but two persons in a canoe, one to steer and the other, who sits at the bow, to fish. As the boat drifts down with the tide, the pole, with the hook attached to it, comes in contact with the salmon, who, when not in active motion, usually lie near the bottom, and are generally quiet as soon as the tide begins to ebb.

"As soon as the Indian feels the fish, he jerks up the pole, and rarely fails to fasten the hook into one salmon, who is then pulled on board and knocked on the head. The whole operation requires a great deal of dexterity and practice, not only to distinguish the difference between a salmon and old logs, with which the bottoms of the rivers are usually covered, but also to get the fish into the canoe; for the salmon is a very powerful fish, and a large one makes a great commotion when hauled to the surface of the water, splashing and thrashing about in a fearful manner."[14]

Salmon taboos and beliefs.[15] The salmon run begins in the Quinault river with the coming of the sockeye in December or January (in exceptional years as late as February or even March). When the first salmon was caught it was carefully laid on the bank with the head upstream. It was then carried to the house and given the wife to prepare. Everyone in the village was then invited to the house to partake of the fish. Above all the fish must not be cut crosswise or cut with anything but a mussel shell knife. It was cut down either side of the backbone (beginning at the head) so that skin and flesh formed a layer about one half inch thick. The entrails were then removed and the heart burned in the fire. If an animal, or even a person, were to eat the heart the run of fish would immediately stop. The head was not severed from the backbone but cooked (or dried) with that portion of the meat. Everyone in the village was given a portion of the first fish caught. This feasting was not observed at the taking of the first of other species.

After this initial ceremony no further rites were observed. But throughout the run the bluebacks (at least) were laid with their heads pointing upstream. Until the butterball ducks (la'e'nopo) came into the river, or a small bird called skoit appeared, the fish must be cut lengthwise and only with a knife of mussel shell.[16] After that the fish might be cut crosswise and the head, backbone, and tail might be hung head down to dry. But the hearts were always burned.

---

[14]*Northwest Coast*, 137.

[15]Gunther has collected and analyzed the rites centering around the taking of the first salmon throughout the area (*Analysis of the First Salmon Ceremony*, A. A. n.s., 28, 1926, 605-617; and, *A Further Analysis of the First Salmon Ceremony*, this series, 2, 1928, 129-173).

[16]At least one informant stated that the same restrictions held throughout the year, but this is doubtful. One informant also stated that none of the taboos held for dog salmon. The Lower Chehalis followed much the same ritual for Cohoe salmon.

The bones of all salmon were thrown on the bank of the river (not in the water). The salmon, returning to the ocean (see below) were believed to take these bones back with them to the salmon home where they again became salmon.

If twins had been born to a couple within the year they could not go near the river, nor dared they eat fresh fish from the Quinault river lest the run stop. The fish they ate must be caught in small streams, such as Moclips river. The older children of the couple were not restricted.

A person who had handled a corpse could eat no fresh fish from the Quinault river or the salmon would stop running.

Evil magic could stop the salmon run indefinitely and any person found practicing such was killed. There were several ways of working the magic. The motive might be jealousy of a person who was having more than his share of luck, or who was taking more fish than he needed. The following acts stopped the run of fish:

Burying a fish in the ground, especially placing it among the roots of a tree or under rotten wood.

Placing the heart in clam or mussel shells and burying them. This was called sipxwanti'tsimul (hiding heart.). The fish would stop running until shells and heart were placed in the river.

Worst of all was the hiding or burying of a fish or the heart of a fish in the graveyard.

It was believed that the ghosts of the dead sometimes came to this world, stole the spirits of the fish, and carried them to the underworld. This also stopped the run of salmon. In this event people persuaded a shaman to go to the land of the dead, where his guardian spirit attempted to steal a fish from the dead and bring it back to this world. The dead, however, were on the lookout for this and it was a difficult procedure. The shaman was often well paid for his services. If he succeeded, the guardian spirit carried the fish to the mouth of the river, placed it in the water, and washed his hands there. The salmon run would begin again within a day or two. Similar magic worked against other fish as well as salmon.

Misp (or Xwoni Xwoni) initiated these things. He would say to the salmon, "Run now"! Then he would bury one or mistreat the heart and say, "Stop now," and they would stop. So it has been ever since. He also told the first men how to treat the fish after being caught.

The following beliefs regarding the life of the salmon contain both fact and fancy. But I leave it to the ichthyologists to determine which is which.

The blueback and steelhead spawn far up the creeks (sometimes staying for a time or even spawning in the lakes). Few of them die after spawning but start their return to the ocean. Once they reach salt water their sores start to heal and they are soon strong and shiny. (One informant stated that all those who spawn die, but that some come back downstream without spawning; these live.) But few dog salmon and humpbacks live after spawning. Most of the black salmon get back to the ocean. The fish which die upriver also return (*i.e.*, their spirits do), and go out to their home under the ocean again.

The old salmon who return to the ocean serve as guides in the run of the following year, showing the younger salmon when and where to come—for they are just like people in that way.

It was believed that the blueback matured in five years, that they then returned to the river where they were spawned.

OTHER FISH

Trout. Although trout were sometimes caught in the dip nets at the weirs, a commoner method was to place a trap called skeli'h in the small streams. These were constructed of small hemlock or vine maple poles, one-half or three-fourths of an inch in diameter, woven across with slender cedar limbs. The trap was conical, being about one and one-half or two feet in diameter at the mouth and tapering to a point at its other end, some six or seven feet away. The cedar limbs were woven at right angles to the poles which ran the entire length. Six loops were placed on the inside which served as ribs to maintain the circular shape.

At the mouth of the cone small straight sticks pointed from the rim inward and toward the center, where they were cut so as to form a small circular opening which permitted access to the trap but made escape difficult. There were no divisions inside the trap; the whole interior formed one compartment. The trap was placed in the middle of the creek with the open end upstream. It was never set to catch fish going up the current. Wattle work fences, resembling those used in weir construction, extended from either side of the trap to the bank to prevent fish from going around the sides of the trap. A rock was placed on top to hold the contrivance on the bottom. It was arranged so that when a number of fish were imprisoned the stone automatically fell off and allowed the trap to float to the surface.

Smelt and candlefish. The people of the lower villages often came down to the river mouth to catch smelt (komo'ɫniɫ) and candlefish (pa'agwa'ls). Both were taken in the surf of the beach, though the candlefish often ascend the river for several miles. There was usually a big run every three or four years, when the water was literally filled with fish. The time of the run varied, usually occurring between January and April.

A dip net (fig. 7) was used in taking the fish. This consisted of a conical net some three feet deep, knitted at its mouth to two poles each about five feet long, which served to hold the mouth open. (This opening measured about one and one-half by five feet.) A handle (tsidja'tcámin), about two inches in diameter and five feet long, was lashed at its lower end to the two poles attached to the net. It curved downward at its upper end. On some a crossbar there served as a grip for the left hand. The fisherman stood at the edge of the surf and held the net under the curl of incoming waves. The fish were carried along by this over-wash and fell directly into the net. A large basket was often filled from a single dip. When the candlefish were in the river they could be taken with the same net or with a net of small mesh secured to a salmon net frame.

Halibut (tcalo's), cod, rock cod (ťoxla'tse), sea bass (ke'toh), and sole were caught with hook and line. They could be taken anywhere along the coast within

Fig. 7. Dip net used in taking smelt and candlefish. (After Willoughby.)

six miles of shore. Calm weather was essential, so the period from June to September was the only time that anyone attempted to take these fish. Flounders might be taken in the ocean in the same way, but more frequently they were caught in the lower miles of the river. The same equipment was used for all these fish. The line was of dried and twisted stems of kelp (xo'tk̓ah) fastened together to make the desired length. A grooved stone sinker (kai'sa‘k) was tied to the end. This rested on the bottom. Several feet from the sinker a short line or leader (tu'lnatcta‘n), about three feet long, was tied to the main line. The lure was tied at the end of this leader. It was simply a rounded plug of newly cut white willow to which was lashed a barb. The hook was a straight piece of bone, with a fork on one end which straddled the plug. The other end tapered to a long sharp point and was so fixed that it formed an acute angle with the pointed end of the plug, to which the line was attached. No bait of any kind seems to have been used.[17] Trout may have been caught in the river and creeks with hook and line, with salmon roe for bait.[18]

A method of fishing on flat shallow beaches has been described by Swan. The Quinault used this method while on their frequent visits to Grays Harbor.

"The turbot and flounders are caught while wading in the water by means of the feet. The Indian wades along slowly, and, as soon as he feels the fish with his feet, he steps quickly on it and holds it firmly until he can reach hold of it with his hand, when he gives it a jerk, and away it flies far into the flats. This process is repeated until enough fish are caught, when they are picked up, put in a basket, and carried to the canoe. They are easily taken by this method of the Indians, as their rough backs prevent them from slipping under the feet. The catching affords a deal of fun, as usually quite a number are engaged in the sport, and their splashing, slipping, screaming, and laughing make a lively time. These fish, like all the fish in the bay, are very fine and well flavored."[19]

Herring appeared in great numbers during the summer. They were taken anywhere within a mile of the beach. The herring rake, common everywhere on the Northwest coast, was used from a canoe. It was simply a long sword-like stick with sharp bones set in one edge. An edgewise sweep through the water impaled the fish on the points and the fish were then shaken off in the canoe. A canoe could be filled in a short time. The rake was not used for smelt or candlefish.

Other sea foods. Razor clams (haitssaw'us) were an important source of food. While there were no good clam beds near the mouth of the river they could be found just south of Point Grenville, less than two hours walk from kwi'naił. The beds between Grenville and Moclips river were usually resorted to for small supplies of fresh clams. But the best digging was to be had at Copalis Beach and in the vicinity of Oyhut. Dozens of families moved to these places every summer to dry clams for the winter's supply. It is said that the shell heaps at Copalis are miles long and

---

[17]Another informant stated that either willow or alder might be used for a plug and that a whole smelt might be used for bait in bass and cod fishing. The hook rested either directly on the bottom or a few feet above. Where bait was used it seems likely that a more elaborate form of hook was employed. Sunny days were especially favorable for ocean fishing.

One informant stated that trolling was known; that Cohoe salmon, cod, and black bass were caught in the ocean in this way. The "spoon" was the white stem of a devil club carved in the shape of a fish, with a bone barb lashed to it.

[18]Swan, *Northwest Coast*, 139-140.

[19]*Ibid.*, 83.

many feet deep. Clams might be gathered at any time of the year, but those dug in May were considered best. A flat digging stick of yew was used. One must always face the ocean while digging, otherwise the clam will be missed or one's fingers get cut.

It requires no mean amount of dexterity and skill to be able to consistently catch the majority of those located, for the clam is more wily than is generally supposed. At the instant that the implement starts to pierce the sand he quickly draws in his neck, reaches the foot down into the soft watery sand below, enlarges it at the end and pulls himself rapidly downward. Unless he can be seized by the neck when the first scoop of sand is flicked away one may as well pass on, for by the time a second scoop is made he will be a foot below the surface. The digging stick was placed about four inches toward the sea from the barely perceptible depression that marks the spot directly above the clam. A single movement shoved the implement downward four inches and removed the sand. The right hand reached quickly downward and seized the neck and the bivalve was slowly pulled to the surface. It was usual to run about over the sand to cause the clams to dig down slightly so that the depressions became visible. This task usually fell to the children, who, upon sighting such a spot, marked a ring around it so that the women would be able to locate the clams more readily. As they were dug the clams were placed in a large open-work basket.

Razor clams were dug with less labor in calm weather, when there were low tides and the surf rolled in and spread out over the velvety sand in wide sheets of water not more than an inch deep. On the strip of beach continually covered with a film of water the clam necks could be seen protruding out of the sand. It was only necessary to seize the neck, give a slight dig and remove the clam.

Mud clams (mita'ks) were secured at the same places as razor clams, but they could be gathered only during a few of the very lowest tides in May. The small hole marking the spot above them served to locate them. A digging stick was not necessary in digging them.

Rock oysters (sklapa'ligwa) were a favorite food. About a mile south of kwi'-naił are several beds of blue clay, visible at low tide, which are hardened to almost the consistency of rock, but not so hard that pieces could not be split off quite readily. The substance was honeycombed with the burrows of these curious molluscs. The old method of gathering them was to split off sections of the rock by means of mauls and wedges. These were broken into smaller pieces and the oysters removed and placed in baskets to be carried home.

Huge black-shelled mussels (kwapi't) abounded on the rocks of Cape Elizabeth and Point Grenville. It was usual to voyage after them in canoes as they were too heavy to carry. In the old days their shells were used for knives and harpoon heads. "China slippers" (tsa'ał) were treated like clams.

Sea anemones were secured at Cape Elizabeth. Crabs were frequently found along the beaches and in the pools of water near rocks at low tide. Herring eggs were not gathered by the Quinault, but they state that the Lower Chehalis of the south shore of Grays Harbor made use of them. I neglected to obtain information on skate, squid, and sea urchins as food.

PREPARATION AND USE OF SEA FOODS

In addition to the material given in the preceding sections, I secured some additional information regarding the preparation and use of various foods which I will give here.

The work of preparing the salmon for drying fell to the women. The fish were "skinned out" in the usual Northwest coast manner by splitting down either side of the backbone so that a fairly uniform layer of flesh about one half inch thick remained with the skin. The stroke of the mussel shell knife was always from head toward tail. If the fish were very large a second layer of flesh was trimmed off. If the head, tail, and backbone were to be dried the entrails were removed and the "blood" along the backbone removed. The pieces were strung on racks which rose in tiers above the fire of alder or maple. Each day the pieces were moved up one tier and at the end of about a week were sufficiently dry to be stored away. Salmon so dried would keep almost indefinitely so long as it was not allowed to get damp. It was eaten either boiled, roasted, or as it was. The heads, tails, and fins were strung on strings and dried. (The taboo on cutting crosswise of the fish evidently extended only to the flesh, not to the removal of tail and head.) Only the gills were not eaten.

The eggs were spread out to dry for a time, then stored in a black salmon or seal bladder, which was hung up to dry. In time the eggs formed a sort of "cheese." The fresh eggs of black salmon were sometimes sprinkled in hot ashes, allowed to roast a few minutes, then dusted off and eaten. The milt of the male salmon was roasted in hot ashes and eaten.

Halibut, rock cod, and bass were dressed and dried in the same manner as salmon. They were usually soaked in water and boiled before being eaten.

Candlefish were dried whole. If their oil was wanted it was rendered by placing the fish in a large trough and adding water. They were then boiled by adding hot stones. The fish were pressed on a flat stone to extract more oil. The oil was used for dunking dried meat and berries.

Clams were prepared for drying by dashing them with hot water until the shells opened. The fleshy parts were then removed and strung on salmonberry sticks and roasted over the fire for a time, then dried in the sun. When thoroughly dry they were strung on cords and stored. They might be eaten without further preparation or soaked and boiled. Fresh clams were sometimes roasted before the fire until the shells opened, then eaten. Fresh clams were also prepared by placing them on hot rocks in a pit and covering them with leaves and sand.

Rock oysters were usually prepared by boiling them for five minutes. The nectar was drunk.

Mussels were always prepared by baking them in a pit for an hour or so.

Crabs were cooked by placing them on a rack a few inches above hot stones. They were then covered with mats and leaves and water was thrown on the stones. They were steamed an hour or two. Clams and fish were sometimes prepared in this same way.

A rather peculiar method of cooking was by means of a bark-lined pit. A hole of the desired shape and size was first dug, then large sections of hemlock bark partially fitted into it. Hot water was then poured over the bark until it assumed the shape of the pit. The bark was then carefully removed and the seams sewed. It was then replaced in the pit, water poured in, and hot stones added until the water boiled. This affair could be used over a period of months. The same method was sometimes employed for the making of a container for the storing of fat or even meat.

HUNTING

Though not as important in Quinault economy as was fishing, hunting was looked upon as a profitable way to spend the month or two following the salmon runs. Game was now and then sought near the permanent villages along the river below Quinault lake, but the upper river and the mountains were the objectives when it was desired to lay by a supply of meat against the winter months. The entire family, or several families from the same village (usually relatives), frequently moved to the mountains during the late summer. Elk (sli'ka'tsi'em), bear, and deer were most sought after, but no hunter could afford to scorn lesser game. Once in the mountains, the family proceeded to erect a semi-permanent camp of poles and brush, and from this as a center the hunter, or hunters, ranged far and near in search of game, while the women and children stayed at camp drying the meat and in their spare time gathering berries and basket grasses and barks.

A somewhat romantic aura surrounded the pursuit of hunting, whether of the sea mammals or of elk and bear, and men were fond of relating their hunting experiences. For this reason they looked with a sort of disdain upon men who were not reckoned good hunters and who found it more profitable to spend most of their time fishing. "A good hunter's camp could be smelled from afar by reason of the odor of decaying refuse and offal—that was the mark of a good hunter."

For weapons the hunter carried only his bow and arrows, supplemented by a mussel-shell knife to be used in skinning and dismembering the game. His clothing consisted of a crude, untailored elkskin, belted at the waist, leggings to protect him from thorns and brush, and sock-like moccasins made from the hock skin of an elk or large deer (the hock forming the heel). If he expected to be long away from camp he took with him a pouch or bag containing a little dried meat or fish. If night overtook him far from camp, he sought a sheltering rock or tree and slept on the ground with only his daytime garb as a covering.

Some hunters used an elk call to lure the male elk within arrow range. This was a sort of double-ended whistle about eight inches long (fig. 8). It was made of a section of elderberry stem, well scraped, its pith pushed out and a plug inserted at the center. To make the proper sound the whistle was held vertically across the lips, the air being forced through the small lateral opening and across the end opening. The sound produced only remotely resembled any sound made by elk, but the males

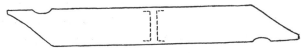

Fig. 8. A double-ended whistle used as an elk call.

responded nevertheless. When the animal arrived within range the hunter aimed for the region of the heart. The elk call was employed as a toy as well. It is said that no other game calls were known.

Elk, bear, and more rarely, deer, were hunted with the aid of dogs. This method seems to have been employed along the course of the river and not in the high mountains. The hunter would take four or five dogs into the woods and set them on the scent of the game. The hunter then took a position at the margin of the river or beside a much-used game trail and waited for the dogs to drive the game past. It is said that properly trained dogs would nearly always succeed in bringing the game within shooting distance. Dogs employed in this manner were kept tied when not needed, lest they chase all manner of game and make them over-wary. It is said that elk rarely frequented the ocean shore.

After the elk was killed it was skinned and dressed. The intestines were cleaned by the simple expedient of turning them inside out. The intestinal fat was left adhering and now was on the inside. Meat and fat were placed in the skin and carried to the camp or village. The bones and parts of the horns were also brought in; the bones to be cracked and boiled to extract the marrow fat, and the special parts of the horns to be used in the making of harpoon points. The cracked bones were also used for this purpose, as well as for awls and other tools. As much as possible of the blood was saved, and together with rendered fat was poured into the only partially filled intestines. The filled intestines were then boiled.

A certain amount of the better (kidney) fat was rendered in wooden bowls by means of hot rocks. This pure white tallow was then placed in the bladder of the animal. It was most commonly used by the women as a facial ointment for beautifying the complexion, and as a cure for chapped skin. More rarely it was used in cooking if there was a shortage of more ordinary fats.

The meat was cut in strips and placed on a frame over the fire, where it went through a combined smoking and drying process. The drying rack was made by driving four forked sticks into the ground, allowing them to project so that the fork was some three feet above ground. Cross poles connected the ends of the uprights. Six or more poles were laid parallel, their ends resting on the cross-sticks. The strips of meat were laid across or hung over these. A long fire was built beneath. Fish were sometimes dried in this same manner. Meat might be partially dried at camp and then taken home and placed on the drying racks suspended from the crossbeams of the house. The dried meat might be eaten without further preparation but was sometimes pounded between rocks and mixed with fat—a product akin to the pemmican of the Plains and Mackenzie areas. Fish was never pulverized.

The skin was seldom tanned in the camp, but was carried home green or dried. Though sometimes the grain and hair were removed before tanning, it was more usual to tan with the hair on, as elk, deer, and bear hides were commonly used as bedding. The summer skins of elk, sea lion, and hair seal were sometimes eaten. The hair was burned off, the skin cleaned, allowed to dry somewhat and then boiled.

Bear (stci'txa'n) and deer (skålle') were hunted in much the same manner as elk, and their meat and fat prepared and used similarly, except that their fat was not in favor as a cosmetic. Elk and deer were hunted in the summer and were seldom pursued "after they began to whistle," *i.e.*, during the rutting season. Bear were hunted in the autumn when they were fat and their skins were prime. Sometimes bear were hunted in the early spring, just after coming out of their winter dens. Bear were also taken by means of a deadfall (see Traps and Snares).

There were few indications of the "bear cult" among the Quinault. If a person were seized by a bear he shouted "Come on, come on and help me!" Then the bear let go and ran away. It is related that Jimmy Chow Chow was once badly mangled by a bear because he could not think of this formula in time. A female bear may now and then be heard talking to her cubs if she does not suspect that humans are about. Many years ago Julia Cole saw a bear whose cubs had recently been killed by a hunter. The bear walked sadly along, swaying her head from side to side, and repeating over and over again "Oh! Oh! My poor children, my poor children!" in a most mournful voice. The skulls of bear (or of other animals) were never erected on poles, nor are there evidences that any dance or ceremony attended the killing or eating of bear.

Marmot (kwukwu'k) were usually sought during the season of elk hunting in the mountains. They were easy to kill. Their skins were much used in the manufacture of bed blankets. A small shoulder robe of four to six skins of the animal was sometimes made. A single skin made a handy seat when one had to sit in a cold or damp spot. The flesh of the marmot was regarded as excellent and well-flavored meat "because they eat grass."

Beaver (stamu'h) were commonly caught by setting a deadfall (stci'ltcin) in the paths frequented by the animals at the point where they leave the water. My informant was ignorant of the exact form of the deadfall or the trigger type, but stated that the weight of the animal sprung the trap; that no bait stick was employed. Beaver skins made excellent blankets. The flesh was dried and when wanted for food was softened by soaking in water until ready for boiling. The four incisor teeth were used in the woman's gambling game (matci').

Land otter (gwa'cups) were caught in the same manner as beaver and their meat and skins used in the same way.

Coon (kwa'las) were captured by setting a deadfall in the paths they used. Meat and skins were treated in the same way as beaver.

The wildcat (sp'a'tca'm) was caught by means of the deadfall also. The skin was a favorite blanket for wrapping about the shoulders. The meat was eaten.

Rabbits (sku'pkhup) were taken in snares (xwa'tsup) made of sinew from the back of the elk.

Mink (sdja'la'pacu) were trapped with the deadfall. The skins were often used as neckpieces. The flesh of the mink was not eaten.

Wolves (tso'pa'h) were hunted with the bow and arrow. Their skins were used for blankets. The flesh was used as food (?).

It is said that neither skunks nor squirrels (sku'dju) were hunted.

44

Of sea mammals the Quinault hunted the whale, sea lion, seal, sea otter, and porpoise.

Whales. Whaling was a dangerous and spectacular pursuit and was hedged about with ritual. To be a whale hunter a man had to possess the right type of supernatural power; he must each season subject himself to a long period of "training" to insure success, and, not the least important, he must possess an ocean canoe and considerable other expensive gear. He must also be able to call together seven other men to aid him. Considering that it called for all these as well as a stout heart, it is no great wonder that only a few men followed whaling. Among the Quinault it is unlikely that more than a half dozen at any one time possessed the necessary qualifications and equipment. About 1850 only Nicàgwa'ts and his brother might actually have been called whalers. To the south of the Quinault there were no tribes which hunted whales, though quite naturally they made use of such animals as drifted ashore. To the north the Queets never troubled with the sport. The Quilleute took to the pursuit to a greater extent than did the Quinault, though they were not so famous in this respect as the Makah or the Nootka tribes.

The canoe used was of the ordinary "ocean" type (see page 67), sometimes manufactured by the Quinault, but more often received from the Quilleute or Makah in exchange for dried salmon, or for sea otter skins. The necessary crew consisted of eight men, six of whom acted as paddlers (and seated themselves two on a thwart), a steersman, and the harpoon thrower. The latter was the headman, and to him the others looked for instruction as to equipment and procedure. A movement of his hand served to order them to rest on their paddles or to paddle briskly in the tense minutes just before the whale was harpooned.

The harpoon was in all respects like that used by the Makah and Nootka.[20] The shaft was an eight-foot length of yew tapered from the middle toward the ends, the point being more slender and shaped to fit the socket of the point. The blade of the point was of mussel shell. The double barbs were of bone, lashed together and to the blade by elk sinew. The wrappings were carefully coated with pitch. The line of braided and twisted sinew was some eight feet long. To this were attached several lengths of inch-thick line made from the slender branches of the swamp cedar, which were first twisted as for withes. These frequently grow to a length of 20 feet without the larger ends being of greater diameter than a lead pencil. Eight to fifteen of these "strands" are necessary to make a line of the required strength. About 100 fathoms of this line were ordinarily coiled ready in the bottom of the canoe. At more or less regular intervals along the central three-fourths of the line, six-foot leaders lead to buoys made of the whole skins of the hair seal.

Whales were most often encountered 12 to 30 miles off shore. The head whaler (harpooner) never aided in paddling the canoe, but stood in the bow and scanned the ocean for signs of the quarry. If a whale were sighted asleep, the canoe approached as quietly as possible. If the whale were swimming leisurely along, the men paddled to within a half-mile or so. The harpooner then gave his orders re-

---

[20]Waterman, *The Whaling Equipment of the Makah*, pp. 29-34.

garding the line and buoys and took his position with one foot on the bow-piece, the other on the forward thwart. The harpoon was held with the backs of the hands uppermost, thumbs not grasping, but resting alongside the index fingers. It is said that a more powerful throw was possible with this than with other grips.

The harpooner now signaled to his crew with the hand. If the whale dove the men paddled briskly. When he came to the surface the crew sat silent, allowing the canoe to drift. When nearly close enough for the thrust, a good whaler would know just at what point the whale would come up. As the animal was ready to dive again the harpooner hurled his shaft and, if the weapon struck, the men backed water to avoid the lashing tail. The harpoon was aimed at a point back of the fin ("like under the arm"). Not all whales lashed about with their tails; some only dashed away. A whale was never struck as he came to the surface. Some whales were very wary and could never be approached within harpooning range.

Almost with the same motion with which he threw the harpoon, the head whaler jumped down to pay out the line and to throw over the several buoys in their turn. When the end of the line was reached one paddler joined the headman, and, like him, braced himself in the bow and held tightly to the end of the line. In the meantime a second man placed himself beside the steersman to aid in keeping the canoe on a course in the whale's wake. The other paddlers did all they could to keep the canoe steady, for during the early minutes, the whale in his agony thrashed about in a fearful fashion, sounding, running at full speed, and often turning sharply about. These were the exciting and dangerous moments of the chase. A single canoe seldom dared venture out for whales. Usually a second was close at hand to lend aid in case the first was wrecked or overturned. Though it was usual to hold fast to the end of the line, it was not always feasible. A lightly-struck or a dangerous whale (one that turned on the canoe) might force abandonment of the rigging or might necessitate following the whale for a long way and at a respectable distance.

If the harpoon hit the proper spot and was deeply imbedded, the whale bled internally; the buoys and the canoe, which he must tow, served to impede his progress and in a few minutes he began to show signs of tiring. The second canoe, if possible, now came on the scene and at an opportune moment a second harpoon was sent to its mark. This infuriated the whale still further, but, already weakened by the first, his violent exertions were of shorter duration this time, and after running a few miles he usually became too weak to be dangerous. Once more a canoe approached and wounded him severely with a long lance or a lineless harpoon. A few thrusts were sufficient to end his life and the rigging was once more assembled in the canoes and the whale towed to the village at the mouth of the river. A strong whale might run as much as ten or fifteen miles before being killed, but, if the whaler's "power" were strong enough, the whale would always run toward the shore instead of out to sea. It is said that so potent were the guardian spirits controlled by Nicagwa'ts that the whales he killed often came to within two miles of the village, and that he never was forced to tow a whale more than five miles.

The head whaler must possess the proper type of guardian spirit, else he would never dare venture after whales. "Ownership" of this spirit was obtained at or shortly after puberty. But mere control of this spirit was not enough; the whaler went through a month of "training" previous to the season of whaling. During this month he was strictly continent and every night he bathed in the ocean or the river. Or he might go out alone in his canoe and practice throwing the harpoon, meanwhile conversing with his spirit. Before his baths he would rub himself with human bones, the bones of the forearm being preferred. These were usually the bones of one of his male ancestors (probably the one who had the whaler's guardian spirit). The skull from the same body was also used, and wrapped in cedar bark or a blanket and carried or placed in the canoe. Contact with such potent elements gave him power to harm other people, so he avoided them. (This is also given as a reason for refraining from intercourse with his wife.) After rubbing himself with the bones, a similar procedure with the leaves of a certain plant was necessary in order to take away the "poison" of the bones. It was desirable to go to a place in the river where bubbles came up as one walked—so that bubbles would come up from a sounding whale and show the hunter which way to go.[21]

After about three weeks of this ritual the whaler notified the seven men who were to comprise his crew. During the succeeding ten days which preceded the actual hunt they, too, were warned against sexual intercourse. If all had followed the proper ritual, and if their wives were faithful while the men were away, success was assured. Should a woman be unfaithful while the hunt was on, the whale would be wary and "wild," and the men would be unable to kill any. This also was true of the hunting of other animals. There were no food taboos for women at such times.[22]

Like all other Pacific coast tribes, the Quinault made use of whales which drifted ashore dead and of live ones stranded on shallow beaches. One of the purposes of the tribal boundary lines at the ocean's edge was to be able to determine to what tribe such a whale belonged. (Tribal boundaries in other parts of the territory were more or less indefinite.) Nearly every winter one or two whales were washed up on the beach in Quinault territory. Certain families received a section about three feet in length all the way around the whale. Families of the upper villages were notified of the event, and their portions were left intact until they arrived. One family would be given the jaw, another the tongue, another the tail, and so on, according to their inherited rights. The finder of a stranded whale received no special share or part.

The blubber was cut into pieces of carrying size. A strong man could carry a section about three feet square. These sections were carried home and placed in a large wooden trough and the fat rendered out by means of hot stones. The trough was of a size to hold a single section three feet square. For a very large or fat whale two boilings were necessary. The scum which formed was removed with the shell of the mud clam. The rendered fat was then stored in large troughs or boxes or, more commonly, in the stomachs of seal or sea lion and in bags made of sections of the whale's intestines. The blubber of the belly side was cut into strips and slabs and dried over the fire, the fat which dripped off being saved. The lean meat was cut into strips and dried like elk or bear meat.

---

[21]One informant stated that a skull was kept in the bag with the harpoon head during the hunt "so that the whale would be tame."

[22]The leader in the whale hunt always received the "saddle," including the back fin, as his share of the whale.

It usually took about a month to render the fat and dry the meat. After all possible oil had been extracted from the blubber, the remainder was more or less roasted and dried and stored away in cedarbark baskets. This, and dried fish, were often eaten together. The oil was a favorite side-dish when camas was served, and was much in favor when dried fish was eaten, the strips of fish being dipped in the fat. Most of the oil was stored against the time of the solstice ceremonies about Christmas. In the dances men would vie with each other in the amount of oil which they could down in a single evening—the contest being always won by those who had the "ocean" or "western" guardian spirit. Tall tales are related of famous old whalers who, in the course of a single evening, could down (and hold down) upwards of a half-barrel of oil! But there was a trick in this. The doughty one would feign to spit some of the oil on the fire. Actually he would vomit it on the fire. A quart or two of oil thus spewed on the fire would cause it to blaze up nearly to the roof, to the amazement and delight of the assembled throng. Thus did he show the power of *his* guardian spirit.

The following account of a famous old Nimrod was told by Billy Mason. Though it deals in a general way with land hunting, its main concern is with whaling:

Nicagwa'ts was a great hunter of all kinds of game except grizzly bear and cougar. He never happened to kill these, but he killed many of all other animals. When he was hunting in the mountains his camp would in a few days begin to stink, because of so much meat and so many fish lying about.

He was short, stocky, and the strongest Indian of his day. Yet he was not a large man. But he was a good man and never quarreled with anyone. In his house there was always plenty of elk meat, whale meat, and oil. He had four wives and many slaves. The slaves he never scolded but called them "brother" and his women slaves "sister." When he went to his father's house at loxe'ls he would dry a great deal of meat and fish. Afterward he would come down here (to kwi'nail) and hunt sea otter. These he went after at night when the otter were asleep Some nights he would kill as many as five or six.

He had much property and many blankets. When the first white traders came he exchanged some of his furs for the things they had. Later on he traded furs for guns. With the guns he hunted sea otter. Once he harpooned the biggest sea lion he had ever seen. He towed it home behind his canoe.

Nicagwa'ts and his brother were whalers, together with a cousin. Sometimes they made their own whaling canoes; sometimes bought them from the Quilleute or Makah. They made their own rope and harpoons. Nicagwa'ts was so strong that when spearing a whale if the harpoon struck a rib the blow would break the rib. And always he was able to stun the whale with the first harpoon—then he had time to throw others. Sometimes he would throw with such force that the thwart under his right foot would give way. They hunted in two canoes, Nicagwa'ts in one, his brother in the other.

Whenever he speared a whale, as he let go of the harpoon his spirit helper would appear. All the men in the canoe would see it. It was the slào'ltcu, the "ocean spirit." Then he would point toward the snowcapped mountain [Quinault mountain?] and say to the whale, "Go toward that white mountain," and the whale would always go in that direction, because he understood what Nicagwa'ts said. After the whale had come nearly to the shore they would kill him. They didn't want to kill him far out and then have to tow him a long way.

When Nicagwa'ts trained himself for whaling he used to go out at night to bathe in the ocean and in the river. He went where no one would see him and no one could hear him talking to himself. He would "talk to the world" (ni·ta·'mmi·xʷ) and tell "the world" what he wanted and ask it to help him. That was when he was coming to be a man, before he was a hunter. He had a skull wrapped in a blanket. He would tell his "Captain" (*i.e.*, the skull, or, more specifically, the ghost), "You had better watch when I go to throw the harpoon at the whale. Make the whale weak—as if he were dead."

Once he was "training" at night out in his canoe. He was practicing with the harpoon. He had along a skull and other bones of one of his (male) ancestors that he had dug up at night, secretly. This night the skull (*i.e.*, the ghost) took hold of the canoe and shook it. Nicagwa'ts did not look around, for if he did he would "get ghosted." He only motioned to the ghost to be still. Then he quit his "training," for he was sure of his helper. After that, whenever he was hunting, the ghost would shake the canoe to show where the game was.

Before he wanted to go whaling Nicagwa'ts would train very carefully. Sometimes for two months he would not sleep with his wife. At night he would bathe at a place in the river where the bubbles would come up to show which way they had gone. He used to rub his body with the human bones (the bones of the forearm) and then rub himself with the leaves of a plant. These leaves removed the "poison" that came from handling the bones of the dead. He kept away from his wife because of the "poison." (Not the true explanation, since the other members of the crew were also continent for a period.)

After he trained like this the animals would be weak and easy to kill when he hunted them. Every summer he hunted whale. He could tell the kind of whale as far as he could see it. Sometimes he hunted for porpoise and would many times bring in as many as ten on a single trip. One time I went with him to fish for bass about three miles out in the ocean. A porpoise came up near our canoe. He speared it easily, though he was then an old man.

He used these same medicines (bones and leaves) for hunting all kinds of game. Every morning and night he would wash with them. He would not tell anyone what he used or let anyone see the bones, but when the summer was over, the hunting all done, and the meat all dried for the winter, then he would copulate with his wife once more, but never would he sleep in the same bed with anyone. He slept by the side of the fire in the middle of the house. He did not want anyone to sleep near him because he had used that "poison" and had handled the bones of the dead.

Now Sammy Hoh and Billy Garfield are the only ones living who have seen that kind of spirit, and they have never hunted whale. But because they have a little of that kind of power they are able to sing the songs that come with the slǎo'ltcu power.

Sea lion. A short distance north of Point Elizabeth a group of rocky islets jut out of the water. These were called lae'lsni·ł ("sea lion rocks"), from the fact that a herd of the animals was usually to be found there. On calm days the rocks could be reached by canoe. Sometimes the animals were stealthily approached and speared as they lay on the rocks. A second method was to come upon them at night, when a man extremely familiar with the ground would be able to kill several before putting the herd to flight. The common method of capture, however, was to harpoon the animals from a canoe. For this a crew of eight men was necessary.

The harpoon used for sea lion was somewhat larger and heavier than that used for salmon and had a single point tipped with a blade (kłaka'n) of mussel or clam shell. The handle (kłǎmǎ'łn) was a fir pole about 10 feet long and without finger grooves at the handle end. To this was attached a line of twisted willow bark about 20 feet long. A single float or buoy of the skin of a yearling seal was attached at the end. As the harpoon struck the animal, line and float were thrown overboard. As soon as the sea lion had tired enough so that the canoe could approach, the line was seized and hauled in until the animal was close enough to be despatched with a heavy yew wood club (skota'). He was then cut up in the water and the sections stowed aboard. A very large animal was sometimes towed home behind the canoe. The skin of the sea lion was seldom used for any article, though the gut was frequently made into bowstrings. The fat was rendered by boiling and then pressing.

The lean meat was cut in long strips and smoke-dried. When wanted for food it was soaked in water for a time and then boiled.

Seal. Usually it was necessary to go from ten to twenty-five miles offshore in an ocean canoe to find fur seal (ma·a'i). The animals were hunted in the months of April and May. The animals were at this time on their annual migration to the islands off Alaska, hence were not encountered along the shore. An ocean canoe was used, but only three men were needed for the venture. The canoe cruised about until a seal was sighted asleep in the sun. Quiet paddling was necessary to get within harpoon range. When struck the animal was hauled in, killed with a club, and hoisted aboard. The skins were used for blankets and robes. The meat and fat were treated in the same manner as with sea lion.

Hair seal (kutcu') were sometimes secured while hunting for fur seal, but were more commonly found on the beaches and rocks of the shore, where they were year-round residents. Their skins were used as floats for whale and sea-lion equipment and as bedding, being usually placed under the rush mats which served as mattresses. The use of meat and fat did not differ from that of sea lion.

The porpoise (skàa'ïnoh, "little whale") was frequently hunted for food. It was usual to go out for them in an ocean canoe. The harpoon used was like that for salmon, the points being of different lengths, though it was somewhat larger.

Sea otter. Even before the first white fur-traders came on the scene, the skins of the sea otter (kakwa·'lakeh) were of considerable economic importance, both for intertribal trade and domestic use. The animals were especially numerous near Point Grenville and the rocks which lie off the point. The animals were very shy and hard to approach. A canoe of the same pattern as the ocean canoe but smaller (called a ło'tk̓) and manned by two men was employed for the hunt. When an otter was sighted the bowman picked up his bow and arrow and got ready to shoot. The other paddled quietly toward the quarry. When the otter was struck he seldom swam away, but gnawed at the arrow, "trying to get it out." This enabled the men to approach close enough to use the harpoon. The harpoon was of the same pattern as that used for salmon. One point was about four inches longer than the other. Both were tipped with mussel shell. When captured the otter was killed and loaded into the canoe. The meat was dried for food. The skins were much in demand among neighboring tribes. Only chiefs could afford to wear blankets of this fur. It is said that sea otter traveled in bands of two to four, but of such a band the hunters were never able to capture more than one on a trip.

BIRD HUNTING

The usual method of capturing ducks involved the setting of nettle-fiber nets, measuring about 20 feet square, between trees on either side of a stream at a height of 15 feet above the water (the height at which the birds commonly flew in going up and down the stream). The fine twine used in the nets made it impossible for the birds to see the trap until too close to change their course. While this net served well enough for sawbills (kàma'tsł) and canvasbacks (stskà'n), it is said that mallards (sluku'kc) were never captured in this way, being wary of the nets. Foggy weather was best for the use of such nets. The mesh was about four inches square.

A second type of net for catching ducks was set in the water. Two poles were set in shallow water about 16 feet apart. A net of that length and three feet wide (*i.e.*, deep) was stretched between the stakes. Rotten fish or otter bait was now placed on the bottom at one side of the net. This side of the net was now made inaccessible by means of brush. The ducks must approach from the other side and, seeing the bait, would dive for it and become entangled in the meshes in trying to get to the surface.

Duck blinds of brush and ferns were sometimes built along the ocean and river shores to enable hunters to lie in wait for ducks. Ducks were often killed by simply throwing rocks at flocks as they flew or swam by. It is said that along Grays Harbor and on Puget Sound ducks were sometimes hunted at night with great torches of resinous wood. The bright light blinded the birds—"made them crazy"—and they could be killed with a stick. The Quinault also hunted at night, but approached the spot where the flock was known to be sleeping and killed the birds with a long pole.

Loon (wa'ɬkale), were classed as a kind of duck. They were shot with the bow and arrow. The flesh was eaten and the skin often used for hats.

The sea pilot (maatssa'tc), a black bird with a long neck, was hunted with the bow and arrow. The flesh was eaten; the feathers were favored for arrows. Pelicans (xwa'hadjt) were hunted by the same means.

Sea gulls were shot when not in flight with the bow and arrow. Their flesh was eaten. They were often skinned and the skin used for a pillow. The rookeries at Point Grenville and Cape Elizabeth were sources of eggs in the month of June.

Pheasant (tamatna') were caught by means of a noose. A clay figure resembling a pheasant was placed on a log and nooses of nettle fiber or elk sinew placed on either side at a distance of about two and one-half feet. The male pheasant, thinking the figure another bird, approached to fight or mate, and was caught. Pheasant were considered the best fowl for eating.

Grouse (ha'msiltcan) were easily secured with bow and arrow. Pigeon (hắmi'm) were killed in the same manner. Snipe (sgi'ɬkgwilk) were hard to kill, but might be taken with bow and arrow or simply by throwing rocks. Crane were used as food also, but crows were never eaten "because they eat everything."

Eagle (gwi'ɬkops) might sometimes be shot, but were usually taken by climbing to their nests and killing them when they came to protect the nests. Their flesh was eaten, their feathers used in a headband of cedar bark in the war dance.

Some kinds of birds were taken by means of a snare with a stick trigger. It is said that the bird spear was unknown among the Quinault.

TRAPS AND SNARES

A number of types of traps and snares were undoubtedly known, but I secured data only on the following:

Bears were sometimes caught by means of a rather elaborate deadfall (stci'lcin), constructed as in figure 9. The top was heavily weighted with stones which were placed on top after the trap was set. Bait of fish or meat was lashed to the horizontal trigger. In attempting to devour this the animal pushed the bar down, releasing the vertical trigger bar. Cougar and wildcat were sometimes taken in such a trap and it was said that deer sometimes stumbled into it.

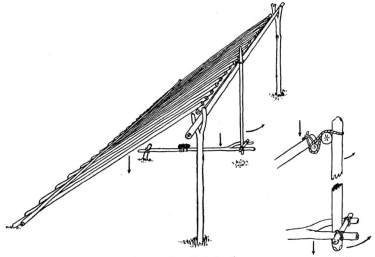

Fig. 9. Deadfall for bear.

A trap for deer and elk (called xwatsa'p) consisted of a combination pit and spring-pole with noose. The spring pole was of yew, the noose of rawhide. The pit was about three feet in diameter and as many deep. The trigger bar, noose, and pit were carefully covered with small sticks and moss. The trap was set in a game trail, and the animal stumbling into the pit pressed down the horizontal bar, allowing the spring pole to fly upward (see fig. 10).

It was said that birds were taken with a miniature deadfall, without added weights, constructed like that for bear. For catching the male grouse a figure like a grouse was modeled of clay and placed at one end of a log. A foot or so away a noose was set so that the grouse coming to "fight" the decoy would be snared.

The Quinault claim that they used no game calls except the double-ended whistle described on page 41.

PLANT FOODS

The Quinault did not use plant foods to any great extent. In part, this is to be explained by the comparative rarity of forms which might serve as staples. The region is almost lacking in the acorn-bearing oaks which furnish a large item in the dietary of the tribes of California. Seed-bearing annual plants and grasses are also

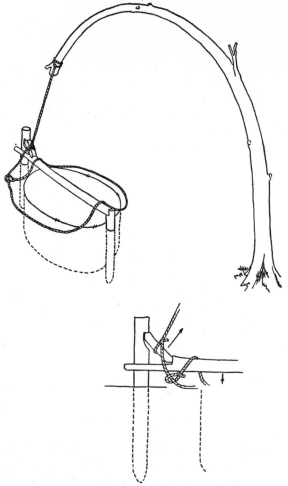

Fig. 10. Pit and spring-pole trap.

comparatively rare in Quinault territory. A few roots and a variety of berries are to be found in abundance but they were gathered and prepared only to add variety to the menu, perhaps to stimulate appetites somewhat jaded by a diet consisting largely of fish.

Of roots used, that of the camas was the most important though it was not as important an item among the Quinault as among the tribes of the Lower Columbia. The plant grows mainly in the open swampy glades or "prairies." Baker's prairie, O'took prairie, and Cook Creek prairie were the chief sources of supply. June was the favored month for gathering the lily-like bulbs, and entire families often moved to these places for a period.

The women busied themselves with their yew digging-sticks and the girls assisted them. Men and boys spent the time in hunting or in gathering plants and woods for special purposes.

The roots were stored in baskets and when a good supply had been secured, the family returned to the home village. Here the roots were washed by placing them in an openwork basket and running water over them. A pit was then dug in the sand, partly filled with rocks, and a brisk fire built on top. A large supply of fresh fern leaves was gathered and when the rocks were thoroughly hot, the fire was removed, the stones leveled, and a layer of fern leaves spread over them. On top of this bed the camas was spread (the size of the pit depending upon the amount of the roots). A thick layer of fern leaves was placed on top and covered with a three-inch layer of sand. The roots were allowed to cook overnight and a fire was kept burning on top of the covering sand during the baking. In the morning the roots were removed, mashed, and made into cakes about twice as large as a loaf of bread. These cakes were buried in the reheated pit between layers of fern leaves and baked for a day. They were now thoroughly cooked and would keep through the following winter. The cakes were wrapped in a grass called pàla'pàla and stored away. Slices were cut off as desired. The Quinault were extremely fond of camas and regarded it almost as a confection. The feeble and ailing regarded the freshly baked roots as very beneficial, and special trips to the "prairies" were often made to satisfy their whims.

Fern roots. Next to camas the roots of ferns were most important among vegetable foods. The main supply came from the ordinary "lady fern" (tsamxai'h) of the region. The roots were secured by means of a digging-stick of the same type used in digging camas. The roots might be dug at any season, but were considered best when dug in August. The roots were roasted in the coals for a few minutes, being continually turned during the process, then removed, placed on a large stone, and tapped with a stick to remove the rough scaly outer layers and the skin. The roots were eaten alone or served with dried salmon eggs. The roots of a small fern called ku'kutsa, which grows on logs, was gathered in late autumn. The roots were baked in the same manner as camas, though only for a half day. They were then bent and twisted to fracture and loosen the skin, which was then peeled off. These roots were usually eaten with whale oil.

Snake head. Both the plant and root of this plant were used. The plants grow everywhere where there is a goodly amount of moisture and a clay soil. The sprouts (a'qàmak) were gathered in April. Often they were consumed raw but a slight cooking in the flames made them more tender. The roots (ska'atos) have at intervals along the stem small bulbous growths about the size of walnuts. These are the parts sought after. They were consumed either raw or boiled and were considered very well-flavored. When boiled they were mashed and served with whale oil or seal oil.

The sprouts are called "Xwoni Xwoni's son." Once a skunk followed this son, broke wind on him, and he thereupon turned into a snake head. The water that comes out of the joints of the plant are his tears. Xwoni Xwoni's sister also became a snake head of a different sort, called tàto'ts. She buried herself in the ground when Skunk defiled her. The roots of this "sister" are eaten, the tops of the "son" used.

Skunk cabbage. This plant was but rarely eaten. Only the white part of the stalk which is just below the ground was used. A few minutes roasting on hot rocks sufficed to cook it. "Sauer kraut" (kwi'itsap'), which is a small, three-leaved, clover-like plant with a white flower, was also used. The Quinault did not have "fields" of clover which they kept clean of weeds as did some of the tribes of Puget Sound, but they gathered the roots of clover. These were baked in a pit like that used for camas, the roots being first wrapped in skunk cabbage or thimbleberry leaves.

Berries and fruits. A great many small fruits and berries grow in Quinault territory and most of them were used for food. But, as in the case of roots, none of these furnished a staple food but only served to break the monotony of a meat and fish diet.

Black huckleberries (nakà'ltcàn) were most abundant, and women and children could pick great quantities in a few days. The fruit was dried either in the sun or smoke-dried over a fire. It was then stored away for the winter. Sometimes it was partly mashed, pressed into cakes, and again dried. The cakes were then wrapped in leaves or bark. Red huckleberries (tao'lom) and blackberries (swha's) were treated in the same way as black huckleberries.

Salmonberries were usually eaten fresh, served with oil of the sockeye salmon. The new shoots of the plant (djanàts), which come up each spring, were gathered when about eight inches in height. Though often eaten raw, they were usually cooked in a pit. When the rocks in the pit were hot the fire was raked out, the sprouts placed over the stones and covered with leaves. After baking a half day, the sprouts were removed and served with fish oil.

Elderberries (sɬo'm) were gathered in July. A considerable quantity could be placed between large slabs of alder or hemlock bark and baked in a fire pit. When cooked, they were stored in containers of alder or hemlock bark which were lined with leaves. More leaves were laid over the berries and the container placed under water in a cold spring. When thus stored, the fruit would keep all winter without spoiling.

Salal berries (skwasa'utcàn) were prepared for winter use by smoke-drying. Cedar was split into thin, narrow strips and woven into an open checker weave, and this frame placed on an ordinary drying rack about four feet above the fire. The frame was now covered with fern leaves and the berries spread on top. Three or four baskets of berries were placed on one such frame. The drying process was kept up for three days. Then the berries were mashed, molded into round cakes six inches in diameter and these again dried. If the berries were wanted for late winter use, an alder dish large enough to hold five cakes was made and the half-dried berries were placed in this and mashed with a stone pestle. The fruit was now dried still more and stored away. When wanted for use, slices were cut from the cake, mixed with water and eaten with oil.

Crabapples were placed in a pit, covered with leaves and baked. Cranberries of both the "bush" and "swamp" varieties were treated in the same manner. Strawberries were eaten fresh. Young women used to pick a quantity, then invite a friend to eat with them. Gooseberries were baked, dried, and made into cakes like other berries.

It is said that the Quinault never ate the inner bark of the hemlock, though the northern tribes of the area used it extensively. Likewise the Quinault never ate sea plants, though they say that the Tillamook and other tribes of the Oregon coast ate kelp and certain other kinds of seaweed.

Wild currants were not eaten. No nuts or seeds of any consequence are found in Quinault territory and none were utilized for food. The kernels of pine cones were I think, not used, though I neglected to inquire on this point.

CLOTHING AND ADORNMENT

CLOTHING

The clothing of the Quinault was simple in type.. In summer the men often went about entirely naked; the women attired only in a grass or shredded bark skirt reaching to the knees. In winter both sexes adopted a blanket-like robe of skins. If the weather was rainy a rain hat and waterproof cape might be worn over the robe. This simplicity of dress is to be explained by custom and climate, and not by lack of knowledge of a more generous wardrobe, since the garments made included caps, hats, neckbands, capes, blankets, rough skirts, belts, apron-like kilts, leggings, and moccasins. But the majority of these were worn only to fit special occupations, types of weather, or the whim of the individual.

Hats worn by the Quinault differed very little, if at all, from those worn by neighboring tribes. Three or more forms were known (fig. 11). The style shown by figure 11c was usually woven of cedar bark in a checker weave, and served largely as a sunshade. Styles shown by figure 11a, b were rain-hats woven in a technique which resulted in an interlocked double layer. The material employed was split spruce roots, with decorative elements of bear or other grasses. Woven into the body of the hat at the crown a skull-cap shaped piece was made to fit the head to hold the hat snugly in place. The figure 11a type was seldom or never manufactured,

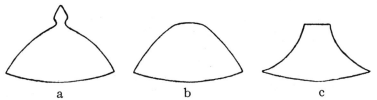

a　　　　　　　　b　　　　　　　　c

Fig. 11.   Hat styles. *a, b,* rain-hat type; *c,* sun-shade type.

but was sometimes obtained in trade from the tribes to the north. Nearly all hats were decorated in some fashion, the woven designs being chiefly those used in other basketry: birds, whales, dogs, wolves, etc. Hats lacking such woven-in decoration were painted with designs in black, white, or red. A leather thong tied under the chin served to keep the hat in place.

Men sometimes wore caps made of the entire skin of such small animals as coon, land otter, mink, etc. To the head section a sort of visor was attached. The tail of the animal was left on and allowed to hang down the back. Caps were also made of the skin of a loon.

Raincoats were made from the leaves of the cattail rush. The leaves overlapped and were sewn across at two-inch intervals with an eyed needle from the wing bone of a sea bird. The thread used was made from the stems of the same rush very finely split and twisted on the thigh in a two-strand cord, which was then doubled and re-twisted. When the sewing was completed a grooved instrument of yew wood was pressed along each thread to make it stand out (and probably incidentally to prevent leakage at the sewing). The garment reached to thighs or knees. The neck and bottom edges were usually lined with the skin of a surf duck (skale'x^w) or, more rarely, with fur. "Mattresses" were made in the same fashion, not woven.

At every season of the year both men and women usually wore a simple headband of bark (fig. 12d), skin, or fur to keep the hair in place. This was tied at the back. To such a headband or to the cap shamans usually attached bear or eagle claws, either in bunches or at intervals. These were attached point downward. But the two kinds of claws were never worn at the same time.

In very cold weather a fur neckpiece was sometimes worn, the skin of mink being preferred.

In winter men sometimes wore a rough hip-length shirt of tanned buck or elk skin with the hair removed. This was fashioned with seams down the sides. The shirt was open all the way down the front, the flaps being fastened with thongs. Along the seams of the sides and at the armholes the leather was fringed. The garment was sleeveless. Often no lower garment was worn, but a simple rectangle of leather might be worn as a kilt, reaching from the waist to mid-thigh. Neither garment was decorated, although a shaman might color the entire garment a black or red.

Leggings were only worn while a man was hunting in the mountains, and then only as a protection against the brush and cold. The only type of moccasin known was a crude type made of skin from the hock section of an elk. The hock formed the heel, the skin below, the foot of the moccasin. The toe was rounded and sewed. The upper was cut to varying heights, up to calf height. From the instep up the skin was split, trimmed, and a half-dozen holes punched in each side for lacing. Moccasins were only worn by hunters and only during the season when there was snow. They were worn with hair inside.

A blanket, or shawl-like robe, was worn a great deal by both men and women. The material was commonly of skins with the fur left on, but a cape woven of bark or grass might serve. In size these robes varied from a single wildcat skin tied about the shoulders to garments reaching to calf or ankle. Blankets were also woven from the yarns of dog wool—a special breed of dogs being kept for this purpose. Both warp and weft might be of this wool, or either of sinew. Rabbit skins were cut in strips, curled and twined with sinew in another type of blanket. Still another type of blanket was made by sewing together bird skins, those of the surf-duck being commonest.

Only chiefs affected blankets of sea-otter skins. Such a robe was made by sewing five or six skins together, the head ends of the skins forming the shoulders of the robe. One sea-otter blanket was valued at one good slave. Robes composed of sewn skins were also made of many other furs, such as bear, wildcat, mountain goat, cougar (panther), land-otter, beaver, seal, and marmot, the latter being a favorite. Usually such garments were held in place by the thongs tied at the neck and chest. In later years, probably about 1800 to 1850, an acceleration of trade between tribes and between whites and Indians resulted in buffalo skins being secured from the peoples of the lower Columbia river, who in turn secured them from the upper reaches of that stream. Buffalo robes were referred to as the skins of "sȧgwiʹlȧmic moos moos" ("Indian cattle"; sȧgwiʹlȧmic being the Quinault word for person or Indian, moos moos the Chinook jargon for cow). The rarity of such robes precluded any but chiefs wearing them.

While a man might go about entirely naked or with a robe over his shoulders, a woman must wear a skirt. The commonest form was a simple affair of shredded bark reaching from hips to knees. In appearance this was much like the grass skirt of Polynesia. The manufacture was simplicity itself: the bark of the red cedar was

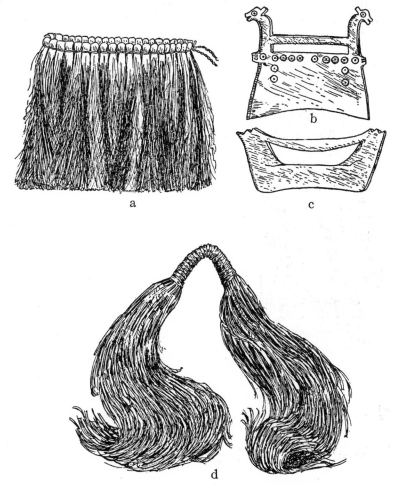

Fig. 12. Woman's skirt *(a)*, head band *(d)*, and bark shredders *(b, c)*.

shredded in 'the usual fashion (see Manufactures), and the segments attached by sewing or weaving them into a plaited belt which was tied at the back (fig. 12a). A variant of the type was made by taking strands peeled from the edges of cattail leaves, and twisting these into long two-strand cords. When enough had been made ready they were looped close together from hem to a belt of the same material, care being taken to get the end loops even. A skirt of this material was favored for rainy weather and for such wet tasks as clam-digging. It was not considered proper for a woman to remove her skirt in public, but when at work with other women or in her own house she might go about entirely naked.

Small girls usually wore dresses of the same type as were worn by older females.

During the rainy season both men and women wore rain-capes, which, with the rain-hats mentioned above, gave quite adequate protection. Two types were known. The simplest was woven of cedar bark, spruce root, cattail, or tule rush and was shaped like a cone, the smaller end having an opening large enough to admit the head. Those made of rush were sewn or crossed by twined elements at intervals, the long heavy stalks serving to conduct the water from top to bottom. The second form of rush cape was made as shown in figure 13. The pattern for a third form is shown in figure 14.

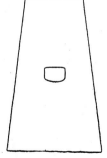

Fig. 13. Women's costume, showing one form of rain cape. (After Willoughby.)

Fig. 14. Pattern of one form of rain cape

BODY DECORATION

Face painting. Both men and women formerly painted the face and that section of the scalp exposed at the part of the hair. Red paint was obtained from a rust found in swamps, or from certain gravel banks. This was baked and mixed with bear oil. Powdered charcoal from alder or vine maple mixed with seal, whale, or fish oil formed a black paint. While it was more common for chiefs and shamans to paint themselves, there were no sex or social restrictions involved. Parts of the body other than the face seem never to have been painted. A variety of designs were known. An individual usually adopted the same design for each day, but there was no sense of ownership of motifs, either by families or persons. Warriors usually painted their faces black. Red was favored by non-warriors. Nearly everyone painted during dance festivals. The following common designs were mentioned:

ƙwaƙwa′xoɫ, "marks on face." Three vertical parallel stripes on either side of the face.

ƙlama′djos. A band (?) across the forehead.

ƙla′mɪnaɫ. A solid wide band from temple to chin to temple. This was used especially (only?) by shamans.

tako′oloƙȧ, "cheek paint." A spot of red on either cheek bone.

Tattooing. Both men and women tattooed the forearms, chest, and lower legs, but only men the face. A woman always performed the operation. In the old days a sharp bone was used to puncture the skin, and moistened charcoal of alder or dogwood rubbed into the incisions. When steel needles came in, the moistened charcoal or soot was rubbed into the attached thread, which was drawn through under the skin. Designs were made either by dots or lines. On the forearm simple lines, rows of dots, "dogs," "stars," and "mountains" were favorite motifs. Series of vertical lines on the calves were often used by women. Old Fisher and "Old Man" Shale were tattooed from temples to chin with the "dog" design. Men seldom tattooed their legs. Quinault women are said not to have employed vertical bars on the chin, though it was frequently seen on women of tribes from the Oregon coast (especially Tillamook) and of Puget Sound. It is said that only high class Tillamook women tattooed the chin. Queets and Quilleute men were much given to lines or patterns extending down the cheeks and around the chin.

Hairdressing. A variety of styles of wearing the hair were known. Men often wore their hair long and flowing, tied with a cord at the neck. Pope once saw a Quilleute chief who was very proud of his hair, which was so long that as he knelt in the canoe it more than reached the water. Or the hair might be doubled up into a club about six inches long, wrapped with cord or cedar bark, so that it stuck straight out at the back. This style was called kwa′xwȧlos or kwa′kuloɫ ("hair in bunch"). Women wore the hair in two clubs or braids which were wrapped. These might be worn in front of, or behind, the ears, and down the back of, or in front of, the shoulders. At the death of a mate or near relative the hair was cut at about neck length.

In summer men wore a headband of skin or twisted bark in lieu of hat or cap. In this were usually placed one or two feathers dyed red; less often feathers were placed all around the band. Shamans wore a headband of mink (saxwa'idjunuks), from which were suspended (usually) four bunches of deerhoof, eagle, or bear claws, which rattled as they walked.

To keep the hair line even, the fingers were dipped in ashes and the scattered hairs pulled out until an even line was secured. Certain persons knew of medicines which were good for the hair. Julia Cole paid Circus Jimmy $15 for the secret. She used the medicine on Katherine Cole's hair after an illness and it came in long and thick. It was applied to an infant's scalp when the child was a month old. It is said that baldness was unknown in the days before people wore the hats of the white man.

The hair was combed by means of a rude comb made of yew, hemlock, bone, horn, or whalebone. A girl kept the combings from her hair until quite a bunch had accumulated, then she tied it to a stone and threw it into the river. It was believed that this would make the hair grow more rapidly. A diatomaceous earth (stábuk) (or a clay?) was used for washing the hair and for washing fur robes as well.

After puberty both young and old of both sexes kept the eyebrows trimmed to a thin curved line. Men removed all traces of beard. The straggling hair of the head was also pulled out. The nails or fingers dipped in ashes might be employed, but it was more common to pluck with tweezers made of a split bone or a pair of mussel or clam shells. Eyelashes and the hair of the armpits and pubes were allowed to grow naturally. A minor ceremony attended the plucking of a pubescent girl's eyebrows. Thus, when Lena Underwood was about thirteen her parents paid Julia Cole's mother $50 to pluck the girl's eyebrows and apply a secret medicine which was supposed to prevent the hair from growing again. The old lady (a Makah) took dentalium shells and crushed them on a hard black rock from the beach. Then she secured a special kind of rock which had always been under water and boiled it until an "oil" came out. This was mixed with the powdered shell and rubbed on the girl's eyebrows. A pubescent girl would beat rocks together "until they sweat" (until a powder formed). Then she took shredded bark, rubbed it in the powder and applied it to her eyebrows to prevent their growing again. A Mrs. Whaler was famous for her beautiful eyebrows and accordingly nicknamed kamtsomá ("good eyebrows"). A youth or a man would ask a girl or woman to trim his eyebrows, while for females the operation was performed by a member of their own sex.

It is believed that males grew much scantier beards in the days before the coming of the whites. Bob Pope stated that his beard grew because a white man named John Wells rubbed something on his face to "make his beard grow like a white man's."

Toe-and fingernails were kept trimmed by filing them down with a bit of sandstone. They were never trimmed by cutting, for this would cut one's life short.

It is said that bad teeth were very rare in pre-European days. Care was taken to not bite things likely to break the teeth. The gum of spruce or fir was gathered, boiled until it was of the proper consistency, and chewed as a gum. I do not know whether this was for the good of the teeth or merely a pastime.

The rare black gum which exudes from hemlocks (called stca'máts) was used by girls as a perfume. Young chaps used to gather it in clam shells, mix it with tallow from the marrow of the lower legbone of the elk, and give it to girls of whom they were fond. The girl would re-melt it and put it away in a section of elk intestine. It was used daily and thought especially good for the eyebrows—sure to make them black and beautiful. It was sometimes rubbed on an infant's chest to cure a cold.

Elk tallow made of the marrow fat finely rendered was universally and daily used by girls as a sort of face cream. The lump was rubbed directly on the face and then the face was massaged with the fingers. A woman who performed this task each morning would have a light-colored, smooth skin until she became old. The tallow was kept in sections of the small intestine of the elk. A section reaching from the tip of the forefinger to the wrist was worth one to two fathoms of dentalium shells.

Elk tallow made from the bones of the lower leg was applied to the hair and scalp every morning by women who took pride in their neatness and good looks.

Jewelry. Both men and women wore a variety of types of necklaces, but I secured very little information on this point. Dentalium shells of sizes too small to serve as "money" were much used, as were abalone shell ornaments. After the coming of the fur traders the blue "Hudson's Bay" glass beads had a great vogue. It is said that when the first steel axe was traded to the Quinault its use was unknown, but a chief bought it and gave it to his daughter, who wore it as the central piece of a necklace.

Abalone shell ornaments were often worn in nose and ears. The ears were often pierced in several places along the rim, as well as at the lobe, and one to three ornaments worn in each perforation. A single ornament was suspended from the nose by means of a string. These were crescentic, oval, or round in outline. Those without pierced septums wore an ornament notched to fit over the septum. It is claimed that dentalium shells were not used as nose ornaments.

Labrets were not worn. It is said that no anklets were worn and that bracelets were not common. I failed to secure information as to whether nose or ears were pierced at any given time in life or whether any ceremony attended the operation. There were no restrictions on the wearing of ornaments for any of the social strata.

Dentalium and abalone (tsa'lelc) were secured in trade from the tribes to the north (Makah and Nootka).

During dance festivals the participants sprinkled the head with the down of duck, geese, eagle, or hawk, but it was not used on profane days. In later years cotton was sometimes used in place of down.

HOUSES

The Quinault were at the boundary of the gable-roofed house of the southern part of the Northwest coast. Only the Queets to the north had this type; beyond these the Quilleute and Makah had the shed-roof type of the Nootka and the tribes of Puget Sound. Houses varied from 30 to 60 feet in length and were usually 20 to 40 feet in width. The long dimension always was east and west. The door was usually in the west end, but might be in the north or south side (facing the river). In a village the houses usually were ranged in a row along the bank (see page 94).

The building of a house required the efforts of a number of men and usually the entire village came to the aid of the family or families wishing to build or re-build a house. Such services were not paid for, the helpers feeling that aid in their own endeavors would be rendered in return. The man building the house, however, fed those helping. First the cedar planks for roof and walls were split out (see Woodworking) and then the posts, beams, withes, etc. were prepared. For the planks large, straight, limb-free cedars were selected and felled with chisels and mauls. Planks two to three inches thick ("3 or 4 fingers") and as long as it was possible to make them were split from these. The posts were usually of cedar also and were commonly small trees left in the round, though actually extra heavy planks or slabs might be used. The single roof beam at the gable was a slender log.[23] All of these timbers were adzed to make them smooth, although the fine adze work of the tribes to the north was restricted to the gable beam and the crossbeams. When all the materials were ready the upright posts were set rather deep in the ground as:

    O   O   O   O

    O   O

    O   O   O   O

The number of posts along the sides between the corner posts varied from a single pair for a small house to four or six for a large house. The center end posts need not reach from ground to gable but might reach only from crossbeam to gable. The corner posts were larger than the others. Crossbeams were placed atop the posts at the ends and usually one or two across the central section. The tops of the posts were cut to receive these. The central beam or beams were finished especially well and were painted with various designs, usually representations of the guardian spirits of the owner(s) of the house. The posts at each crossbeam supporting the ridge pole were also carefully adzed and usually decorated in painted designs. The other posts were decorated less commonly. Poles or sections of split cedar were atop the crossbeams directly above the posts. To these and to the ridge pole were lashed the rafters.

The wall planks were placed vertically and were dug into the ground a foot or more, the depth depending on the length of the plank, for the tops of the wall planks were evened and set so that they would rest snugly against the lower roof plank. All wall planks, even those at the ends of the house, reached from ground to roof. Wall planks did not overlap, nor were they lashed or fastened in any way. Roof planks were laid horizontally and single planks usually extended the length of the house, though on large houses two lengths were necessary, the joint being covered with a plank placed vertically. Each plank overlapped the one below it about two inches. The planks were held in place by cedar withe lashings which passed around the rafter, across the upper edge of the lower plank and under the lower edge of the upper plank and fastened to a vine maple pole laid atop the planks paralleling the rafter. The overhang of the roof at the eaves was about two feet. The two planks at the peak overlapped and were fastened only at their lower edges.

---

[23]The ridge pole was raised by means of a "scissors" (*i.e.*, two poles crossed and lashed).

This was to allow them to be spread apart to admit light and allow the smoke to escape. No opening was left as a smokehole. Sticks of the proper length resting on the crossbeams and placed against the planks kept them in place when opened. The opening was usually closed when the occupants of the house retired for the night and was opened in the morning. The peak planks were usually in several sections so that a larger or smaller aperture could be opened. Cracks in the walls were chinked with moss or closed by adding strips or narrow planks.

Highly amusing to the Quinault is the following legendary incident:

Bluejay (the buffoon) built himself a house. When he came to the roof he started laying the planks at the peak. The result was that all the planks overlapped the wrong way. Soon afterward there came a violent rainstorm and the water poured in at every plank. Thereupon Bluejay seized his bow and shot arrows at every place there were leaks.

The door in the house was usually in the central plank of the west end. It was oval in shape, the bottom being usually a foot or two above the ground. In some cases the top of the door was rounded, the sides straight, and the door extended to the ground. The door itself was a plank cut to fit the opening snugly. (But some were simply oblong sections of plank large enough to cover the opening and were hung on the outside.) It was "hinged" or suspended at the top with strips or thongs of elk hide and usually swung outward. Doors were not carved or painted. At night a large plank was placed over the door on the inside and barred with a stout brace.

In front of the house a plank platform was constructed, with a plank seat built against the house. Here the old men of the village were wont to gather, especially on sunny days, to gossip, hear news, and discuss local affairs. Here a man went each morning to see what kind of a day it was going to be. And here men merely sat "to watch the earth" (námela'itctàn), as it is expressed. The platform was also a work area. Women were not forbidden the platform, but they seldom stayed there. Not even slaves were excluded.

The floor of the house was at the ground level, no excavation being made for the house beyond leveling and clearing away the débris of moss and rotting wood which accumulates in this rainy region. The floor was earth sprinkled over with sand, which was renewed now and then.[24]

A bench or platform at a height of about four feet extended around the four sides of the house. This was about four feet wide, usually made of two wide planks. This was the sleeping platform, "wide enough for a couple to sleep side by side." In front of it, two feet or less above the floor, was a bench or platform which served chiefly as a seat, though in cold weather people might sleep on this so as to be near the fire. The sitting posture, even on the bench, was with legs doubled under, not hanging over in our "chair posture." A wide shelf was suspended three feet or so below the eaves. On this dried meat and fish and other food which tended to mold were stored away, chiefly in baskets. The space under the platforms was also utilized as storage space (fig. 15).

Ordinarily two to four families occupied the same house. Each family had its fire so that the fires were built near each end, or near the corners if there were more

---

[24]The Lower Chehalis and Clatsop were said to have built, now and then, rectangular, plank-lined, underground houses roofed over with a gabled plank roof.

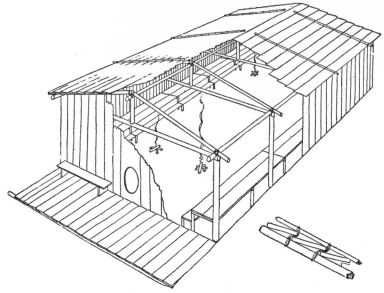

Fig. 15. Plan of house.

than two couples. In cases of polygyny each wife had her own fire. The head or chief wife (na'tcil) had her fire at the northeast corner. There was no special placing of secondary wives. In the morning the chief ate his meal with the head (first) wife, in the evening with the second.[25]

The head (the eldest, the "owner") of the house occupied the rear wall of the house. Slaves slept anywhere except in the spaces allotted to others. Above each fire a drying rack (with one or more tiers) was suspended. Here were dried fish, meat, and wet clothing.

In one corner of the house a section like a tiny room was planked off on the platform. In this stayed pubescent and menstruating girls.

It was said the entire house was sometimes lined with tule or cattail mats for warmth. Some houses were divided into two rooms by means of a plank partition.

Wood, chiefly dry spruce and fir limbs, was collected during the summer and stored under the platform. This dry wood was burned mixed with the wet wood gathered in winter. Kindling was the foregoing and pitch wood.

Now and then a lean-to three fathoms or so square was built against one side of the house. Its roof planks ran vertically. It was without wall planks. It served as a place to store wood and as a work place during rainy weather.

When people were going to be away from home for several days or more they "locked" the house by barring the inner door and going out through the roof.[26]

[25]I secured the following names for parts of the house: na'me'djȧk, "on the end" (the northeast corner); xwȧttso'sȧk, "crossways" (the southeast corner); pene'edjȧk, "upper end" (the east end); aḑwetsi'idjak, "lower end" (the west [door] end); me'txȧlaxʷ, "middle" (the middle of the north side); ȧt̓alne'edjȧk, "back end" (the middle of the south side); pote'edjȧk, the platform at the east end where the head of the house stays.

[26]Houses were never burned at the death of the owner but were often torn down and rebuilt in a different spot.

OTHER TYPES OF HOUSES

The very poor, ne'er-do-wells, and those who did not expect to remain long in the village sometimes built houses of bark. The framework was like that for the ordinary plank house but the walls and roof were of slabs of cedar bark. The bark of cottonwood and hemlock might also be used, though rarely.

When camping on the beach, especially during the summer season of clam-gathering, mat-covered lodges were used. A light frame of poles, with a gable roof (?) was set up and the mats lashed to this.

While hunting in the mountains during the summer a variety of shelters were constructed. A rectangular house of bark laid on a framework of poles was one form. A conical bark lodge was also known. A brush shelter was made by placing four forked poles in the ground and laying poles in the forks. Other poles were laid across these. Brush (hemlock, vine maple boughs, etc.) was laid across the top and leaned against the sides. A wedge-shaped shelter was made by lashing together two pairs of poles and placing another pole across these as a ridge pole. Brush was leaned against this frame on two sides and one end. A lean-to of bark was also known. As often as not no shelter was erected, camp being made under the friendly protection of a large tree whose boughs hung low, offering both shade and protection from the rain.

SWEAT HOUSES

It was said that on the Columbia river each village had its sweat lodge. North of the Columbia the sweat lodge was known but was not common. One such was at a village on Chenoise creek (Lower Chehalis). Among the Quinault only the village of la'lcił boasted such a lodge. It was a rectangular pit about five feet wide, seven feet long, and six feet deep. The roof consisted of planks laid across the pit and covered with earth. The floor was covered with sand. The door was an opening in the roof planks at the river end of the lodge, covered over with mats. Stones were heated outside, then placed at one end of the lodge. Water in which some herbs had been placed was sprinkled on the stones to form steam. The bathers rubbed themselves with the leaves of a fern, then blew on those parts of the body which were afflicted with pain. "The breath went clear to the bone." Two to five men usually sweated at the same time and it was something of a game to see who could stand the most heat. When they had sweated enough they emerged and plunged into the river. Men did not sweat-bathe oftener than once in two weeks. The sweat lodge was cared for by a man who knew the proper medicine to use. Women used the lodge less frequently than men.

HOUSEHOLD MISCELLANY

Bedding consisted of a "mattress" of several layers of rush mats and blankets of marmot, wildcat, wolf, or other skins sewed together. A person lay directly on the mats and covered himself with blankets laid fur down. A rolled-up mat or a bundle of feathers served for a pillow.

The fire-fan (po'kstaktán) was made of the tail or wing of an eagle, the feathers being spread and interlaced with cord. Eagle wings served as brushes and small brooms. A broom was also made by tying a bunch of boughs together at the butt ends.

Fire tongs were made by splitting a stick and tying the pieces at one end. A wedge inserted near the lashing kept the tongs open. A similar tongs was employed for handling the stones used in stone boiling.

Sand was sprinkled around the fireplace in a fairly deep layer, some new sand being added each day. The sand was completely changed about once a month.

Some decorated the walls of the house here and there by means of a few horizontal bands of red and black.

MANUFACTURES

Although Quinault material culture is definitely inferior, both aesthetically and practically, to that of the tribes to the north the objects manufactured were more numerous and of better quality than those made by more southerly tribes of the area. Many of their handicrafts have been sketched in other sections of this study. I will describe here only those features not touched upon elsewhere. The main activities requiring skill, patience, and the expenditure of a vast amount of real labor were the building of canoes and houses. With nothing beyond a few bone and stone tools they built large, fairly comfortable carpentered houses of planks and hewed large seaworthy canoes from massive logs.

Large trees from which canoes or planks were to be made were carefully selected on the basis of straight trunk, absence of limbs and knots, and straightness of grain. Since many of the large cedars are hollow, the selected tree was tested for soundness by chiseling a hole some distance in. The cutting was done with maul, chisel, and wedge. A platform several feet high was built around the tree to enable the workmen to cut above the taper of the roots. Cuts were made entirely around the tree in two rings a foot or more apart and when these were an inch or so deep the intervening wood was split out and the operation repeated. The lower cut was carried in horizontally, while the upper one slanted downward. The direction of fall was regulated by a straight face at one part of the cut.

For a canoe, the desired length of log was cut or burned to the proper length and then split down the center from the top end. For planks a cut about three inches deep was made and wedges driven in. As the split opened other wedges were driven in along the sides and "prys" or bars of wood several feet long and flattened at one end were used as levers. Planks were usually four fingers thick. There were men who were specially adept at the felling and splitting of trees. Their services were usually secured when such work was to be done.

CANOES

Most of the canoes used by the Quinault at the present time are of the "shovel-nose" type, though a few with sharp bow and stern are still used. All my informants agreed that in the "old days" (say before 1850) no "shovel-nose" canoes were used, though the Chehalis, the tribes of Puget Sound and of the Lower Columbia used them and the Quinault knew of them. It seems likely that the introduction of gill net fishing on the Quinault reservation caused the adoption of the foreign type, for the handling of clumsy gear is much easier from the heavy, steady shovel-nose than from the easily-overturned canoes of earlier days. When the Quinault reservation was formed members of tribes from all over western Washington moved there and this probably stimulated the introduction of the shovel-nose type. In fact, the Quinault claim that the shovel-nose canoe was introduced by Humptulips who came to reside on the Quinault reservation (see fig. 16).

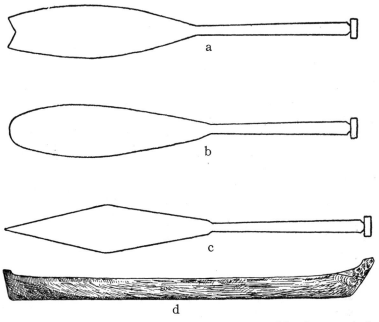

Fig. 16. Types of paddles, and a river canoe. *a*, type used in river travel; *b*, ordinary type; *c*, ocean type.

My informants differ as to the number of types of canoes used in pre-European times. Some claim that "ocean" and "river" were the only types used; others give as many as five: (1) ocean or whaling; (2) sealing or small ocean; (3) river; (4) small river or ducking canoe; and (5) sea otter type. To this elaborate series may be added a "racing canoe," which seems to have been a slightly modified sea otter canoe. Those who classify the canoes under two categories say the sealing canoe was only a small ocean canoe and the ducking canoe a small river canoe. Actually all canoes were built on a single basic pattern with modifications in size and slight changes in pattern to suit the purposes for which they were intended.

Thus an ocean canoe was of a size to accommodate the eight men and the large amount of gear essential to whale hunting. Its bow was of a size and form which would cleave the high seas of the open ocean and its sides sufficiently high to exclude most of the side slop of tempestuous waters. In sealing fewer men and lighter gear were needed and a smaller canoe of the same pattern served well enough. River canoes were stout and sturdy, with thick bottoms which would not soon wear through or split when being poled or dragged over gravelly beds. In hunting ducks or sea otter only one or two men were in the canoe and speed was more to be desired than seaworthiness or strength.

All these types of canoes were built after the general plan of the "southern" or "Nootka" pattern. The chief differences from the "northern" or "Haida" canoe is a straight (vertical) instead of a projecting stern, flaring but straight sides and a flat bottom instead of a generally half-round cross section. The differences between the two types is illustrated by Waterman.[27]

Although almost all adult male members of the Quinault were, and still are, capable of fashioning canoes, certain men were experts in this line and would be sought after to build for their neighbors and relatives. In the old days a man might be given food products or clothing in payment. In recent times canoes are often bought outright for cash.

An ocean canoe (lo′ḵłeł) was usually six or seven fathoms (35-42 feet) long and as wide as a man's reach minus the distance from the fingertips to the elbow. Five fathoms was the average length of a sealing canoe (alo′kȧ, "canoe"). Its width was as great as that of the ocean canoe. A river canoe (sȧna′xwił) was about three fathoms long, though some were made a half-fathom longer or shorter. A small canoe of this type, but only as wide as the length of the arm, served as a ducking canoe and was called alo′kȧ. The shovel-nose (sḵe′ih) is usually about three fathoms in length. I do not know whether the racing or sea otter canoes had separate designations. They were probably made about the same length as the river canoes but were narrower and more sharply pointed than river canoes.

All these types were made by the Quinault themselves, but the greater part of the large ocean canoes and many of the sealing canoes were secured from the tribes to the north. Both Quilleute and Makah manufactured them to some extent but the Nootka were the acknowledged masters of the art. Many Nootka ocean canoes were traded to the Makah who traded them to the Quilleute and they in turn to the Quinault. The Quinault traded them to the tribes of the Columbia and of the Oregon coast at least as far south as the Tillamook. Furs, dried clams, salmon, dentalium shells, and slaves might serve as media of exchange. Among the Quinault a man of the village of oe′ni·ł (?) named gwi′te, who was the son of a Lummi slave named tsa′mstap, was the most famous maker of canoes.

Manufacture of a canoe.   Regardless of size, all canoes were constructed in substantially the same way. Naturally a man would know the location of a number of trees which might be suitable for the size of canoe wanted. If a log of the proper sort could be found on the river banks or the ocean beach this might be used instead of a tree as it saved the bother of felling a tree. To test whether a tree was solid throughout a small hole was chiseled in the trunk to a considerable depth. The tree might be felled either by burning and chiseling or by chiseling and splitting (see page 66). When felled the top was burned off to form a log of the desired length. Wedges were inserted in the log at its upper (top) end and the log split down its center.

---

[27]1920, p. 11, fig. 2.

All canoes, large and small, were formed from the half of a log so that a considerably larger log was needed for an ocean canoe than for one of the smaller types. Obviously a single log sufficed for the hulls of two canoes. Bow and stern pieces were fashioned separately and attached later. The butt end of the log was always used for the bow of the canoe for the reason that the wood of that portion has a higher specific gravity. When only one man is in the canoe it manages much more easily if the bow is relatively heavy. The canoe swings less easily with each stroke of the paddle than if the bow is light and rises out of the water.

After the log had been split fires were built at intervals or continuously along the split surface. These were carefully watched so that they did not harm the outer margins—the parts which formed the gunwales and sides of the canoe. Fires were of little service near the bow and stern where the canoe was narrow, as the danger of burning the shell was great. After the fire had burned for a time it was put out and the charred wood removed with an adze. A second method of removing the wood from the inside of the canoe was to cut notches across the inside width of the canoe at half-fathom intervals. These were cut several inches deep, the wood split out, then a new series cut. As the bottom of the canoe was approached the notches were cut closer and closer together and more care used in the splitting.

One informant claimed that the outside of the canoe was shaped first, another that the wood was removed from the inside before the outside was formed. Judging by the one or two canoes I saw in the process of manufacture I assume that both outside and inside were fashioned more or less simultaneously. As the work progressed the workman frequently sighted down the center line of the canoe to make certain that both sides were assuming the same relative forms. The sides and bottom were left relatively thick and attention was concentrated on the shape of the craft. When the shaping of the canoe had been accomplished to the satisfaction of the workman he bored a series of small holes here and there to test the thickness of the wood. Before this the thickness of the shell was tested by "feeling" with one hand on the outside, the other on the inside of the hull. The holes were left open until the canoe was finished, for it was very important that the two sides be of even thickness so that the boat maintain an even keel.

With the holes as a guide the workman now carefully adzed the entire hull to its final form. For an ocean or river canoe the sides were left two fingers, the bottom three fingers, thick. The heavier bottom gave the boat steadiness. For the lighter "ducking" canoes a thinner hull was favored. Present-day shovel-nose canoes are made somewhat heavier.

Next the bow and stern pieces were shaped and fitted in place. Holes were bored in these and in the hull of the boat and bow and stern pieces securely lashed by sewing with strong cords of spruce root or cedar limb withes.[28] The gunwales were trimmed down and evened to give the boat a neat appearance. The holes which were bored to gauge the thickness were then plugged and the entire surface of the boat smoothed down a bit by rubbing it with the skin of the dogfish. The boat was now partly filled with water and hot stones put in until the hot water and steam penetrated the wood and made it pliable. In the meantime thwarts were pre-

---

[28]Shovel-nose canoes were not fitted with bow and stern pieces.

pared which were somewhat longer than the original width of the boat. The hull was now spread to accommodate the thwarts, which were lashed or pegged in place. The water and stones were then removed and the craft was ready for the water.

In the case of the larger canoes it was usual to build up the depth of the boat somewhat by adding separate gunwales, usually four to eight inches in height. This was to compensate somewhat for the loss of depth entailed in the spreading of the canoe. These were held in place, holes drilled through them and into the hull and wooden pegs driven in to secure them. The gunwales of some of the smaller canoes were sometimes built up slightly. A river canoe was built as deep as three times the distance a man can reach by spreading thumb and middle finger.

In modern times steel tools have made the use of fire unnecessary in canoe construction. Modern axes, chisels, adzes, and augers make the building of a canoe a much simpler task than in the old days. The flat-bottomed row boat has displaced the dugout canoe to a certain extent, but for trips beyond the comparatively quiet waters of the river's mouth the canoe is still preferred.

As in other crafts there was a certain amount of individual variability in the procedure of canoe building. Some men, for example, drilled a line of holes along the center line of the canoe almost at the start of the hollowing-out process. Measurements from this line served as an aid in keeping the sides of like form and dimension. Some slightly charred the boat before the launching and at intervals thereafter as a means of preventing the wood from decaying. Even in pre-European times paints were sometimes used on canoes, red on the inside and black on the outside being the favored colors. These paints were made by mixing soot or red ochre with animal oils.

Care and repair of canoes. The red cedar of which all canoes were made is a very durable wood but it splits easily. Rough usage in the rapids and the effects of the sun frequently caused the canoes to crack. Now that canoes are fairly easy to manufacture they are frequently allowed to remain in the water when not in use, but in the old days it was usual to drag them out of the water if they were not likely to be used for a day or two. They were commonly covered with mats or skins to protect them from the sun's rays. If the canoe was not likely to be needed for a longer time it was hauled high on the bank of the river and turned bottom-up. Cedar is very water-resistant but at bow and stern the end grain is exposed to the water and in time these parts became rotten. Fairly large sections were then cut out and new pieces fitted in their place. If a shiftless man had a canoe with part of one end broken out he might weight the other end so as to cause the damaged end to stand high in the water, and go on for years using the canoe.

With time the grinding of the canoe on the bottom and the action of the water caused the outside of the canoe to assume a frayed or "feathered" appearance. The canoe was then taken out of the water, thoroughly dried, and a thin layer of the outer wood removed by careful adzing and polishing. With reasonably good care a canoe would last as long as ten years or more.

Cracks and seams were repaired by drilling pairs of holes along the split. Through these spruce root or cedar limb withes were passed and tied tightly. I am not sure whether the sewing at each pair of holes formed a unit or if the sewing was of a spiral nature. If the seam did not close by tightening the sewing, wedges were driven under the "stitches" and allowed to remain. In any case the seams were made watertight by smearing with pitch.

Paddles. The Quinault had three, possibly four, types of paddles (fig. 16a-c). The commonest form was, like most others of the Northwest coast, slender in outline, the handle being comparatively short and the blade long in relation to the whole. The short bar which formed the handle was usually of a separate piece. The tip was gently rounded. This form was called xwa'pi (fig. 16b).

For use with ocean canoes a slightly longer paddle with a long tapering point was the vogue (fig. 16c). It was called kaiále'x xwa'pi (northern paddle) and according to tradition was not as ancient a form as the type first mentioned. It seems fairly certain that the ocean canoe is an element derived from the tribes to the north and it is logical to assume that the special form of paddle used with it is likewise a northern element.

The third form of paddle was like the two preceding except that the blade was wider at the lower end and terminated in a curious double tip (fig. 16a). Traditionally this was the form of paddle used with the "shovel-nose" canoe and came into use when that form of canoe was introduced by the Humptulips and other Lower Chehalis or Chinook tribes which moved to the Quinault reservation during the latter part of the nineteenth century. Disregarding tradition, I am fairly certain that the crescent-tipped paddle is linked with the crude shovel-nose canoe, just as the sharp-tipped paddle is associated with the ocean canoe and was never used with inland types of craft. It is commonly said that this crescent-tipped paddle was specially serviceable while going up-river, the tip, like the split pole of the Klamath, serving as an efficient grab in the mud. It is also said that the concave tip gave an advantage by spreading over roots, stones, logs, and so on. A pointed paddle is hard to fix on a slippery concave surface and is more likely to slip as the forward thrust is given than is a concave-pointed paddle which gives a two-point bearing.

Paddles were made of yew, ash, or soft maple. The first was considered the best for all around use but the last had the advantage of being lighter in weight. A man would make a paddle about the length which he could measure by spreading his arms—*i.e.*, a fathom. This closely conforms to the rule in vogue among the Eastern Woodland peoples, where, I believe, a paddle was made one to two inches longer than a man's height. A paddle for use in the stern was made slightly broader and longer than the paddle used by the bow man.

One very reliable informant claimed that a fourth type of paddle was known—the double-ended paddle (tsali'n xwa·pi, "two or double paddle"). His testimony was borne out by one other, but very unreliable, informant. Three informants claimed that this type was unknown among the Quinault and stated that they had never heard of such a form. However my original reliable informant volunteered the information and elaborated it by stating that the double-ended paddle was used only with small canoes which were low, usually with the ducking canoe. He added that he had not seen one in about 50 years and that it was used mostly by young fellows in their horseplay. My informant's grandfather told him the Quinault had always had paddles like that. I would be inclined to credit them with this type of paddle except for one thing: It is well known that from about 1820 on it was not unusual for trading ships to take Indians from Northwest coast tribes along as seal hunters in Alaskan waters. Here many of these Indians must have seen Eskimo and Aleut using the double-bladed paddle in the kayak. A Quinault might have returned home and tried the new form of paddle as an experiment or to show his sophistication. On the whole it seems safest to seriously question the claim of the sincere old man who said that his people made use of the double paddle.

Canoe poles. Ascending the rapid reaches of the river, in the more turbulent rapids and sometimes along the shallow margins of the ocean and bays the pole supplanted the paddle as a means of propulsion. Indeed, in the swifter rapids it would be impossible to force the canoe against the stream by means of the paddle. Two men poling the canoe might pole on the same or opposite sides, it mattered little. The same end of the pole was always used as the handle, *i e.*, the ends of the pole were not reversed with each stroke.[29] Poles were made of young hemlock and were usually 10 to 14 feet in length. They were carefully seasoned, the butt tapered down, and the tips hardened by charring them somewhat.

Sails. There is a reasonable doubt as to whether sails were known to the people of the Northwest coast in pre-European times. The fact that many of the tribes, including the Quinault, made make-shift sails of thin boards sewed together inclines me to the belief that the sail is aboriginal in the area. My Quinault data add nothing new to the problem. They employed cedar mats most commonly but also knew the wooden sail. The sail was carried from a short mast which was lashed to a thwart. I believe that upper and lower crosspieces were employed, at least with the mat sail. No attempt to tack or to sail with a side wind was made and the sail was always carried at right angles to the boat. If the wind were not blowing from the stern the sail was taken down.

Bailers and other equipment. The Quinault had only a single type of bailer (kle′ktcotȧm) for canoes (fig. 17). Usually they were made of alder or of soft maple. In size they varied from 10 to 14 inches. No bailers were made of bark.

Fig. 17. Bailer.

Since most canoes commonly had some water in the bottom, either from rains or minor leaks, it was customary to cover a part of the bottom with brush laid several inches deep. This kept the cargo dry. Passengers who were not paddling, usually old people and children, sat on this brush to avoid getting wet.

On ocean voyages, when there was a danger of rough weather, inflated seal skins were taken along to tie along the sides in case the canoe began to ship water. These served to lift the canoe sufficiently to lessen the danger.

[29]I believe the reversing method is commonest in the Eastern Woodlands.

Navigating the canoe. Like all peoples of the Northwest coast the Quinault were expert canoemen. It is rather difficult to give a description of the fine points essential to management of a canoe so I confine myself to a few specific remarks. Near the finish of the stroke the stern paddler altered the direction of his stroke and the plane of the paddle. If he desired to turn the canoe about, the side of the canoe might be used as the fulcrum, the paddle like a lever. On ocean voyages, when the sea was running high, care was taken not to cross the larger waves directly at right angles. A slightly diagonal course kept most of the keel in the water and eliminated the danger of breaking the canoe.

It was customary to always land ocean canoes stern foremost. This had a practical significance in surf landings, for the high bow, facing outward, prevented high waves from swamping the boat during the time of waiting for the proper wave. Among a number of tribes of the area this bowpiece is called "head" and the two tips "ears."

	Bowpiece	*Tips*
Quinault	stȧ′skss (head or nose)	k̇welan (ears)
Quilleute	disosit (nose)	ollȧxa·t (ears)
Makah	kwȧqu′b (sits at the bow)	ihi′qaȧł (ears)

It is interesting to note that the Yurok of California call the curious yoke which adorns the bow of the better canoes "ears"—a point which rather conclusively proves its historical kinship with the bowpiece of the north in spite of lack of resemblance in form or function.

The tribes from Kwakiutl to Tlingit use a rather different type of canoe from the tribes to the south but still retain the practice of landing their canoes stern foremost. Since this practice is quite unnecessary with the high projecting stern of the northern canoe, it implies that the specialized stern of the north is a rather recent innovation.[30]

RAFTS

Rafts were seldom or never used on Quinault river, but were useful for crossing rivers when making overland journeys. Thus a raft was always kept on Raft river (hence the name) at the point where the trail to Queets crosses. Rafts were usually made of two or three logs lashed together with cedar withes. The craft was made of logs of a size and length so that it would support two men.

A family moving their house from one place to another on the lake or lower reaches of the river would place the planks across two canoes, thus forming a sort of raft-platform, on top of which other things might be loaded. I am not certain whether sea trips would be thus ventured even in the calmest weather.

BOWS

Bows (k̇u′łȧk) were of the usual type of the Northwest coast—short and wide with recurved ends and a thickened, narrowed grip. The root of a young white (yellow?) cedar made the best bow, but yew and vine maple were also employed. It is said that only cedar bows would serve wi.hout sinew backing and even these

---

[30]Cf. Olson, *Adze, Canoe and House Types*, p. 22.

were usually backed to add strength and spring. It was difficult to find a piece of yew sufficiently straight and free from knots to yield a bow, as the tree runs to twisted and knotty forms. Yew bows were so fashioned that the white layer of wood next the bark formed the back of the bow.

Wood of any of the three kinds mentioned was carefully seasoned before the shaping, and then was laboriously fashioned by means of shell knives or beaver teeth, ground down with sandstone, and polished with the skin of a dogfish. The commonest length was from the tips of the fingers to the middle of the chest. At its widest part it was about three fingers wide. The tips were steamed or soaked in hot water for about 10 minutes and the ends were bent toward the back at a point about four finger-widths from the tips. Hot rocks were next applied at the inside of the curves and the wood slightly browned to prevent a return to the original form. At this juncture the bow was further seasoned by burying it in sand and building a fire above. This baking process was kept up for one to two hours. The bow was now ready for its backing of elk sinew. A glue made by boiling raw skins of seal, sea lion or elk or some part of a sturgeon (the head?) served as the adhesive. The sinew was laid on, glued, then another layer applied, and so on, until it formed a layer one-sixteenth to one-eighth inch thick.

The bow string was usually of sea lion gut, dried and twisted, more rarely of elk sinew. At one end of the bow it was wrapped several times around the notch and made fast with a series of half-hitches or some other knot. The other end of the string was formed into a loop large enough to slip along the bow and tied in a non-slipping knot. A man who took pride in his possessions might decorate each end of his bow with a woodpecker scalp. Painted decorations on the front of the bow were a rarity (fig. 18).

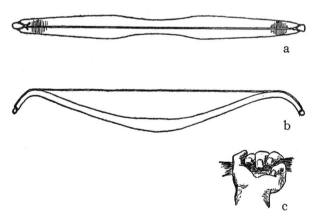

Fig. 18. Bow.

ARROWS

The Quinault used the usual type of Northwest coast arrow with bone instead of flint points (fig. 19). The bone points varied in length from four to six or eight inches. Arrows with foreshafts were not known. The proper length for an arrow (ḳuta'iåks) was the measure from the armpit to the tip of the thumb or to the tip of the middle finger. For the shaft either cedar or the wood of a small bush (called ko'xosimal) which bears white berries was employed. The stems of the latter are

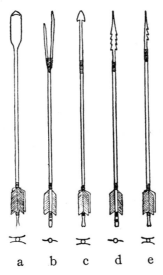

Fig. 19.   Types of arrows.

very straight and when seasoned are tough and springy. Shafts were straightened by burning them slightly in the fire at the proper places, or by steaming and straightening. The method of feathering was rather crude: In one type the feather was not split along its rib but tied on with the rib lying along the shaft. Two such feathers were used, one on either side of the shaft (fig. 19a, c, e). For ordinary radial feathering the feather was split along the rib and the two halves of the same feather used on an arrow (fig. 19b, d). The feathers were the length of the measure of four fingers width. The ends were secured with a lashing of sinew or cherry bark. Eagle feathers were preferred but those of the "shag" were also used. It is said that straight feathering was the usual form, that spiral feathering caused an arrow to wobble in its flight. The arrow was notched for the bow-string, but not deeply. Between feathering and notch the arrow was flattened to give a better grip. The section from the notch to the feathering was wrapped to strengthen the shaft and to give a friction grip.

Types of arrows.   Three types of arrowpoints were used for ordinary hunting, all of them of bone. One was an awl-like point notched along one side (fig. 19e), another a similar form notched or serrated on both sides (fig. 19d), the third a conventional arrowhead shape (fig. 19c). The "tang" of all types was elongated so that it was in reality a sort of foreshaft. The end to be inserted into the shaft was flattened in a long taper and inserted into the split shaft and lashed with sinew. The points might be made from the bones of whale or bear or the horn of elk.[31]

For such small game as rabbits, ducks, and other birds a double-pointed arrow with wood points was sometimes used (fig. 19b). In form this resembled a salmon spear, the two spreading points being of different lengths. These points were of wild cherry or salmonberry, hardened at the tips by burning. This type was referred to either as kuta'iáks, or a word meaning "burned points," or tsamo'ih ("double" or "two points"). One point was about an inch longer than the other and the two points diverged to an inch or more apart. A blunt-pointed arrow (áxwep) (fig. 19a) was sometimes employed for the hunting of small birds. It was also made for small boys because "they could not hurt anyone with it." The whistling arrow and the harpoon arrow were unknown. Figures 18 and 19 show the bow, the various types of arrows, and the method of holding the bow.

Arrow release. In shooting, the bow was usually held in a horizontal position or nearly so, though in the thick woods a man shot in any convenient way, sometimes holding the bow vertically. The bow was grasped with the thumb and little finger of the left hand on the front of the bow, the three remaining fingers clasping the back (fig. 18c). Sometimes even the third finger was held on the front of the bow. The arrow was grasped between the thumb and the second joint of the index finger and the "pull" was directly on the arrow, not on the string (the "primary" type of release). The marksman "aimed," *i.e.*, released the arrow, from just in front of, or a little below the eyes. The arrow passed between thumb and forefinger, or between thumb and middle finger and over the forefinger of the hand that held the bow. Thus the arrow passed above the bow if it was held horizontally, on the right side if it was held vertically.

To nock the bow the end with the permanent tie was placed in the instep of the left foot, grasped and sprung at the center with the left hand and sprung at the upper end with the right hand, the thumb and forefinger being employed to slip the loop of the string on or off. Another method was to place one end of the bow below the right knee, grasp the center with the right hand and pull while the thumb of the left hand slipped the string on or off.

QUIVERS

Quivers were made of the skins of wolves or wildcats. A single skin made a quiver. The skins were removed in the style known among trappers as "cased," *i.e.*, the only cut was made from hock joint to hock joint and the skin was pulled over the body and head. The holes at the eyes and mouth were sewed and the head part used as the bottom of the quiver. The hair side formed the inside. A leather strap for carrying was all that was added. The quiver was carried under the left arm with the strap over the right shoulder. The skin might be more or less tanned by rubbing brains into it and working the skin to soften it. Bow and quiver and a basketry kitbag were the essential elements of a hunter's equipment. In recent times, after the introduction of firearms, the quiver was discarded, powder and caps were carried in receptacles in the kitbag, and a steel knife was carried at the belt.

---

[31]One informant claimed that points were sometimes made of a stone called salo'h (jasper ?) which "chipped like ice." The shaping was roughly done by flaking and finished by grinding on sandstone.

FIRE MAKING

The fire drill (dji'tstcup', "twirl fire") was a simple shaft made from the root of the alder (małåp k̓c'łap). The hearth was of the same material with the usual series of pits and grooves. Both pieces were carefully selected for texture and dryness. Underneath the hearth finely shredded powder-dry cedar bark (k̓wi'lol) was placed which quickly took fire from the spark born in the twirl-dust. Ordinarily fire was produced by twirling the drill between the palms but the bow drill was also known. In this method the bowstring was given a single turn about the drill, which was pressed down by means of a block with a depression for the shaft. When the tinder had taken fire the glow was nursed into a flame by blowing on it and adding bits of fuel. One informant stated that iron pyrite and flint were used for striking fire. When safely started the fire-fan was employed. This was simply the wing or tail of an eagle or other large bird. The tail feathers were spread fanwise by being twined or laced apart.

During the rainy months of winter it was difficult to keep drill, hearth, and tinder dry enough to yield fire. The "fire carrier" was an ingenious device which made it unnecessary to make new fire while journeying. This was made of finely shredded cedar bark tightly braided. Once started burning this would burn like a piece of punk. A braid two fathoms long would last a long day's journey, sunrise to sundown. It was carried with the burning end held in a split stick projecting from the pack. Women carried fire inside a pair of clam shells with a piece of dried fern root as punk.

For traveling on dark nights torches were made of long pieces of pitchwood (kwaåle'ł) often found in the Douglas fir. A piece an inch in diameter would be split three or four times to form the torch. Such a torch would not blow out except in a very high wind.

Fire tongs for picking up coals, brands, and cooking stones were made by splitting a one-inch stick. At one end they were bound together with bark strands and a wedge inserted to spread the tips.

SLING AND STONE THROWER

The sling (łampł) was known, but chiefly as a toy. It consisted of a wide thong or a strip of cedar or willow bark. A curious affair, called by the same term, was the splitstick stone thrower (fig. 20). A curved stick some 18 inches long was split for about eight inches and the inner sides whittled away to form a slot. It was then lashed at either end of the split. Flat pebbles or small stones were wedged into the slot (fig. 20a) and thrown with an overhand motion much like that used with the atlatl. The atlatl was unknown.

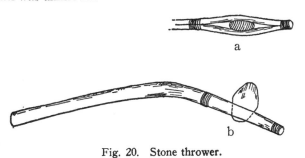

a

b

Fig. 20. Stone thrower.

The chief tools for woodworking were hammer, chisel, wedge, and adze. The hammer (fig. 21) was of tough stone of pestle form, the side being the striking surface. A large maul of stone (without wood handle) (fig. 22) delivering blows from the lateral surface was used in driving stakes, *e.g.*, for the salmon weir. These and other stone implements were shaped, for the most part, by the pecking process and finished by grinding on sandstone. There was almost no flaking of flint, quartzite, or jasper, though the process was known. Flakes and a few rudely chipped points have been found in the midden at the site of kwi′naiɫ.

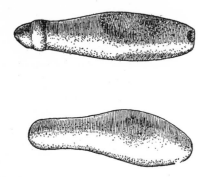

Fig. 21. Hammers of stone. (After Goddard.) Fig. 22. Mauls of stone. (After Goddard.)

The chisel (ƙlá′mɫàn, "dig tool") consisted of a shaft of yew with a bone or stone edge set into one end. The other end was wrapped with elk thong to prevent splitting. The adze was of the "D" type,[32] the handle being much like that on a carpenter's saw (fig. 23). The blade was of some tough stone, horn, or a section of legbone of bear. The stroke was always toward the workman. The adze was used for smoothing planks, finishing canoes, and so on. There was little refinement in woodworking among the Quinault and finishing touches were with chisel and a rubbing down with sandstone or ṭhe skin of the dogfish. All tools were sharpened with sandstone.

Fig. 23. Adze.

Wedges were of elkhorn or the hard tough knots found in rotten logs. The latter were wrapped at the butt with elk sinew to prevent their splitting.

Planks were split from logs either in the desired thickness or in double-thick slabs which were re-split. A number of wedges were driven into the end of the log.

---

[32]Olson, 1927, plate 1.

As the split opened wedges might be inserted at its apex. As everyone who has worked with the coast cedar knows, the wood splits so readily that no great effort is necessary to split off long boards or planks which are almost perfectly uniform in width and thickness throughout their length.

Knives for light work, such as skinning, cutting fish or meat, and light wood-working, were simply whole mussel shells sharpened on sandstone.[33] Material for whetstones was found at several places along river and beach.

The drill was a simple shaft a foot or so long with a point of bone. The bow drill (hàgits) was sometimes used.

The digging stick (tsa'xwap) was of yew, of cedar or spruce limbs or the limbs with tough ends found in rotten logs. The length was about three feet.

In addition to the stone hammer a maul was sometimes made by taking a section of the trunk of yew or other hard wood and cutting it down to the desired weight. An attached section of limb served as a handle.

SKIN DRESSING

The Quinault were far from being adept in the art of tanning skins. As in most of their other arts and industries they were content with only a little more than the necessary fundamental knowledge. This was true even in, *e.g.*, wood carving, though they were thoroughly familiar with the much superior products of the Quilleute and Makah. Leather serves poorly in a wet climate and this is probably the explanation of the slight use made of skins, especially of leather with the hair removed, on the North Pacific coast.

Aside from skins for drums and a few other objects the Quinault used most skins with the hair left on. The tanning process was as follows: The flesh was removed by laying the skin on the ground and scraping it with the edge of a sharp stone (probably a knife-like section of sandstone) or an edged bone. Raw brains were worked into the hide and it was then pulled and rubbed. The glue was broken up by main strength rather than by chemical process. The finished product was pliable and white. The flesh side of fine robes, such as sea otter, were further tanned by smoking, but this process was employed more as a means of coloring than of tanning. Only winter (*i.e.*, prime) skins were tanned; summer skins were often eaten, especially those of seal, sea lion, and elk. No tanning was done by means of barks. The hair was removed from skins by the simple process of allowing them to lie in water for several days, when the beginnings of decay and softening of the tissue made the hair "slip."

BOXES AND DISHES

The elaborate boxes and dishes of the northern tribes were not made by the Quinault, but several simpler types were made. None of these were carved and if painted at all the colors were black or red in very plain patterns or simply all over.

---

[33]One informant stated that this was the woman's knife, never used by men; that the man's "knife" was of elk horn, some eight inches long.

One type of box was made with bottom and sides in one piece, kerfs being cut where sides and bottom met as shown in figure 24. The corners were sewed with cedar or spruce root or pegged. Invisible sewing was not known. An overlapping cover was made in the same way.

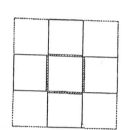

Fig. 24. Pattern for wooden box.   Fig. 25. Wooden platters.

A similar type of box was made by cutting kerfs in a board for the three corners, steaming and bending, and pegging or sewing the fourth corner. The bottom was pegged. The edges of the cover were sometimes inlaid with sea otter teeth or with shells. Such boxes were never used for cooking or the storing of oil (oil was kept in stomachs and bladders). Furs, trinkets, personal effects, and so on were usually kept in them. The size varied from small affairs perhaps eight inches on a side to large storage boxes several feet in each dimension.

Platters which served as individual dishes were usually of a simple but conventional form (fig. 25), carved of soft maple. For feasts, great platters of the same type were carved from sections of log and were sometimes as much as ten feet long.

A box for storing berries was made by taking two oblong pieces of the smoothed outer bark of hemlock, laying them in the form of a cross, and bending the ends upward. The bottom was thus double. The corners were then sewed. Either cooked or raw berries were placed inside, covered with leaves and the entire box submerged in a stream or pond. It was said that berries so stored would keep throughout the winter.

Boxes, bowls, dishes, and platters were frequently carved from solid pieces of alder or soft maple. These woods were preferred because they imparted no taste or odor to the food. The shaping was done chiefly with mallet and chisel, the inside bottom corners being rounded. Large cooking boxes were as much as 18 inches deep, and two feet square. Cooking troughs several feet long and about six inches deep were also used for boiling. The cooking was done by means of hot stones handled with tongs of the splitstick type.

Box-like containers made by this process served as water buckets and urinals. Handles for boxes were made of slender cedar boughs twisted into a rope.

Spoons (fig. 26) were carved from soft or vine maple. Early in the nineteenth century trade with the Columbia river tribes resulted in the bringing in of buffalo skins and horns and after that time a few horn spoons were made. One informant stated, however, that horns of mountain goat and sheep were known earlier. Various shells, especially of the mud clam, were also used as spoons.

Ladles for oil were simply round or oval bowls carved from soft maple.

Fig. 26. Wooden spoon.

DYES AND PAINTS

I secured only the following data on these features:

Oregon grape root was crushed, then boiled to secure a yellow dye. The material to be colored (chiefly grass for baskets) was allowed to soak in this for a considerable time.

Grasses, barks, etc. were dyed black by burying the material in the black mud of swamps for a week or so.

Alder bark was boiled to produce a red dye. For dark red, hemlock bark was used. A weak dye of hemlock colored fish nets a neutral tone. It also served to preserve the net and "make it lucky."

Red paint was made from a substance (iron oxide?) found in the gravel banks. This was ground and dried. Black was from the charcoal of alder or vine maple. Both were mixed with oil for use. For painting objects of wood, etc., these were mixed with the juice of cedar bark and the albumen of salmon eggs. The paint brush was made from the tail or wing feathers of eagle.

WEAVING

I was told that only the Ozette and Quinault among the tribes of the coast between Grays Harbor and Cape Flattery kept the type of wooly dog whose hair was used in weaving. My informants, however, gave inadequate and conflicting accounts of the method of weaving, but I give the divergent opinions for what they are worth.

The dogs themselves were said to be fairly large, though some were small. They were kept in a special pen (to keep them from crossing with common curs?) and were never fed fresh meat but only dried elk meat and dried fish. Before they were to be clipped they were fed in some special way. The hair was about three inches long. In color they varied: black, white, brown and "wolf-colored." Their ears stood up in wolf fashion.

They were sheared each time the hair attained its full length, usually twice a year. Before being clipped the dogs were washed, a white clay or diatomaceous earth being used to remove grease and dirt from the wool. The shearing was done by holding a tuft of hair at a time and cutting it close to the skin with a carefully sharpened mussel shell knife. As the tufts were cut they were placed one by one into a cleft stick to keep the hairs aligned. (No carding was done.)

Twisting of this hair into yarn was done simply with the fingers (Pope) or by means of a spindle which was rolled down the thigh. The spindle whorl was eight inches or so in diameter. A third informant stated that a spindle (without whorl) which had a hook at its tip was used to pick up the tufts of hair out of the split stick, the spindle being merely twisted by the fingers of the right hand. The yarn was then rolled into balls. Few (or none?) blankets were woven with both warp and weft of this yarn, twisted elk sinew being woven or twined in as the other element.

The weaving was done on a simple frame. One informant stated that the yarn was simply laced back and forth horizontally, but this is unlikely. A second informant claimed that the warp was wound round and round the frame with both rear and front warp being woven into the same section of fabric. I could not ascertain if the process of reversing the warp was known.[34] One informant stated that the warp was simply suspended over a bar, the lower ends hanging free (Tlingit style). The "weft" of the fabric was usually of elk sinew, the cords being woven in or, more commonly, twined in as pairs. In the latter case they were placed one to one and a half inches apart, the dog hair yarn being packed together as tightly as possible. The sinew strands were scarcely visible in the finished product. The body of the fabric was usually white or brown, a black or brown border being the only pattern attempted. It was said that the wool from fifteen dogs would suffice for a blanket about six by eight feet.

The familiar rabbitskin blanket of western North America was also made. The skins were cut into strips and these twisted hair side out, a spindle being sometimes employed. The strips were either woven as a simple cross weave or, probably more usually, used only as the warp, the weft consisting of elk sinew threads twined in at intervals. The skins of ducks were sometimes cut into strips, which were twisted and woven in the same fashion as the strips of rabbit fur.

BASKETRY

Materials. The Quinault used a wide variety of grasses, barks, and roots in the manufacture of baskets, mats, nets, cords, etc. I give the following as an incomplete list of these materials and the method of preparing them.

Spruce roots were dug during the winter. Roots from pencil size to three inches in diameter were made use of. They were cut into four-foot lengths and the bark removed by holding them over the fire for a few minutes, then peeling.

They were then split, beginning at the small end, into quarters, sixths or eighths, with mallet and chisel. These sections were then split into layers about one-sixteenth of an inch in thickness by holding one piece in the teeth and stripping or pulling off the thin piece with the right hand, the left following down the section at the point of the split. The roots split fairly readily between the rings, provided the process is begun at the point of the triangular piece (the center of the root). These pieces of varying width were then reduced to the desired width by further splitting.

---

[34]See Olson, 1929.

For watertight baskets the fibers must be almost square (*i.e.*, about one-sixteenth by one-sixteenth or slightly larger). The strands were then soaked in warm water for an hour or so, then scraped by holding a shell in the hand and pulling the fiber between the edge of the shell and the thumb. The fiber was then stored away, or stored before scraping. In either case it was soaked before using. This material was used especially for hats, water baskets, berry baskets, or other waterproof containers and also for openwork carrying baskets.

Open weave baskets were sometimes made of split cedar limbs, and the unsplit ones could be used as warp in others. Young cedars growing in swamps have the most slender limbs. The bark was ordinarily stripped from these and, if split at all, they were simply split in half, beginning from the tip end.[35] The process was like that employed in the second splitting of spruce roots. They were kept in water until wanted. Such limbs were also used for ropes, first twisted somewhat to form a withe, then twined with others to form, *e.g.*, a whale harpoon line. They were also used as single strand lines and were very much used for lashings of all sorts.

Another wood used in basketry was that of the vine maple. Straight knot-free sections, two or three inches in diameter, were chosen and split in quarters or eighths. Only the sap wood of these sections was used. Each piece was then split in half along the line of the rings, then each of these in half, and so until strips of the desired thickness were secured. The pieces must be green and be kept wet during the process. This material was ordinarily used for large, heavy-duty baskets, such as those for gathering clams, carrying fish, wood, and so on.

A number of types of baskets were made of cedar bark and it was often combined with other materials. The bark was gathered between the time the geese flew north and their journey south (April to September)—that is, while the sap was running and the bark was loose. Young trees up to eighteen inches in diameter, which were free from limbs for some distance, furnished the best bark. A knife-like bark peeler of horn, bone, or hard wood was used to break the bark loose at the base of the tree.

Strips twenty feet or so long could then be pulled off by merely pulling the loosened bark outward. These were laid on the ground with the inner bark upward. At the top end of the strip the inner layer was separated from the outer. The inner could then be easily removed by merely peeling it off. The outer bark was allowed to remain in the woods. The inner bark was dried for a day or two, then folded at intervals of about eighteen inches and stored. When wanted, it was dampened and split into the desired thicknesses and widths.

Shredded cedar bark was used for towels, the infants' diapers, head pad and bedding, for hiding the discs in the sláha'lam game, for women's skirts (fig. 12*a*), and for many other uses. The process of shredding was as follows: a yew canoe paddle or an edged board was lashed between two uprights at waist height. The bark was slid across this, tree side down, and beaten with a scissor-like stroke with a bark-shredder of whalebone (see figs. 12*b*, *c* and 27). This process removed some of the outer fiber of the bark and softened what remained. The strip was then twisted and split until it was almost as soft as cloth.

---

[35]One informant stated that cedar limbs could be split down sufficiently fine for watertight baskets woven like those of spruce root.

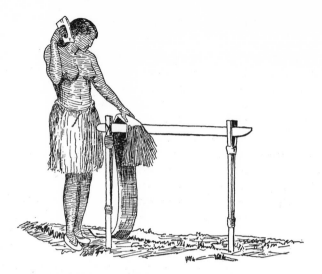

Fig. 27. Shredding cedar bark. (After Willoughby.)

Other materials used in basketry were: Mountain grass or swamp grass (k̓ulȧ'-lstap); a raffia-like grass from the shores of Grays Harbor; tule, used for packsacks and coarse baskets; nettle fiber, usually for nets.

The following techniques were known in basketry:[36]

1. Checker work; in cedar bark and vine maple. (See pl. 3f.)
2. Twilled work; in the same materials (see pl. 3c).
3. Plain twined (see pl. 3e).
4. Crossed warp, twined weave (see pl. 3d). This was called xȧ'łap (lace).
5. A weave employing one inert and two active weft elements with a soft (bark) warp; wrapped twined weave (see pl. 3a).
6. Coiling technique (see pls. 3g and 4a). This type (spu'ttcu) was a sewing of spruce or cedar root strands around a multiple-rod foundation. Looking into the basket the coils followed a counterclockwise direction. It was said that only a few women made baskets of this type; that the Skokomish and Klickitat made them more commonly.

Basketry decoration was by means of several techniques: overlay twining and variations in the color of the material being the commonest. Mountain (or swamp) grass (see above) usually supplied white, but was sometimes dyed. Various dyes and colors were used (q.v.). The tops of several types were sometimes fringed with scallops (tsi'łȧn, "handle") made of spruce root or cedar limbs. Pairs of handles were also used.

Baskets were used for storage of foodstuffs and clothing, for carrying (by women), as water buckets, and for cooking. I know of no significant variations from nearby tribes in weaving methods, types of weave, types of basket, or other feature.

---

[36]The designations used are those from Mason, *Aboriginal American Basketry* (U. S. Nat. Mus. Rept. for 1902, 171-548, 1904).

MATS

The Quinault did not make the large cedarbark mats of the northern tribes. They did, however, make a small mat some twelve inches square. Two such were lashed together on three sides to make a sort of hand bag for the fire drill, the hearth, and knicknacks.

The usual type of mat was made of the leaves of the cattail rush, made in the same fashion as the raincoat (see Clothing and fig. 28). A basket was also made of this material, sewed in the same way as the mat. Figure 29b illustrates another technique of mat-making.

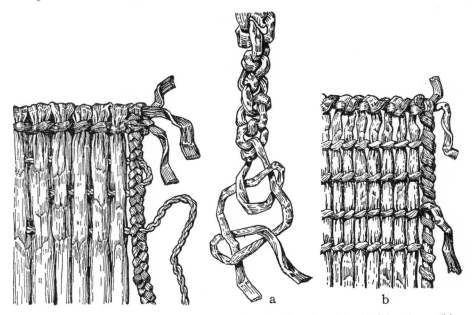

Fig. 28. Mat of cattail rush.   Fig. 29. Samples of braid *(a)* and mat *(b)*.

CORD, NETS, BRAIDS, KNOTS, ETC.

I will give a few (though incomplete) data on these topics. Cord was sometimes made from the down of the fireweed (never from the down of cattail); but this was never used in weaving. A strong type of thread or cord for fish lines, for sewing up mats, for weaving baskets, etc., was made by splitting the edges from cattail leaves and twisting these on the thigh into two- three- or four-strand threads (fig. 30). A beach grass called k̓lo'om was sometimes used as one strand, combined with a strand of rush, for a two-colored thread. Nettle fiber was used chiefly for nets. The stems were shredded in the same way as cedar bark. This separated the pith and pulp from the tough strands. The latter were then dried, cured, and twisted into cord. A net twine was also made from a raffia-like sea grass called ła'kstapc (drifted grass), which was got in trade from the Chinook. Other types of braids are shown in figures 29a and 31.

Fig. 30. Samples of cords and braids.   Fig. 31. Samples of braids.

The following knots were known:

The half-hitch.

The square knot (notci'łáł łáms, "help each other knot").

The sheet bend (łima'nis łáms), used in making nets.

A half-hitch slip knot.

Nets were woven by the men, but the fiber was prepared by the women. It was said that no shuttle except a stick with a fork at each end was used in weaving the net. Others simply wound the cord around a plain stick or used the ball itself for passing the cord. Mesh measures were a simple rectangle of bone or wood. Gill nets were unknown.

MONEY, VALUE, TRADE

Before the days of the traders most values were measured in terms of strings of dentalium. The Quinault secured these in trade from the north. They knew that the Makah and Nootka gathered them by means of a long pole with small sticks at the end which entered the open mouth of the shell. Ordinary shells were called xwe, exceptionally long ones ƙuna'łxʷ. The Nootka were said to eat the flesh of dentalium.

The unit of value was a "string" which was slightly over a fathom in length; the string was supposed to sag to a black dot tattooed on the middle of the chest. The largest shells ran 40 to a string, the smallest 44 or 46. The strings of smaller shells were worth less. One informant said that the number of shells over the unit length determined value. Thus a string of 40 with shells large enough so that there were four over the measure was worth four blankets, if five over, five blankets, and so on.

The following is a list of miscellaneous values:

1 "string" of 40 without shells over: 1 blanket.
1 "string" of 40 plus 1 foot: 5 or 6 blankets.
1 Hudson's Bay blanket: $8 or $10.
1 "trade" blanket: *ca.* $1.50.
1 sealing canoe: 10 to 15 blankets.
1 slave: 15 to 20 blankets, or 2 sea otter pelts.
1 gun: 1 slave.
1 ocean canoe: 1 slave.
10 strings, of a fathom each, of blue Hudson's Bay trade beads: 1 blanket.

A certain amount of trade was carried on between the various Quinault villages, but it was of a minor nature compared with exchanges of goods and services for mutual benefit (see Occupations). Some trade was carried on with near-by tribes. The northern groups, especially Makah and Nootka, were the sources of ocean canoes and dentalium. These flowed south chiefly from tribe to tribe, although trading voyages were undertaken. In exchange for these the southern groups exchanged dried salmon, dried clams, and the like. With society, religion, and material culture on a lower level they had little to offer the groups to the north except food products. Travel was more often for the sake of visiting than for trade.

Trade was greatly stimulated by the founding of the trading posts on the Columbia in the early part of the nineteenth century. Quinault territory was rich in fur-bearing animals, particularly sea otter. A brisk trade was carried on between Quinault and Makah on the one hand and Quinault and the fur traders on the other. Some of the chiefs made one or more trips each year to the Makah, trading furs for ocean canoes and slaves. A subsequent trip to the mouth of the Columbia was for the purpose of trading furs and the sale of slaves and canoes to the natives on the Columbia—at a profit. In return were received guns, powder, steel tools, and trade blankets.

TRAVEL AND TRANSPORT

Nearly all travel was by canoe, most of it up and down the Quinault river. It was a two- or three-day trip from kwi'naiɬ to the lake. The canoe was poled much of the way, one man at the bow and one at the stern being most usual. At log jams portages were constructed, skids being used for sliding the canoe. Log jams were usually burned during the summer in order to keep the channel open.

Ocean travel by canoe was limited to the quiet summer season or to short trips on calm winter days. Whaling and sea lion hunting were hazardous because of the danger of storms, as well as by reason of the nature of the game. Canoe voyages were made as far as the Makah villages in the north and the Shoalwater Bay villages in the south. In ocean travel there was usually a steersman who gave orders and watched for exceptionally large waves. In crossing large swells care was taken not to cut at right angles lest the canoe break or split, but an angling course was taken. Canoes were usually landed stern foremost; always so in surf landings. In rough weather voyagers always ran before the wind.

Rafts were sometimes used in moving from one place to another. The house planks might be lashed as a raft, or placed across two canoes. Rafts of three or more logs were used in crossing streams and were kept available on small lakes as well.

Because of the boisterous nature of the coast it was not always possible to travel by canoe on the ocean. A trail, with canoes at Shoalwater Bay and Grays Harbor, ran from the village of Chinook on the Columbia to the Makah village of Neah Bay. For the most part it followed the beach, but at cliffs and jutting points trails were cut through the forest (map 1). Rafts were kept at rivers where there were no villages. Elsewhere, as at kwi'naił, the traveler could always claim his right to free ferriage.

There were also fairly well defined trails from the forks of the upper Quinault river to favorite hunting localities. Trails also ran from the village pini'lks to Baker's prairie and from nokedja'kt to the Queets river and to a village on the Humptulips river.

Along these trails, and elsewhere on land, goods were packed. Women usually carried in baskets especially constructed, using a tumpline across the forehead. Men carried with the tumpline across the shoulders, *i.e.*, the strap passed across the chest. A man carrying a heavy load might use two straps, one across the forehead, the other across the chest. The packstrap (carrying strap or tumpline) was about 15 to 20 feet long, braided rope-like except for a plaited section about two feet in length at its center. This section was woven or plaited two to three inches wide (fig. 31c, d). The material was of beach grass, cedar, or willow bark.

On rare occasions light loads were lashed to the backs of dogs.

A makeshift method of carrying meat was by making two hoops of cedar limbs and lacing them across with strips of cedar bark. The meat was piled on one, the other placed on top and the hoops lashed together with cedar bark. A wide strip of bark served as a carrying strap.

Men hunting in deep snow sometimes used snowshoes (kwi'tau). I secured no details beyond that these were oval hoops of vine maple, lashed across with thongs of elk skin.

THE SOCIAL STRUCTURE

The Quinault were without any formal tribal organization. They considered themselves set apart from neighboring groups largely because they occupied the fairly definite area of the watershed of the Quinault river and because their language differed in dialect from those of neighboring tribes. To a certain extent nearly all the members of the tribe considered themselves blood relatives, though this was never formally expressed. Rather, it was thought that if one could trace his ancestry back far enough he would find linkages with all others of the tribe. This attitude appears by implication through a study of the genealogical tables and must underlie the relative rarity of intratribal marriages—there being a rigid taboo on marriages between kinsmen no matter how remote. So great was this incest horror that it undoubtedly inhibited marriages between persons who might conceivably be kinsmen but who were not definitely known to be relatives. These attitudes, perhaps more than anything else, gave the Quinault a sense of tribal unity.

There was no clan system or traces of it, nor any other formal type of social unit. Nor was there a sense of village unity. Kinship, that is, blood relationship, was the chief, almost the only, tie which bound individuals to each other both within and outside the tribe. Intertribal marriages were more common than matings within the tribes. The kinship bond was strong and effective no matter how remote the genealogical relationship. The result was that every person counted his kinsmen in hundreds. The duties of aid, of hospitality, of blood revenge, of not quite formal visits between relatives seem to have held between an exceptionally large number of persons. Close blood kinship, however, naturally counted for more than remote relationship.

In theory there were three social classes: nobles, commoners, and slaves. In reality (except for the slaves) these were subdivided and blended into each other. Anyone could properly claim kinship with members of the nobility and thereby make out a somewhat dubious case for his own good status. Wealth counted for almost as much as blue blood, and it was possible to raise one's standing through the acquisition of wealth. In time even lowly origin would be overlooked or forgotten. But slave blood carried with it a lasting stigma.

B. M. was regarded as a chief because of his descent from chiefs. But gossip had it that his wife had slave blood in her ancestry (through her father's mother). His children are therefore referred to as skåttso'ms sådjilke' (half slave) and not regarded as of noble blood. This gossip, however, was retailed only by those who disliked the family.

I record the following designations of social class and rank:

snu'gwap or stodja'k, noble or chief.

ca'netam, ali's, or qa'xetam, rich man, with almost the same meaning as the preceding.

tcasali's, newly rich.

tols kwitita'lmix^w, from people of good blood, but not nobles.

keli'c djaȧdjȧ', poor people (though not of poor blood).
tolskwɛhmiɫta'lmix^w, "from not of good blood," *i.e.*, common people.
skwȧttso'ms sȧdjilke, half slave (with slave blood on one side of his ancestry).
skwȧ'ttsȧs, "one eye" or "half blind," *i.e.*, partly slave blood.
gwȧts or eskutsȧs, part slave (or slave?).
sadjilke, slave.

There were no formal rules regulating marriage beyond the general one that a person might not marry a blood relative, no matter how remote the relationship. Conversely, one might marry anyone not a blood relative. B. M. married his mother's mother's sister's son's son's daughter; but there was great opposition to the marriage, especially on the part of his parents. After more than 40 years it was still a source of discussion and gossip. I heard of one case where a man married his mother's sister's daughter. The couple were almost ostracized by their fellow tribesmen. People scarcely spoke to them. In the old days this marriage would not have been permitted.

The extent of the incest group, as much as anything else, was undoubtedly a factor in bringing about an exceptionally large percent of extratribal marriages. A check of my genealogical tables yields the following data on marriages of Quinault with: Quinault 22, Lower Chehalis 12, Queets 10, Hoh 6, Makah 5, Quilleute 3, Wynooche 4, Humptulips 3, Satsop 3, Skokomish 3, Nisqualli 2, Nootka 2, Copalis, Puyallup, Yakima, Chinook and Clatsop one each. This gives 58 marriages with outsiders to 22 within the tribe. The proportion of the former may have been smaller in pre-European days, before intensified trade and concentration on reservations brought about closer contacts. But that the same tendency existed in early times is indicated by the number of intertribal marriages a century and more ago.

I have no record of a marriage between residents of the same village, the native theory being that all members of the same village were relatives, though this was not explicitly formulated. It follows that members of the same household did not intermarry.

THE KINSHIP SYSTEM

The manner of expressing relationship does not differ markedly from that designated as "Salish" by Spier,[37] and conforms closely to Lowie's Lineal in all but the speaker's generation. The chief difference from the more usual Salish type is the use of the sibling term for cross and parallel cousins only when employed as a collective term for siblings. Other sibling terms than those employed for cousins are customarily used.

The Quinault employed kinship terms more frequently than names in address. The incomplete list which I give is set down as it was dictated to me by H. S. A few supplementary terms were furnished by J. C. In ordinary address the prefix ȧns (my) was used, though it might be omitted. Seemingly it was customarily omitted when addressing a son or daughter. The prefixes tsis (she), tis (he), tsai (they) could be used preceding ȧns (my) for a slightly more formal type of reference.

---

[37]Leslie Spier, *The Distribution of Kinship Systems in North America* (this series, vol. 1, no. 2, p. 74, 1925).

Thus, tisȧnkuta'n (he, my younger brother) would be used when speaking of him. The dead were never mentioned without the prefix ȧnts[u] (my gone?) preceded by the personal pronoun. Relatives by marriage were usually referred to by the same terms used for blood relatives preceded by the word qwe'lex (by marriage) or were referred to or addressed as ȧnqwe'lex (my-by-marriage-[relative]).

I did not have an opportunity to check the actual use of kinship terms by the genealogical method, but many of them, particularly "cousin," "aunt," "uncle," "niece," and "nephew," are used very loosely.

Beyond the rigid rule that no blood relatives may marry, there were few rules governing the conduct of kinsmen. There were no parent-in-law taboos nor proscriptions on matter-of-fact conduct between siblings. A girl was permitted to converse and be friendly with lads and young male relatives of her own age-class. Toward unrelated males she maintained an aloof attitude, not even speaking to them. A married woman might speak with anyone, but she was careful not to arouse her husband's jealousy.

Parents, uncles, and aunts were the most potent influences in the bringing up of children, but any elder had the right to admonish youngsters or even youths and young women.

The following is an incomplete list of the kinship terms:

ȧnka'h, my mother.
ȧna'l, my father.
ȧntsuk̇le'tsimal, my deceased parents.
ȧnnux'kȧ'ktȧn, or k̇le'tsimal, my parents.
ȧnku'lau, my aunt (if the connecting parent is living). This term was somewhat flexible.
ȧnsi'xwȧn, my aunt, my uncle (if the connecting parent is dead).
ȧnsi'l, my uncle (if the connecting parent is living).
ȧnstcitcȧma'an, my stepfather.
ȧnsmata'xwȧn, my mother-in-law.
ȧnklauc lȧnsma'taxwȧn, my brother's mother-in-law.
ȧnstci', my grandmother, my great aunt (*i.e.*, mother's or father's aunt), my step-grandmother, my stepmother's mother.
ȧnstco'pȧ, my grandfather, my great uncle (*i.e.*, father's or mother's uncle), my step-grandfather, my stepfather's father.
ȧnstsamla'tci, my great grandmother (lit., "my double grandmother").
ȧnstsamla'tcopȧ, my great grandfather (lit., "my double grandfather").
ȧnsk̇eta'htcopah, my most remote grandfather (lit., "my longest grandfather").
ȧnsk̇eta'htci, my most remote grandmother.
ȧnȧmȧ'n, my child.
ȧnstso'xwail, my youngest child (?).
kuto'n, son.
kume'l, daughter.
ȧnstcitcai'ail, my stepchild, my stepson, my stepdaughter.
ȧnsixwa'l, my nephew, my niece (if parent is living), my husband's sister's child, my wife's sister's child, my husband's brother's child, my wife's brother's child, my brother's wife's child (male speaking), my sister's husband's child (female speaking).
ȧnstcexwa'l, my nephew, my niece (if parent is dead). I am not quite certain that this term is correct as some informants claimed that only the uncle-aunt terms changed upon death of the connecting parent of speaker. (Another informant, a Queets woman, gave ȧnsȧno'-tcial as the term for nephew, niece, cross cousin, parallel cousin; but I am not certain that it is correct.)

àne'mats, my grandchild.
àmstsamḷa'emats, my great grandchild (my siblings grandchild?).
àne'àh, my older sister.
ànkuta'n or ànkuta'àno, my younger sister, my younger brother.
ànklau'c, my older brother.
ànukwuḷkle'ts, my sibling, my cousin, parallel or cross, male or female. This is used for all
    cousins, no matter how remote. (Lit., "we are all one"?.)
ànstca'n, my brother-in-law, my sister-in-law. The reciprocal term.
ànstcistcan, my sister-in-law (female speaking?).
antcitcwànà'h, my brother-in-law (female speaking).
ànsidja'ltatc or ànsdja'ltatc, my brother-in-law (male speaking).
ànkaxtcitciwanonàmàn, "my brother-in-law before" (after spouse of the speaker is dead).
ànkaxtcàanàmàn, "my sister-in-law before" (after spouse of speaker is dead).
hanànstàxwe'nop or tisànstàxwe'nop, my husband (lit., "he my mate").
lanànstàxwe'nop or tsisànstàxwe'nop, my wife (lit., "she my mate"). When a man has sev-
    eral wives this implies his favorite wife.
tàxwenop, my spouse (the vocative form).
ànnukla'ah, my deceased wife.
antitcigwi'nmih, my deceased husband.
tàstàànsxo'xmix^w, my "divorced" spouse.
ànstcan, my husband's brother's wife, my wife's brother's wife.
àntsamatuh, my husband's sister's husband, my wife's sister's husband.
ànsxo'koł or ànsk̓wi'n, my kinsman.
ànsxo'kooł, all my kinsmen.
ànqwe'lex, my kinsman by marriage (e.g., my wife's sister's brother).
ànxwe'ɛlex^w, my kinsman by marriage (who is a young child?).
ànqaxkwelekmàn, my child's parents-in-law (after child is dead).
ànscà"o, my co-wife.

THE HOUSEHOLD GROUP

The labor of building and maintaining a house, the tradition that a house should be at least six fathoms long, and the social prestige which went with a large house naturally tended toward the formation of household groups larger than the family. The traditional or pattern number of families in a household was four, but the actual number varied from two to six.

The head of one of these families was rather indefinitely regarded as the "owner" of the house. This position was the result of seniority, wealth, or prestige. His actual authority was negligible but his word carried weight. He òccupied the rear part of the house (see Houses), the other families occupying the sides or front corners. There was no very formal allocation of space, however. The household group was a democratic one, almost communistic in many respects, though each family had its own fire for warmth, cooking, the drying of meat, etc.

At the death of the "owner" of a house the remaining inmates often tore it down and rebuilt it near by, though this was not always done. There was no definite rule as to the inheritance of houses. Authority might be assumed by the eldest remaining head of family—a brother or cousin—or it might pass to an eldest son. The actual title to the house usually passed to the eldest son, or, failing sons, to the next of kin, such as brother, cousin, or nephew. This statement must be qualified by the fact that the ownership of the house was not so much individual as collective. In a way the head of the household was regarded as "owning" only the end or corner which he occupied, while the others "owned" their sections. The headman could not deprive the others of their shares in the estate.

There was considerable diversity in the makeup of the household group, but almost invariably the inmates were kinsmen, or kinsmen through marriage. A man and his married sons, a group of brothers, uncles and nephews, cousins, or combinations of these were the commonest relationships between the heads of families. Wives, children, parents-in-law, slaves, and hangers-on completed the household group.

I give the following examples of household groups to illustrate their diverse makeup. These, however, do not quite represent normal conditions, since the date is about 1875, after the decimation of the tribe and its concentration in perhaps four villages.

1. na′tcȧpah and his wife.
2. so′ɫmic, wife, and children; his aunt and her husband; a widow.
3. soɫa′itȧn and wife; his mother; his wife's mother; a widow; a slave.
4. xopȧ′tȧn, a widower.
5. po′xolanux and wife; his brother and wife; his three unmarried sisters; his three unmarried brothers.
6. xȧla′skȧn and his two wives; his mother; his wife's mother.
7. se′senoh and his wife.
8. xe′klaiɫ, his wife, and two children.
9. wake′nas and wife; their four children (married); grandchildren; his wife's father; a number of slaves.
10. xȧlma′ɫ, his wife, and two children; slaves.

THE VILLAGE

As everywhere on the Northwest coast, the village community was the fundamental larger social unit. The tribe was merely a loose aggregation of villages, without formal organization or any form of centralized authority, with nothing beyond territorial, cultural, and linguistic unity to bind its members together. There were no tribal meetings or councils, nor, except for potlatches, ceremonies at which all members of the tribe were present. And ordinarily at the potlatches other tribes or village groups were also present.

The interests and loyalties of the individual were in a descending scale down the list: family, household, village, kinship group (within and outside the tribe), tribe. This may seem a natural attitude, but I wish to emphasize its contrast with the attitude found among such groups as Tlingit, Haida, and Tsimshian, where the greater part of the interests of the individual centers around his clan group or the moiety rather than around village or other social group.

Quinault villages were about twenty in number, scattered at random between river mouth and lake, with a handful of people living above the lake and at Moclips. Except at the mouth of the river, favorable spots for salmon weirs determined their locations. In size they varied from a single house occupied by one or more families to villages of perhaps eight or ten houses.[38] Clusters of houses not more than a hun-

---

[38]One informant claimed 28 houses for the village of kwi′naiɫ, but I am certain that this is an exaggeration or that it refers to the period after the concentration of the tribe there.

dred yards apart were counted as separate villages. Thus me′tsugutsałán and kwi′-naił stood so near to each other that a stranger could not have known that they were counted as separate towns.

The houses within a village were ranged in a random row ten to twenty yards from the bank of the stream, the long dimension of each house oriented to the east-west, with the door of each at the west end. There was no concept of ownership of land either by individuals, households, or village groups. The household group "owned" the land where the house stood—until the house was moved. In each house was one man tacitly recognized as "owning" the house. He was its head, but there was no idea of house chiefs. He was merely the senior partner in a flexible and fairly loose corporation.

Much the same may be said of the village as a whole. In every village was a man regarded as "chief," but his authority grew out of the respect he commanded by reason of wealth, birth, age, or personality. There was a strong tendency, however, for the position to be hereditary, the "office" usually passing to his eldest son.

To the casual observer the main evidences of human occupancy at such a village consisted in the houses themselves, the anchored canoes, and the salmon weir stretching fence-like across the stream in front of the village. To the inhabitants themselves the weir was the most important feature of the village. Upon its construction and maintenance depended the very existence of the villagers. Like the houses, it was built by community effort. It was owned by the community and maintained by community effort. At intervals along the weir were fishing platforms where the fishermen stood in manipulating the dip nets. Each head of a family (or each household) had his platform where he fished year after year and where his father had fished before him. The village "chief" usually controlled the rights to the platform most favorably located, where the water was deep.[39]

The village chief usually owned the largest house. To his house-platform usually came the other men at daybreak, to discuss matters of common interest, to decide what should be done during the ensuing day. To his house now and then he called the entire village to admonish and advise, seldom or never to command. He had certain duties as well. He was expected to aid the unfortunate, to feast his village-mates now and then. If a potlatch was to be given, the bulk of the expense in food and property gifts fell on him. He was the leading man, the "father" of the little community.

OCCUPATIONS

Strictly speaking, there was no idea of fixed or hereditary occupations. Through practice or innate ability a person became specially skilled in certain pursuits. Certain men emphasized hunting over fishing. Others were known for their skill in splitting planks, others for their pre-eminence in canoe-building, and so on. A woman might become very adept in basket-making. In the native mind these skills were due in part to the possession of certain guardian spirits. Thus a man who was

---

[39]Although in theory these platform locations were owned by individuals, it was seldom so in practice. The eldest son merely inherited the right as a trustee. His brothers shared in it. It was at best an indefinite type of individual ownership. Besides it was impossible for one person to man the platform both day and night during the fishing season, so two or more men shared the labor and the catch.

skilled at climbing trees and cutting off the dead limbs for firewood owed a part of his ability to the fact that coon was his guardian spirit. No man could hope to hunt whales unless he had the "ocean" or west guardian spirit.

Specialists naturally exchanged their goods and services for the goods and services of others. There was little or no idea of work for "wages."

AUTHORITY AND OFFICE

Though the Quinault frequently spoke of "chiefs," the term was a relative one. The chief was referred to as snu'gwap or ali's (lit., "rich man") and this term perhaps expresses as well as anything the native attitude: the rich occupied positions of influence in the community. Linked with an ill-defined emphasis on good blood, in practice it was assumed that to be a chief was to be a rich man, to be a rich man was to be a chief. In each village there was a man who owned the largest house, who had the largest number of wives and slaves and the greatest amount of property. His fellow villagers looked to him for leadership and advice. Ordinarily these were his relatives. Lesser individuals of good blood were sometimes also called snu'gwap ("chief's family"?). The most influential of these constituted an indefinite group and were called djatci'las snu'gwap ("close together chief"?).

Outside of his own village the authority of the chief was practically nil. The highest chief of the tribe was merely the wealthiest man of an important village. The following ranking was given me: the head man at la'lcił had many slaves, a number of wives, and lived in a large house. He was probably the highest "chief." Below him in order were the chiefs of kwi'naił, no'skałàn, t'o'nans, and nokedja'kt. The leading men of very small villages were not classed as chiefs. Over the people of his own village the chief exercised a sort of paternal authority. People did as he told them or as he advised them more out of respect than of fear. One informant (Mason) stated that the chief might order that an offender be ducked in the river but this was the only instance of a claim of power to punish. Public opinion carried more weight than a chief's word. I once heard Mason upbraid a young man for not taking proper care of an injured uncle. But it was a shaming of the offender rather than the giving of an order and was purposely shouted in tones which all the neighbors might hear! The fellow gave no sign that he had heard.

Although the chieftainship was not a formal office there was a strong tendency toward inheritance of the position. Normally the eldest son of the chief succeeded. He was expected to undergo an exceptionally rigorous puberty ritual. In the absence of male heirs the position passed to a brother or cousin. Or a son of the chief's daughter came to be regarded as chief. The Mason family trace their position through Mason's father's father's mother's father, who was the chief at Montesano. This in no wise indicates matrilineal succession, but is merely a status in the community determined by blue blood. A chief or a noble family in reduced circumstances still wielded some influence because of noble lineage. On the other hand a nouveau riche (tcasali's) might come to be regarded as a sort of chief. A Hoh man who was very successful in the pursuit of whales and sea otter came to be known as the djàlki'nalis (slave chief) because of his slave origin. The term was used in derision, but only behind his back. In no case could a woman become a chief, though a woman of high class or of dominant personality exercised considerable influence in the community.

No chief could, *e.g.*, stop a man from fishing. In case of a quarrel between two men the chief might intervene, but his word did not carry authority in a real sense. If a man was a murderer or a persistent troublemaker the chief might advise the people that he could be killed with impunity; or he might even order his slaves to kill the offender. But in the latter case the chief had to make a payment to the relatives. In cases of blood-feud or those involving blood-price the chief acted as mediator, though the amount to be paid was determined by the injured kin or by the village "speaker." In cases of friction between tribes the leading men would try to reach an amicable settlement. Those who were guilty of fomenting trouble might be warned by the chief. If they persisted, the chief would publicly condemn them and their fellow tribesmen might then kill them without starting a blood-feud, though the relatives were in some instances compensated.

It was customary for the village "chief" to call a village assembly now and then, at which he admonished and advised his fellow townsmen, particularly the young men.

It was said that old Tàxo'là spent much of his time on the bench in front of his house. Both winter and summer he would be there, watching for the arrival of visitors so that he would be the first to greet them, to invite them in, to hear what news they brought.

The speaker. Several of the leading chiefs of the tribe (the leading men at the larger villages) had specially designated men whose duty it was "to speak the chief's mind" to the people of the home village and to carry on negotiations with other villages or tribes. Such were called sukuna'àgwam or tca'àtalak. The speakership was not a definite office, though a man once appointed speaker functioned as such until his death. The office was not hereditary. A new speaker was chosen by the chief on the basis of "stage presence," a loud voice, thorough knowledge of tribal customs, familiarity with the potlatch formalities, ability to speak several languages, and the ability to soothe injured feelings in case of a blood-feud. The spokesman received no pay for his services. Often the ranking man of a minor village filled the position for the chief of a larger village. The speaker was often consulted by the chief and was his adviser in many ways, particularly during the time the chief was planning a potlatch.

The joker. As among the neighboring tribes certain individuals assumed the status of joker or buffoon. There might be one at each large village, though ordinarily there was but one in the tribe. The position was definitely not an office, neither was there either hereditary or other transmission of the prerogative. At the death of the old joker, or shortly before, someone else merely began to rib people and he thereby came to be regarded as the successor. Though others were commonly the butt of his remarks, he himself was fair game for similar sport. For obvious reasons most of the joking was carried on within the hearing of others.

During my visits Austin Chapelis was the joker. One might say to him, "Hello, my slave;" or in derision, "Here is the man who always tells the truth. He is not even afraid to speak his mind ₀o the chief." Once a visitor came walking down the beach with his trousers rolled up. When he was within hearing A.C. said, "He comes on horseback; he has white-legged horses." While Hoh Williams was government policeman A.C. never tired of teasing him. One day H.W. said, "You always make fun of me before the people. Why don't you let me alone? Don't you know that Chapelis was not your father? Mai'åko (a slave) is your father." At the time A.C. was sitting in his beached canoe. He was so flustered that he started paddling on the dry gravel, much to the glee of the bystanders. When next he saw H.W. he said, "Where is that son of ne·'pincl (a slave at Hoh)?"

No matter what the joker said to one, one must take it in good part and above all not show anger. J.M. always avoided A.C. when possible, because the latter once remarked that the former was really a berdache. Before J.M. was married A.C. said to him, "Why are you going to marry that girl? You are part woman. How can you do anything to her?"

A woman never acted as joker. Unknown were buffoons who spoke in inverted speech or who did the opposite of what they were told.

SLAVERY

Slaves were either war captives or the descendants of such. This being the case persons of high rank in another tribe might be taken prisoner and end their days in slavery. All persons captured in a war belonged to the chief who was leading the party. He might keep them or sell them. Most slaves held by the Quinault were members of near-by tribes, indicating that there was no extended "trade route" along which slaves were traded. Such trading as there was seems to have been mostly from north to south. Slaves secured at Neah Bay were sometimes re-traded on the Columbia. Slaves owned by various wealthy men are mentioned as coming from Tulalip, Oyhut, Humptulips, Lower Chehalis, Willapa, Chinook, Lummi, Hoh, and Klallam. Nicagwats owned a woman from a Nootka tribe called kaiuᴋut and a man from the Nootka groups known as xåcᴋwe'aq. Since the Quinault never warred with most of these groups it is clear that most slaves were acquired through purchase. It was said there were no Quinault slaves because the Quinault had not engaged in war for a long time.

Persons captured in war were seldom ransomed by their relatives. Ransom involved the payment of two or three times the person's value as a slave, or the trading of several slaves for him. There was no fixed valuation of slaves. A man was valued according to his ability or strength, a woman according to her skill in handicraft. Old persons were not worth much. A female slave had about the same value as a male.

Although slaves were regarded as property, certain features of common humanity crop out in regard to their treatment. A slave worked for (and often with) his master at woodcutting, hunting, fishing, and so on. Female slaves gathered wood, carried water, cooked. To an undetermined extent the products of a slave's labor belonged to him. It was expressed thus: "A slave might be very lucky in his hunting and trapping. He might get more furs than his master would accept. In time he might buy himself free." Thus, xȧcќwe′aq saved up a surplus of furs two or three times the value of a slave. This he gave to his master. Then he went home and his owner said nothing. Slaves were allowed to keep their winnings from gambling, though they often gave them to the master as a matter of course. Slaves recently acquired were frequently sold or traded, but old servants of the family or those inherited from one's father were seldom disposed of.

Slaves belonging to the same master were sometimes given permission to marry, but no wedding ceremony was involved. Johnson Wakinas' father had a slave named Lȧmcȧn (from Tulalip) who won a race horse in a gambling game and gave it to his master, together with ten muzzle-loading guns. Then he married another slave named Vȧk, whose master lived at Oyhut. The two had not received permission from their masters, however, so it was regarded as a mere love affair. Lȧmcȧn ran away to Oyhut repeatedly in order to be with his love. This displeased his master, who told his nephew to lie in wait for him at Oyhut. The nephew stabbed him. Wakinas' father killed several slaves because they persisted in trying to escape. (J.W.)

Now and then it happened that a female slave had children by her master, but they were still regarded as slaves. Some say that Bob Wing is the child of Tyee Man's father by a female slave who had kinsmen among the Chehalis and was a distant relative of Billy Mason's.

One case came to light of a male slave marrying a free woman and the memory of this union blights the reputation of a leading family. It is a subject to be mentioned only in whispers—or to be thrown in the face of a member of that family in a bitter quarrel. Reference to such a blight in the genealogical tree is made by using the term "one eye" (skwa′ttsȧs) as applying to such and such a person. No matter how many generations back the thing lies, it remains as much a disgrace as though it had occurred recently.

Bob Wing and Joe Wing (the children of Lȧmcȧn and his slave paramour) are still regarded as slaves, and as belonging to Tyee Man. Joe, however, resides at Shoalwater Bay. Bob's children are likewise regarded as slaves, and in native theory their children will also be slaves. So far as I could learn these are the only slaves still held by the Quinault. Probably most, if not all, the others returned to their tribes during the period of readjustment between 1850 and 1900. Slaves were nearly always given names, or nicknames, taken from their tribal or village designations. A woman from the kaiuќut (Nootka) was called kai; a man named xȧcќwe′aq came from a Nootka group of that name; a Klallam woman was called ќlallah. It is said that slaves were not buried in the cemetery. Slaves about to die were usually taken out of the house and placed in a hollow among the roots of a tree. A blind slave was forced by his master to stay under a canoe, where were buried several of his master's children, until he died there. This is the only instance that I learned of, of anything like human sacrifice. Some say that no child born of slave parents could have his head flattened.

Since slaves constituted a real form of wealth and were valued highly (ten guns, a horse, fifteen and twenty blankets being values mentioned), only the wealthy (chiefs) owned slaves. It is doubtful if they ever constituted more than a very small portion of the population. Johnson Wakinas' father is said to have owned "about thirty" slaves, but this number is certainly exceptional. Probably few persons owned more than one-tenth this number.

Old Tàxo′là's father owned a slave later called Dan, who was of a Nootka tribe. He was captured when only six and traded to the south. He was raised almost as one of the family and Tàxo′là's wife later "adopted" him. Tàxo′là and this lad were sent every morning to their plunge—for a slave might seek for a guardian spirit on equal terms with a free man.

BERDACHES AND HOMOSEXUALS

Berdaches were uncommon and were not linked with shamanism. A "female" who lived some 50 years ago was regarded as an hermaphrodite, but she lived with and reputedly had sexual intercourse with another woman. A Queets berdache was said to have had all the essential male organs of normal size but he did woman's work (cooking, basketry), sat down like a woman, and spoke with the voice of a woman. His sexual life was limited to intercourse with old women. This led to his early death, for it was thought to "poison" a young man to have sexual relations with an old woman.

His sister was also a berdache. One Quinault female was masculine and bore a man's name. Though her organs were those of a normal female she had sex relations with other women. She followed the occupations of a man. The Quilleute and Ĥumptulips also had berdaches among them.

No social stigma seems to have been associated with such aberrations. The males were known as keknatsà′nxwix^w (part woman) and females as tàekxwà′nsix^w (man acting). Homosexuality was not practiced except by berdaches and their mates.

THE CYCLE OF LIFE

BIRTH CUSTOMS

Pregnancy. The cessation of the menses signalized pregnancy. The period of gestation was thought to be nine lunar months.[40] There was no taboo on sexual intercourse during this period, but the couple ordinarily refrained during the last month or so. There were no dietary restrictions except that the woman ate no raspberries, strawberries, or thimbleberries lest the child have a birthmark. After about the sixth month the woman was careful to do no hard work. Both the father and mother took care that they saw nothing strange or horrible. If either was frightened by an animal an attempt was made to kill the animal and a piece of its flesh was eaten, provided it was an edible creature. Seeing a crippled animal or person was apt to cause the child to be similarly affected. Both parents must be especially careful not to laugh at anything unusual. One of my informants went to a vaudeville show in Tacoma where he forgot himself and laughed loudly. One of the performers was a contortionist. He was concerned lest his unborn child be affected. The sight of an animal which squeaks might cause the child to be sickly, or cause the child to be fretful and to imitate the cries of the animal. To cure this some of the hair of the

---

[40]S. H. stated that it was nine months for a girl, twelve for a boy.

animal was burned and the ashes rubbed on the child. During pregnancy the husband avoided killing the following animals: mink, coon, bear, land-otter, eagle, hawk, and sea gull. Neither of the couple handled mice, woodrats, or crows, or other animals which steal, lest the child grow up a thief. There was no rule against the woman eating the flesh of animals which had suffered. No medicines were employed for barrenness and none used as contraceptives. Spring was regarded as the most favorable time for children to be born.

For five or ten days before delivery was expected the woman usually remained in the house. During this time she drank a great deal of hot water "to make her warm inside." The leaves of a certain grass were eaten to insure a quick and easy delivery.

Delivery. When labor pains began a midwife was called in. The expectant mother was given an infusion of salmonberry bark to drink. If the labor pains were severe or prolonged the patient was given a brew made by mixing soot from around the smokehole with hot water. There seems to have been no such aids to birth as massage or pressure on the abdomen. During delivery the woman lay on her bed, or if she chose, sat on the bench in front of the bed platform. Some midwives were able to manipulate the child, turning it in case the limbs were twisted so as to impede the birth. If the child were born feet first it was regarded as proof that the couple had indulged in sexual intercourse during the entire period of pregnancy. The husband was usually present at the birth but took no part in the care of the patient. A shaman was called in if the birth proved very difficult. The umbilical cord was cut an inch from the body and tied. The midwife or a helper held the other end to prevent its return to the womb. The afterbirth was expelled by gentle pressure on the abdomen. Both the father and mother repeated a prayer "to the world" for the welfare of the child. The child was bathed immediately, but was not pulled or its limbs manipulated in any way. If the infant was disfigured by a birthmark resembling an animal it was certain that it would not live long. The placenta and the mats, clothing, etc. used at the birth were taken by the midwife to a spot some distance from the house and burned. The placenta was called the "baby's grandmother." In the villages near Quinault lake the father usually took the placenta and lashed it at the top of a tree. The midwife was usually paid a blanket as a fee, in recent years five or ten dollars.

The child was not put to breast for about a day, the mother's milk not being considered good until then. The day following the birth the new parents called in their friends and relatives, each of whom brought the child a gift, such as a blanket, beads, cedar bark, or some other object of moderate value. A small feast was spread and the infant was given a name by a grandmother or grandfather. This name was used until the child was eight or ten, when a new one was given. This second name was used until a final name was given at about the time of puberty. Infants were nursed for at least a year, sometimes for three years. Boiled fresh fish minced in warm water was a part of the diet after a year.

Five days after the delivery the mother bathed herself, but remained in the house for another five days. The couple refrained from sexual intercourse for about a month following the birth.

After the birth of a first child the mother did not comb her own hair for five months lest it become thin. There were no such restrictions at subsequent births.

Twins and monsters. There was no horror of twins (tsaile' sxwił), though the parents had to observe a number of taboos. For twenty days neither parent could fish, lest the fish stop running. The father of twins must refrain from hunting for two years, lest he frighten away all game. There were no food taboos observed, the couple being supplied with fish and meat during these periods by relatives and friends. The father of twins sometimes camped in the woods for a month following their birth.[41] It was believed that twins lacked the fontanelle, that they were born with the bones of the skull fused. Twins were never separated, lest both die. If one went for an armload of wood, the other followed. They occupied the same bed. If girls, they both married the same man. They were never referred to as "twins," but as "wolves" (tsopoh), lest they become ashamed. It was believed that the twin born first invariably grew to be a smaller person than his fellow. I heard of one instance of a husband threatening to kill his wife because he considered one of her twins the child of another man. None of my informants knew of triplets being born to Indian women.

It was believed that women sometimes gave birth to animal-like children. These were referred to as skuku'm (monsters). An illegitimate child born in 1925 was said to have been of human form below the waist, hair seal above. The head was long and "looked as if it was full of water." The mother was said to have killed it. Another woman gave birth to a creature "like a monkey" and a few years later to one "like an alligator, which made sounds like a land-otter." Several generations back a woman gave birth to a creature which was hair seal below the waist, with a sturgeon-like head. It was said that until recent years such monsters were always killed and their bodies burned far from the village and far from salmon streams and ocean, lest their ashes reach the water. This was the only type of burial involving cremation, though the Quilleute were said to burn all infants who died shortly after birth. The mother of a monster often died (*i.e.*, was killed by the creature), or was crippled or made blind.

CHILDHOOD

During the first month of a child's life the limbs were pulled and rubbed daily that they might be straight and strong in later life. Every day the child's body was rubbed with water in which an octopus had been cooked. This made the muscles strong "so that they could grab like an octopus." The eyebrows were rubbed to make them curved, and the nose was straightened. The ears were massaged to make them lie flat to the head "so they would not have ears like mice." When the umbilical cord dropped off the mother kept it until the child learned to walk, when it was tied to a string and placed around his neck "to keep him from getting into mischief."

---

[41]One informant stated that the parents of twins must refrain from eating fresh fish for a year and that during that time they must not cross a salmon stream; that during the year they lived back in the woods, camping beside a small creek.

At puberty the cord was removed, but placed in a safe place and kept throughout life.

Every child of good birth had its head flattened. Persons with undeformed heads were called ƙwico'sos (flea face) and were thought to be mentally inferior. Only orphans or the children of ne'er-do-wells grew up with heads not flattened. There was no rule against the flattening of the heads of slave children. The flattening was done as follows: A bundle of shredded cedar bark or ashes wrapped inside cloth was shaped like a small pillow, placed on the forehead and lashed tightly in place by thongs tied to the sides of the cradle. The pad for flattening was applied within a few days of birth. The lashings were tightened from time to time and the process lasted over a period of months.

While the head was being flattened the child was always carried in the cradle. This was a trough-like affair some thirty inches long hollowed out of red cedar. The inside was padded with shredded cedar bark which served as both mattress and diaper. Holes in the bottom served for drainage. The bottom of the cradle was rounded so as to permit of rocking. At the foot end a handle was carved to make for ease in handling. The cradle was carried on the mother's breast by means of a carrying strap which passed around the neck. Indoors the cradle was suspended from a curved springy vine maple pole attached to the wall. Strings from the corners of the cradle passed to the tip of the pole. A few scallop (laȧma'gwȧn) shells on a string rattled when the cradle was rocked. The skins of coon or wildcat served as blankets. Lashings which passed through holes in the rim of the cradle kept blankets and baby in place.

Children who were still nursing were usually carried at the breast to be near the source of food. Nursing mothers wore the robe or blanket pinned over the right shoulder and under the left arm. The child was carried inside the blanket, secured by a carrying strap which passed over the point of the right shoulder of the mother and under the child's neck. The other end of the strap passed under the left arm of the mother and under the child's buttocks. The ends of the strap were carried on around and tied at the back. Larger children were carried on the mother's back, inside her blanket, and were likewise secured by a carrying strap. During the first year the infant's hair was never combed, lest it cry continually and later insist on following the mother about everywhere.

A child was regarded as wholly irresponsible until four or five years of age, when "his sense comes" (tukolȧ'mmana). From that time on he remembered what he saw and heard. Children under that age were never punished. From about the age of five until twenty the child was talked to and advised every night by his father or grandfather. This was thought to "give the child the mind of his father or grandfather." Only low class people whipped their children. A child who was abused would likely grow up to be a rough parent who abused his own children. A well-brought-up child would live to be a credit to his parents, who would feel badly if he misbehaved.

Naming. Some informants stated that a child was named when one day old; others that no name was bestowed until the child was a year old. The latter probably was the usual custom, though there were undoubtedly some differences between the various social strata. A very young infant was referred to as skana'ił (baby), a young child as xa'kảo. When the child was about a year old the grandfather (or both grandfathers) usually gave a feast at which one of them bestowed his name on the child, at the same time often assuming a new one himself. Or the child might be given the name of a grandparent or more remote ancestor who had died some years before.

Some time before maturity a person usually acquired a nickname which referred to his appearance, to some act he had performed, or to something which befell him. This might be given by a parent, some other relative, or a companion. Nicknames were usually derogatory in nature, such as Big-nose, Rough-back, and so on. Sometimes these appellations displaced the real name. Members of the upper class, however, detested being called by their nicknames and only the village or tribal joker would use their nicknames in their presence.

When a person reached the age of puberty another name was usually bestowed, though it might be given earlier. This name was generally that of a living ancestor who had asked that the child be so named or had assented to it. In such cases there was no taboo on the name when the elder died. When B.M. was given his father's father's name his father gave a three-day potlatch, inviting all the peoples of the west coast from the Makah to the Chinook. Girls usually received a new name at puberty. The parents invited in all the adult females of the village, as well as a few old men. Food was served the guests, who spent the day singing the songs of their guardian spirits, or love songs. Toward evening the father or mother made a brief speech, announcing the new name. If the parents were people of means each guest was given a present.

I give the following example of a series of names: Bob Pope had three names. Na'ảmetux (close to the clouds) was given him when he was very young. koxo'djak (no meaning) was a name taken from his mother's father when Pope was about thirty-five. Kwa'tsagwił (middle of the canoe) was his father's name. When he assumed it (many years after his father's death) he gave a great potlatch and announced his new name at its end.

Personal names were regarded as family property (through either maternal or paternal lines) and no person would be given or allowed to assume a name not in the family. It was claimed that really new or original names were never bestowed. A man would not assume the name of a relative who had recently died. Several years must elapse before the name would be used, unless the name had been given to another during the elder's lifetime. The giving of a name did not make a previous one obsolete. The name received when a child might be used throughout life.

The following will illustrate the types of names customarily given. Some are nicknames by which individuals were known, the real names having been almost forgotten. But there seems to be no great difference between the types:

Men

łe'kmałtcu, "Owns the harbor"
xwảti'ảls, "Light-colored forehead"
djaxwanu'x, "Shaking all the time"
pe'koh, "Spotted skin"
lu'mlethu, "Red cloud" (from a guardian spirit)
tsảko'tsi, "Owns both sides of the river"
ta'knił, "Salal leaves"
kwatsảgwił, "Middle of the canoe" (Bob Pope's name; derived from his raven
       guardian spirit.)
xałma'ł, "Slow to get ready"
tsa'ảkotcản, "Muscles"
taukwinaił, "Full-blood Quinault"
pa'uhtsitcản, "Rough back"
mả't'litc, "To hold something"
klo'kgwak, "High legs"

Women

xwả'tłnal, "Thick lips"
kwiło'tcản, "Striped back" (a nickname)
xu'kảnis, "Teeth"
me'tsugutsałản, "Middle of the point" (from the village of that name).
kả'lảmnał, "Flat lips" (a nickname)
ƚlamts, "Red nose" (a nickname?)
pało'soh, "Thick face" (a nickname?)
tcảtsgwalolmixw, "Trouble maker" (a nickname)
kwi'xòtsi, "Creek tumbling like a waterfall"
xwe'tsảlgwas, "Person who ran away"
ƚwakaloxwas, "Salty when something is boiled"
kuntu'h, "Grouse"
tảpả'tckảs, "Thin nose"
djolo'ł, "Always crazy"
xwu'tsak, "On the corner side"
t'ảpả'cks, "Snot on the nose"
dje'ảlảmuh, "Weeping breasts"
na'ảmayah, "Worker"

ADOLESCENCE

Aside from a festival at which a name might be bestowed, and the rites attend-
tending the quest for a guardian spirit (*q.v.*), there were no special ceremonies attending the adolescence of a boy. A girl's pubescence was not the signal for ceremonies of major importance, which it was among the tribes farther north. Instead
it was merely a period extending over nearly a year during which the girl was regarded as unclean, possessed of supernatural powers, and during which her actions
would influence her entire later life.

At the onset of the first menses the girl was usually removed to the village of
no'omo'łapctcu (little Moclips) or to no'omo'łapc.[42] These places were special re-
treats. The latter was preferred because no red salmon run in the creek there and
the danger of stopping the sockeye run was avoided. In some instances, however,
the girl was permitted to remain in her home village. In any event she was placed

---

[42] The modern village of Moclips. The name referred in a vague way to menstrual blood.

in a tiny room (said to have been but four feet long) arranged in one corner of the house on top of the sleeping platform, partitioned off from the rest of the house. She remained in this room for ten days at the first menses and for five days on the four successive months during which the rigid restrictions were followed. During the five months no hunter might look upon her, lest he lose his luck. She must not speak to the others of the household and must not look at the fire, lest she age quickly and her eyes fail early in life.

At the first menses the girl fasted for five days but was allowed water to drink. For the remainder of the five-month period her diet was severely restricted and she spent nearly all her time within the cubicle. She was allowed to eat but once or at most twice a day. Ordinarily her only food consisted of five bits of whale fat and five small pieces of dried salmon. If she ate more it was believed she would become gluttonous; if allowed warm food, that her teeth would decay. If she ate fresh meat no hunters would be able to secure game. If she ate fresh fish the salmon run would cease. If she ate fresh berries Thunder (the thunderbird) would send a storm with thunder and lightning.

At the first menses the girl remained within the dark cell for ten days without going outside. For subsequent menses during the five months, the period was five days. She was provided with a water-tight basket of water and a small basketry cup for drinking. No one else might use these. The cell was so small that she could not lie straight, in fact she was warned against sleeping with outstretched legs lest she become pot-bellied. She was not allowed to gaze on others of the household or have conversation with them. She was not permitted to work during the entire five months, even basket-making being forbidden.

At the beginning of the period of seclusion the girl's face was painted with red ochre mixed with oil. Her hair was combed and plaited in two braids which were decorated with dentalium and allowed to hang in front of her shoulders. Each morning her face was washed by another and new paint applied. Her face was rubbed briskly with a cedarbark towel to prevent her becoming wrinkled. Once a week or so her hair was combed. If she washed her own face she would soon become wrinkled, if she combed her own hair she would become bald. So far as I learned there was no use of the scratching stick or the drinking tube.

An older girl (a sister or a friend) acted as her companion and helper (sakona'-ume'enàh, "watcher"). During the intervals between menses the girl bathed herself according to a definite ritual. Each morning, accompanied by her companion, she went to the stream (which was not a salmon stream) and waded out until the water reached her waist, then squatted down until the water reached her neck and sat with her hands folded under chin. She sat thus for a time, then waded ashore and again waded out. The fifth time she remained in the water a considerable time. Before the first plunge she rubbed her face and body with a red fungus which grows on rotting wood. At the end of the bath she washed this off, this being the only time she might wash her own face. On the way back to the house she was careful not to look back at the stream.

After her fifth menses had passed the girl's mother invited the women and a few old men of the village to a feast. The day was spent in singing songs, dancing, and feasting. At the end each guest received a present. Her long stay in the dark cell was now over. But her companion remained with her constantly, and she continued her daily baths. She was now regarded as eligible for marriage, and ordinarily did marry within a short time. During subsequent menses she was careful not to bathe, or even wet her feet.

A married woman also was under certain restrictions for five days at the time of the menses. She stayed inside the house, kept away from the river, and refrained from eating fresh meat or fish. At the end of the period she purified herself by bathing. If her husband was hunting at the time he would move out of the house and camp in the woods. If a hunter so much as saw a menstruating woman he had to bathe and purify himself for ten days. There were no restrictions or rituals in case he were merely fishing. There was no menstrual lodge. It was known that a woman's menses tended to come at the same phase of the moon, but there was no belief in a causal relation. Just before and during menstruation a woman drank quantities of a hot infusion of salmonberry bark.

A couple once brought their pubescent girl from Queets and stayed with some relatives at a Quinault village near the lake. Soon the sockeye stopped running. Then people knew that her five months were not over and that she had stolen and eaten fresh salmon. They started down the river taking the girl with them. When they came to the big log jam the Quinault seized her, tied stones to her body and threw her in the river. No one said a word about the occurrence, but since that people have been very careful to carry out the puberty rituals.

MARRIAGE

Young men ordinarily did not contemplate marriage until the all-important supernatural power had been acquired, but girls were regarded as fit for marriage as soon as they had completed the five months of seclusion. From that time until marriage the girl was closely watched lest she have affairs and become pregnant. Marriage was largely regulated by the parents, yet the wishes of the young were seldom violated. The caste system was not as rigid as among the tribes to the north, but matings between commoners and the higher class seldom occurred. Marriages between slaves and non-slaves were unthinkable.

When a young man took a fancy to a young girl he spoke to his parents about it and they began the negotiations. Or the parents of a young man visited various villages looking for a suitable mate. Kinship, no matter how remote, was a definite bar to marriage. All those of a village were usually kinsmen, so marriages were commonly intervillage. The Quinault tribe numbered at most only a few hundred. The result was that genealogical kinship could be traced between the majority. There was, therefore, an exceptionally large percentage of intertribal matings.

Divorce. In case a couple could not get along they ordinarily separated without any ado. There was usually return of the marriage gifts by both sides. The wife merely returned to her parents, taking along her personal effects, such as clothing, baskets, dishes, digging stick, and so on. The children usually followed the mother, though the man's children by a former marriage remained with him. To a certain extent the husband might exert pressure on the wife and her kin if he did not wish her to leave, but he could not force her to remain. The husband might ask advice of the chief, who might advise "Send her away if she doesn't suit you. It is better so than to have trouble." Common grounds for divorce were adultery, laziness, bad temper, barrenness (if considered the fault of the woman). There were no restrictions on future marriages.

Adultery. Sex relations between the unmarried were not regarded as serious offenses. If the parents of the girl learned of such, however, they usually insisted that the couple marry. The young man's parents were expected to exert pressure on him. A pregnant girl was forced to name her lover and her male kinsmen then sought him out and forced him to marry her. If he refused, they might kill him. The child was reared as if conceived in wedlock. If a man married a pregnant girl and he was not the father, the child was killed at birth. A child born before marriage was raised by the girl's parents, but if she subsequently married she usually took the child. Illegitimate children were not regarded with contempt.

If a married woman had an affair her husband, if he cared for her at all, might kill her lover, and sometimes his wife as well. If a husband learned that his wife was carrying on a flirtation, he made a point of warning the man before the affair became really serious. A man would kill even his own brother if he were the culprit.

When a young man (or his parents) had decided on a proper mate his parents paid a visit to the girl's parents to discuss the matter. Usually the young man remained at home on this occasion. No definite arrangements were made until the kin on both sides had time to talk the matter over. If the match satisfied everyone the boy's parents and possibly other kinsmen went to the girl's home to make the final arrangements, usually taking with them the gifts which validated the contract. These were not exactly a bride-price, as the idea of purchase was not uppermost, and among commoners they might be very minor items. A fairly well-to-do commoner might give ten blankets, a canoe, and a few other items. The party stayed at the bride's home a day or two and were feasted and entertained. The girl and her kinsmen then accompanied the groom's kin back to his village. The ceremony usually took place the following day.

For the ceremony the two kin groups seated themselves on either side of the house (or in two lines if outdoors). The girl's father then led the bride across to the other group and seated her beside the groom. Some of his kin usually brought gifts which went to the parents of the groom, who ordinarily gave most of them away to their kin. The bride's father then walked back to his own side. He then made a speech saying, *e.g.*, "I have brought my daughter over here, and now, my good people, you will have her as a mother to your village." He exhorted the couple to be happy together, to live in such a way that they would be respected, etc. The groom's father answered in kind, and the ceremony was complete. In the meantime food was being cooked, but before it was eaten there were songs and dances. After everyone had eaten, the bride's kinsmen went home, leaving the girl behind.

The ceremony for members of the nobility followed the same pattern but was more elaborate.

Elopement was a type of marriage resorted to in case objections had been raised by either parents, but was more frequent among commoners than among the upper class. The father of the girl might pursue the couple and, if his objections were strong, might kill the man. But ordinarily the elopement was regarded as proof of strong affection and the couple were permitted to marry. The groom or his kin had to make gifts to the bride's parents as in ordinary marriages. Elopement with a married woman was a serious offense and the injured husband had the right to kill the man without fear of retaliation by his kin. It was regarded "in the same way as stealing." But the husband might only say to her, "If you want that man for a husband it is all right, but you can't stay in my house and have him for a lover."

A famous elopement took place some four or five generations ago. Gwa'xwoⱡáp was a young commoner who made a trip to Montesano. There he happened to catch a glimpse of the daughter of pe'kuh, the chief. It was a case of love at first sight. She was but recently free from the puberty restrictions, yet already many men of high class had come to her parents seeking her hand. Despite the fact that she was constantly watched the two managed to steal away without being observed, and fled to his father's place. Her father had no idea who had taken her and sent his kinsmen and slaves searching for her. At Oyhut the news leaked out. But the chief was afraid to punish the young man because his father was a powerful shaman. The descendants of this pair became leading chiefs among the Quinault, Tȧxolȧ' being one of them

Polygyny was permissible but ordinarily only chiefs or lesser nobles had (or could afford) more than one wife. The greatness of certain chiefs was measured almost as much by the number of their wives as by the number of slaves they owned. The first wife exercised no authority over later ones, and it was stated that she could not prevent her husband from marrying a second. Sororal polygyny was the normal type, it being considered that if the second wife were not the sister or kinswoman of the first that the latter's children would have to submit to scoldings from a woman who thought nothing of them. A great chief who had ten or twenty wives (one chief of some generations back was said to have had thirty) of course married outside his wife's kin group. Sisters were less likely to quarrel than co-wives who were unrelated. Old chiefs sometimes took young girls as additional wives, but among commoners marriages were usually between age-mates.

In case of death the surviving mate was expected to re-marry into the same kin group, but there was no compulsion. A man was expected to marry his deceased wife's sister, but he paid the "bride-price" as for the first. The parents of the widower sometimes arranged the second wedding, though a man of middle age or past was allowed to conduct his own negotiations. The death of the husband obligated one of his brothers to marry the widow. If there were no brothers, or none without wives, another kinsman (e.g., a cousin) took the widow. In any event the kin of the deceased were obliged to care for her and her children unless she preferred to return to her parents, or until she remarried. If the widow married outside her husband's kin group against their wishes, trouble and bad feelings might arise. She was regarded as belonging to that group, as was the husband to the wife's group. The kin of a man leaving widows were expected to care for or marry all of them.

The widow or widower was expected to wait a year before remarrying and during that time to remove the taint of death by daily bathing. The widow of S.H., however, remarried (to J.M.) within a few days of her husband's death. A person who lost two mates was regarded as "poison" and it was thought that the third would also die. Potential mates therefore avoided marrying anyone twice bereaved.

Residence was pretty uniformly patrilocal but varied with circumstances. A young man seldom had a house of his own so the young couple usually moved into the house of the groom's father. But if the father had a number of wives, or if several elder brothers were already settled there so that the house was filled to capacity, the new couple might take up their abode with the bride's people. A young man of means might build a house of his own, or might join with his brothers or other kinsmen in the undertaking. The length of time that young couples remained with the parents varied. Houses were frequently torn down at the death of an elder and this usually broke up the household into several new units. The bonds between these new units, however, remained strong.

The following accounts of ceremonies, and of thwarted love, throw some sidelights on marriage and courtship:

A young man who lived at a village near Quinault lake wished to marry a girl from a near-by village, but her parents objected. He was without means and, moreover, was an inveterate gambler. He finally went to Bald hill in search of a guardian spirit. He built a fire there. From where he was he could look down on the lake. A group of girls, his sweetheart among them, paddled across the lake to gather salmonberry sprouts. She saw his fire and sang:

O neȧnskwȧlȧm cuk eł nȧh sȧgwilxʷcioł ȧłnȧgwih, O it seems to me that my heart flies to you.

When he heard her he sang in answer: kwemȧtcit łitciłtitcin natci łexelmȧntȧn, As soon as I came to the top of this hill she felt sorry about me.

Then he ran down to see her, forgetting about the vision he was seeking.

Johnson Wakinas' parents had made the preliminary arrangements with the chief and his wife at Montesano (Wynooche). Before they went over to bring the girl to kwi'nał for the ceremony they sent a messenger to announce the day of their arrival. A number of kinsmen made up the party. In front of the village the people shouted as in the potlatch ceremony. The canoe was beached a short distance from the village and the speaker went on to the girl's house with the gifts which had been brought. He talked to her parents, holding up the blankets, beads, etc. The parents were satisfied and then stated how much they were prepared to give in return. Then the chief came out and invited Johnson's father and party in, stating he didn't want to see them camping out. They were put up in various houses, staying two days. A month later the girl's people together with the people of many Lower Chehalis villages came to kwi'nał, bringing the girl with them for the ceremony. There were so many that they brought their own food. The next morning the people gathered outside, the Quinault on one side and the others in a row a hundred feet away. The Chehalis speaker then arose and said, "We want to see our young son (the groom) now. This girl we brought with us, she is now a mother of your tribe." The Chehalis then staged a dance, and then the Quinault danced. Some of the bride's party sprinkled dentalium shells along a "trail" to the seat prepared for her beside the groom, and she followed along behind them. The Quinault women were then told to pick up (and keep) the dentalia. After they had done so, all the Chehalis came over and each took some article of clothing or some other object from each Quinault. This mock-scramble was known as sxwi'tsnamił (taking things away). A feast for everyone present followed. The next day the bride's party returned home.

Once or twice a year the near kinsmen of the groom accompanied him and the bride on a visit of a few days to her parents, taking along food and gifts. Her kin were expected to make similar return visits on occasion. These visits were continued through the years.

Chief Peter of Neah bay (Makah) wished to marry a certain Quinault girl. He came down the coast with a fleet of ocean-going canoes, and they paddled up and down the river in front of kwi'nail singing songs. At a signal all the canoes were beached in front of the girl's house. In the chief's canoe were guns, blankets, beads, and so on. His men then carried the canoe, with the chief and the goods still in it, toward the house. When close enough he hurled his whaling harpoon at the house with all his might. It pierced through a plank. This was evidently regarded as a good omen, for it was said that he would not have taken the girl otherwise. The father of the girl now came out and was told that the whaling outfit, the canoe, all the goods in it, and several other canoes were his if he would yield the girl. It was stated that this form of payment was unknown to the Quinault.

A rather worthless young fellow who had no property but sponged on others was courting the daughter of the chief at the village of pini'lks. The girl looked with favor on him because he had a powerful guardian spirit. He used to come to the outside of the house and talk with her while she was in her puberty cell. Finally he persuaded her to elope with him, and loosened two of the wall planks so she could escape. On the appointed night he came carrying a large bag made of cattail rushes which he had stuffed with moss. "We'll run away, but I'll leave this bag of furs and blankets for a payment," he said. She felt the bag and decided that her parents ought to regard its contents as a reasonable gift. So they left the bag in the cell and started away.

But a female slave belonging to the chief was suspicious and kept close watch of her. She heard what was going on and awakened her husband; the two followed the runaways and overtook them on the trail to Baker's prairie. She persuaded the girl to return. The suitor continued to haunt the village but the slave warned him that he had best stay away. In the spring a Makah chief came and took the girl away, giving her parents four ocean canoes, five slaves, and a quantity of dentalia. Her father gave in return a considerable amount of property and three slaves, who were to be her servants.

A year later she was far along in pregnancy and she and her husband returned for a visit so her mother could attend her in childbirth. (The couple ordinarily went to the girl's home for the birth of the first child.) Her former suitor heard of the visit and came to the village. He had told her, "I will never allow anyone else to have you for a wife, because my guardian spirit is strong." She heard that he was about and was afraid of what he might do. She finally persuaded her mother to return to Neah bay with her. As they went down the river the rejected lover stood on the bluff below the village of la'lcil. The girl hid under the blankets in the canoe as they passed, but he "shot" his "power" into her and before they had gone far she felt a pain in her back. That night she told her husband, "I have a pain as if something had hit me." Soon her labor pains began and a stillborn child came forth. She bled profusely, blood even running from her mouth. As she died she told them what she was sure had happened. They took the body back to her home village for burial.

The young man, in the meantime, had run away to Grays Harbor. The dead girl's father sent two of his slaves down there to kill him. They found him, but pretended friendship, first telling him they were running away to their home on the Columbia. He believed them, and the three hunted and fished together. One night after they had hunted snipes on the beach the three made a bed, with the young fellow sleeping in the middle. While he slept one of the slaves ripped open his abdomen so that his intestines came out. His "power" was great, however, and he was able to raise himself up. But the other slave stabbed him in the back. The slaves hurried back to their master and told what they had done.

DEATH AND MOURNING CUSTOMS

The Quinault followed a number of burial practices without much real preference for any one type. Probably the commonest method was burial in a canoe which was raised several feet from the ground on a platform consisting of four posts and crosspieces. In some cases the body was placed in a rude box in the flexed position and a second canoe inverted over the box. In other cases the body was merely wrapped in mats or blankets and placed in the canoe, which was left uncovered. Another variant of the same method was to cut a canoe in half, placing one half in an inverted position over the other. One or more holes were cut in the upright canoe. Perhaps originally intended to prevent water from filling the canoe, the custom was interpreted as signifying that the canoes used in the land of the dead were so perforated. A related idea was that the canoe so treated was "killed" and so went to the other world, where the deceased might use it. In some cases the canoe was not elevated. Often the same canoe was used as a receptacle for several coffins or bodies, but ordinarily the individuals buried together were members of the same family, or at least close kin. Another ancient burial method was the placing of the body in a box on four posts. In some cases a small gabled grave-house was erected over canoe or coffin. Or the body might be placed directly in the grave-house. In some few instances the canoe or grave-box was placed in the branches of a tree—a variant of platform burial. In rare instances (*e.g.*, if a person died while on a hunting expedition), the body was placed in a hollow tree or in the hollow at the base and the entrance blocked to prevent animals from eating the corpse. Still another form of burial was in a shallow grave in the earth. There was no special type of burial for shamans, except that those who had been much given to evil magic were buried a short distance removed from the graves of others. Usually the body was placed with the head to the east—the direction of a road to the land of the dead. Otherwise there was no very definite orientation. The body was usually lashed with knees against chin and hands interlocked around the knees, and was placed face downward in the grave. Only children born monsters were cremated. The face of the dead was never masked.

When a sick person felt that his end was near he called his spouse, a close kinsman, or a friend and gave a few directions as to the disposal of such of his goods as were not to be placed with the body. As soon as death occurred several men were hired to care for the body and to prepare the grave. Burial took place within a day or so. The body was taken out through the roof, or through a hole in the wall made by removing a plank or two. Nowadays the body is removed through a window. It was believed that if the body were carried through the door the other members of the household would soon die of the same disease, "because they go in and out of the house by the door." The fear of the ghost also constituted a reason for removal through wall or roof. Now and then slaves were carried out of the house to die outside, so that the house would not be contaminated.

Usually only those hired to dispose of the body went to the grave. Near relatives took care to remain very quiet for some days; because when a person was in great sorrow the soul left the body very easily. The ghost of the newly dead was believed to hover about ready to seize the souls of living relatives.

Soon after the death one or more shamans were called in to drive out the ghost and the sickness from the house. This practice is still adhered to, the Shakers coming to the house and driving out the evil by means of bell-ringing, singing, and dancing. Between the time of death and the burial, friends and relatives came to the house to view the body and to comfort the members of the household by weeping with them. Those visitors who were relatives of the deceased received small gifts for this service, those not kinsmen received nothing. Those who handled the dead body ate no fresh fish for a month, and during that time purified themselves by bathing each morning.

The property of the deceased was disposed of in various ways. Blankets, a few utensils, a man's bow and arrows, and the like were rendered useless, *i.e.*, broken or torn "so they would go to the land of the dead" and placed in or alongside the grave.[43] Dogs, and in the later years, horses, were kept by the kin as mementos. A man's canoe was usually not destroyed (old ones were used for burial) but kept by the family. Slaves were not killed at the death of the master, but remained with the families. A man usually indicated before dying "what he wished to take along." It was stated that food was never placed at the grave. Guns were never placed with the body lest the ghost return and use it to kill a surviving relative. There would be no visible mark except a black spot on a person so killed. A man's shamanistic rattles were placed in a hollow tree some distance from the village.

About a hundred years ago a man named k̓le'el died leaving a wife and small son. Three days after he was buried he returned to his house, appearing as well as ever. He said to his wife, "In the place where I went there are plenty of fish but I couldn't catch any because I didn't have my driftnet. So I have come back for it. Where is it?" She pointed to it and he took it and started out the door. But his wife seized him and said, "You mustn't go back! Here is your little son crying continually for you. Stay with us; don't go back." The dead man turned, looked at his son. His head nodded quickly several times (a gesture of affection) but he went out without speaking. He went back to his grave and climbed into his grave-box; then he really died. Some people followed him, but he was already dead. The next day his son fell ill and died within a few hours.

A ceremony of purification of the house was performed within a few days after the death of an inmate, particularly if several members had died of the same disease. A member of the household gathered spruce and cedar boughs and the branches were burned near where the dead person had lain so that the smoke and crackling would drive away the sickness and the evil. As soon as the smokiness began clearing away and it was possible to enter the house, the boughs were taken out in the air and the objects of the house were beaten, while the phrase, oxo'xk̓loh kwi'tax djatso'-tsamph, Go! Go! Don't turn back again!, was repeated over and over. This ceremony was performed every day, usually in the evening, for a month or so. During the same period the ashes of the fireplace were strewn (daily?) around the house to prevent the return of the ghost—ghosts being very much afraid of ashes. The branches of currant were strewn within the house to give it a clean, fresh odor.

A short time after the death a near kinsman gave a minor potlatch, distributing some of the goods of the deceased and feasting the guests. Those who had conducted the burial were paid at this time, usually by the kin of the deceased, less commonly by the kin of the surviving mate.

---

[43]Another reason given for this custom was to prevent vandals from stealing the objects for their own use.

For a month or so the relatives did not go near the new grave. Following this period the nearest of kin went morning and evening and, standing a short distance away, sang songs of mourning, or merely wailed and wept. The cemetery was, at most villages, some distance away, frequently across the river from the settlement. But some graves were erected within a hundred yards of the houses.

The adult relatives of the dead cut the hair in mourning. The members of the immediate family cut it at the top of the ears. Close kin not of the family cut it necklength, more distant kin, at the shoulders. It was stated that even distant cousins cut the hair. Since nearly everyone would ordinarily be in mourning during the year for some near or distant relative the hair remained cut most of the time. For the death of one very much loved a mourner might cut the hair several times. If all one's near relatives died he cut the hair very short. There was no sacrifice of finger joints or other bodily mutilation during mourning.

There was a definite taboo on the name of the dead for about one year. It was a deep insult to mention the name of the dead to one of his relatives. Since many names were taken from natural objects it was necessary to change the names of some of these from time to time. A Makah girl married a Quinault man named k̓a′mkȧn (black salmon; also "fish"; also "food"). She became homesick and hanged herself. His name as well as that for the fish was then changed to tsi′łan (food).[44] After some years the original names were restored. The theory was that mention of the name of the dead renewed the sorrow. The relatives of the deceased might start a quarrel over such a case. If the name of the deceased even resembled that for something or someone else these words were avoided. An old Quinault woman had a son named tcȧme′h, who died. A Queets man was named tȧdja′mc. The old woman gave him the name of tsoti′sȧm to take the place of that which resembled (!) her son's name. Usually, however, another name, in place of the one which resembled that of the deceased, was chosen from the family array of names. The taboo on the name of the dead was rigid (within the tribe) for a year. But among the close relatives the taboo was maintained almost indefinitely. Thus, when I asked S.H. the name of his first wife (who had been dead ten or twelve years) he claimed not to remember and called on his second wife to inform me.

Those with means usually carried out the ceremony of reburial on the first or second anniversary of the death of a relative. There was no set time for such a ceremony and the less wealthy might postpone it for even five years. Invariably involved was the giving of a potlatch (see Potlatches) with the chief mourner acting as host. The ceremony was known as tsa′nstastȧm (move again the body). The bones were carefully collected, wrapped in new robes and blankets, and placed in a new box, together with new things such as implements, dentalium shells, etc. The box was then buried in the ground. Those who handled the bones were paid a considerable sum (twenty to thirty dollars in recent times) and there was also another payment made to the persons in charge of the original disposal of the body. There was no decorating of the bones, or ceremonial "eating" of them at this ceremony.

---

[44]This instance was one of two cases of suicide known to one informant. The other involved a case of love between a lad and a girl who were relatives and therefore forbidden to marry. The young man shot himself. Burial for suicides was the same as in more ordinary deaths.

There were few taboos on other members of the village after a death. After the first month there were few restrictions on the mourners. A widow was expected not to remarry within a year, but some remarried within a few weeks.

It was believed that if a person during his lifetime ate the flesh of an animal killed by a predatory animal that the "robbed" animal would dig up or molest his body after its burial. A.J.'s stepmother's mother's grave was dug into (it was one of the few cases of inhumation) by a wolf and the flesh eaten. The bones were collected and again buried but the wolf again dug them up. This happened four or five times, and in the end even the bones were eaten. It was believed this was because she had at some time eaten a deer or seal which the wolf had killed.

I was told that the dead were buried above ground because the dead sometimes returned from the land of the dead.

PROPERTY AND INHERITANCE

Like most peoples of the Northwest coast area the Quinault were property-minded and esteemed wealth as much as they did blue blood. The same word (ali's) meant both "rich man" and "chief" or "noble." But the social importance of rank and wealth was definitely less than among the tribes to the north. This more democratic structure no doubt resulted from or was encouraged by the small size of the villages (about four houses on the average) and the bonds of kinship within the village and, to a certain extent, within the tribe. Formally the social structure was rigid, with sharp distinctions between nobles, commoners, and slaves. But in everyday life society was essentially democratic, with all classes sharing in the labor, working together. Property as such certainly assumed more importance in the period following contact with European traders. Life was enriched by the comparatively easy acquisition of guns, blankets, horses, iron tools, and so on. Potlatches were certainly given more frequently than formerly, and the potlatch more than anything else tended to create a consciousness of social strata, or of wealth prestige.

Although the Quinault set great store by property and wealth there was not the amount of reserve goods found among the northern tribes. A house, a few slaves, a few canoes, furs or blankets, strings of dentalium, and supplies of food—these constituted the elements of wealth, even for the rich. Of these, slaves were as important for ostentatious purposes as for the services they performed. The greatest incentive to the accumulation of goods was the potlatch system, though this applied mainly to the rich, the poor not having the right to give feasts. Yet the potlatch system by its very nature prevented the accumulation of really large amounts of goods. When a man had amassed a sizeable amount of wealth he was expected to give a potlatch, and, conversely, if he planned to give a potlatch within a year or two he must needs begin to accumulate for it.

The Quinault were not rich in material goods other than foodstuffs. Their concepts regarding property other than of personal possession were poorly defined. A rich man accumulated wealth in order to give it away. Most personal goods were placed at the grave when death occurred. I have discussed the rules of ownership and inheritance of most forms of property elsewhere (see Death and Mourning Customs, Houses, The Household, etc.). I will state briefly, however, the main concepts of ownership and inheritance:

There was no idea of ownership of land beyond a "use-ownership" of the house site. Houses were nominally owned by one man but his title was but partial, being shared by others of the household. A man owned canoes, personal effects, implements, and dogs. When at the point of death he might make a verbal "will" regarding their disposition. Most personal effects were destroyed. Remaining things were randomly divided among the surviving members of the family (or according to his wishes), with a tendency toward the eldest son receiving the lion's share. The slaves of a rich man would be divided almost equally among the sons. If there were no sons in the family then the wife or daughters, brothers, and other kin received the property. Women owned little beyond the articles of their own manufacture. Some of these were placed at the grave, the remainder usually being given to the daughters or other female kin. Every person "owned" certain spirit songs. These were sometimes "given" to others before death. They were not inherited. The "owned" guardian spirits were likewise not inherited, being individuals in themselves. But they often voluntarily went to surviving members of the family.

HOSPITALITY AND ETIQUETTE

No man of standing would refuse hospitality to visitors. In fact one's prestige was enhanced by a reputation for entertainment. As soon as visitors—they were usually near or distant kin—from another tribe or village arrived, regardless of the hour, preparations for a meal were immediately begun. The other villagers, hearing the bustling about, would get up and repair to the host's house to share in the meal and get news and gossip. If visitors had no relatives in the village they went to the house of the most influential man ("the chief"). Even those with kin in the village were half expected to visit the chief first. There the old men would gather to hear the news. It was said that the Copalis people never let their fires die out, for they were always expecting visitors. Certain low class commoners, ne'er-do-wells, abused the rules of hospitality and definitely planned on spending the greater part of the year at the houses of their various relatives.

The family of kla'màts were low class. For weeks every year they lived in the house of old wake'anas at la'lcił. Then they would go to kwi'naił and live with old Tàxo'là. They had kinsmen among the Queets also and always spent some time there. Wherever they had relatives, there they would go to stay. They owned no house and very little property other than the canoe in which they traveled.

It was usual for the men of the village to gather before breakfast at the house of the most influential man. There they sat about on the platform or bench in front of the house. They gossiped, discussed what should be done during the day, and so on. At the end of this "conference" it was customary for one of them (usually one who had fresh salmon or meat in his house) to invite the others to his house for food.

ETIQUETTE

I made few queries regarding formal rules of etiquette and conventions of conduct. It was customary to enter a house without knocking or announcing oneself. The ordinary door was suspended from above and could be opened from the outside.

When lovers (or in some cases spouses) met they exchanged no word before nodding the head very rapidly as a greeting.

A girl had a lover who at sight of her came running toward her, nodding his head. This amused her so much that she made up a song which ran:

sin	tactcitla'n	nee	ma'álcxosá
what	news bring (you)	this	nodding head

(You come nodding your head and running as if you were bringing news.)

Swearing. Oaths ran to a pattern involving the use of terms comparable to our Anglo-Saxon monosyllables and used in much the same way and spirit. The only one I recorded was xa'kȧn atskutc xȧntcitcu'gwȧls, which translates freely as "Ouch, by a vagina, I hurt myself." A man swore at or tried to insult another by using a number of words regarded as vile or obscene. Less pornographic insults consisted in stating that the other was a slave or the descendant of one, and so on.

BLOOD PRICE

The principles of weregild were quite consistently carried out. Murder (sle'-kwih) usually involved a real blood feud, the relatives of the murdered man wreaking vengeance on the murderer. Only rarely would the relatives be molested. The murderer's relatives had no right to carry the feud further. In many cases the murderer or his kin might settle the affair by the payment of a blood price (slala'ktih). This was ordinarily higher for a noble than for a commoner and might be one to three slaves. Some shamans were thought to have the power to kill by means of sorcery. A man who fell ill without obvious cause might receive word through his guardian spirit that so-and-so was working black magic or causing the illness by more direct action by means of his "power." If the man died his relatives would then demand that the shaman pay. Powerful shamans suspected of several such killings were put out of the way. It is said that women never killed men, but even so no payment would have been necessary. A man who had killed several was regarded as a public enemy and a designated man might be paid to put him out of the way. If a man killed the slave of another he must pay a slave or a money-equivalent to the owner.

Justifiable homicide was recognized, but involved payment nevertheless. A husband had the right to kill his wife's paramour taken in *flagrante delicto*. The kinsmen of the culprit could still demand payment but the price was less than for ordinary murder. If payment was refused the kinsmen did not have the right to kill in revenge.

Motive played but small part in the compounding of a crime. If a man killed another accidentally he must pay the kinsmen or be killed by them. The killer's relatives could not continue the feud. In case of accidental injury the injured man must be compensated according to the seriousness of the injury. This was called sla'lakut (payment to make friends). If payment was refused the injured man perpetuated a quarrel until he was paid. Injuries which arose out of quarrels must likewise be compounded. The tribal or village "speaker" frequently acted as go-between for the parties in cases of both injury and homicide. His function was to avoid bitter blood-feuds and he might even set what he considered a fair price.

WARFARE

There was no sharp distinction in the native mind between feuds and warfare. The Quinault had little national sense and seldom if ever made war as a tribe. Feuds which transcended the immediate kinship groups might become intervillage, but even when the quarrel was with a group of another tribe, other villages were not necessarily involved. It is doubtful if they felt that it was any of their concern. There are some traditional accounts of trouble between villages within the tribe, of group feuds with other tribes; but there are no accounts which picture the Quinault, as a tribe, at war with other groups. Neither are there any indications that they made raids for the purpose of securing slaves, though many of their slaves were war captives secured in trade. In part this decidedly unwarlike, even timid, attitude is to be explained as the result of the tribe being scattered over a long stretch of river, of small villages bound together by an indefinite sense of a certain kinship bond between members of different villages. There was little sense of tribal solidarity, hence little tendency toward uniting in a common cause against a common enemy.

There was no separate class or caste of warriors. All adult males not too old to be active served as warriors. There was no special war chief. The headman of the village gave orders and led. If he were too old to take active part his place was taken by a younger man who acted under orders from the elder.

There seems to have been no idea of war honors of a formal sort. No glory attached to war activity. War was a necessary evil, engaged in to avenge a wrong. The sole war trophies seem to have been the heads of the slain. These were placed on poles on the margin of the village, the special place reserved for them being referred to as lakwailostán (heads on pole).

Perhaps about 1800 the people of kwi'naił enclosed the village in a palisade. From that time on it was also called atsa'lep (within the palisade). The palisade (kàla'xàn) consisted of posts about 16 feet long set into the ground about three feet. The posts were made of 18-inch cedar and cottonwood split in half and set round side out. The posts were strengthened by lashing hemlock poles about four inches in diameter just below the tops of the posts. Several openings in the wall served as gateways. These were closed by means of doors which were barred from the inside. Around the inside of the wall a cedar plank about 18 inches wide was placed as a shooting platform. It was placed at such a height that the head and neck of a man standing on it were above the top of the posts. The plank rested on stout pegs set into holes chiseled into the posts. In times of danger sentries (suxwanaxwàme'ànà, they who watch) paced back and forth along the platform. Several other villages were also palisaded.

The following were the ordinary weapons of war. A war spear (skewe'ḵlàm), about eight feet long; the handle was of yew, the point of whale bone or mussel shell. A war club (tci'toł) of whale rib, of the familiar Northwest coast type, was ordinarily carried. It was slung from the wrist by means of a stout leather thong so that the hand might be free for manipulation of spear or bow and arrow. Clubs of the same pattern were sometimes fashioned of stone. Bow and arrows completed the list of weapons.[45] War knives of iron were fashioned after contact with the fur traders.

Armor consisted of a sleeveless shirt (gwatke'lks) reaching to mid-thigh. It was made double, of the heaviest elk skin, and laced up the front. It is said that an arrow shot from the strongest bow would scarcely penetrate the double thickness. Rod and slat armor of wood or whalebone (baleen) was sometimes worn in addition. There were no protective devices for head beyond the ordinary hat, or for neck, arms or legs. The shield was unknown.

In time of war the active participants painted the entire face with a black paint made of cedar charcoal mixed with elk fat. The war headdress was a twisted rope-like headband of cedar bark dyed red. Undyed eagle feathers were placed upright in this. Eagle feathers were used because it was thought that they "helped" or protected the wearer.

A war party usually carried a crude drum (tambourine) made of deer hide (with the hair removed) stretched over a hoop of vine maple. Rattles made of the shells of a bivalve were employed. I failed to inquire about special war songs or dances. I was told that when strangers were seen approaching, the women and children of the village were sent into the woods to hide, on the suspicion that the newcomers might be enemies. It was said that all encounters were on land, never from canoes.

The following is the legend of a minor war between the Quinault and Queets. It serves to illustrate motivation and the lack of national sense.

Some people of the village of łałe'lap went to a village of the Queets for gambling games. The Queets lost heavily and out of spite killed a Quinault. His companions came home and related the incident to Tsa'álak (broken in pieces), who was a village headman. He said, "Well, I guess we will have to fight with them. Everyone get ready and we will go in two or three days." They went to the Queets river and watched until a canoe-load of Queets came down. They were relatives of the Quinault. From them the Quinault learned the village and house of the guilty parties. Then they went to that village and killed some of the inmates of that house. But the other Queets of the village, instead of being satisfied with an evened score, started to fight. Several Quinault were killed but the others killed a number of Queets, both men and women. The children were thrown into the houses and the houses fired.

The Quinault went home and built a palisade around their village. Each side made several more forays and before the affair was finally settled several of the Queets villages were involved. The Queets lost rather heavily and finally the war ended.

The following story relates to a feud which assumed the proportions of a minor war between the Quinault of one village and the Ozettes (a sub-tribe of Makah).

Nicagwats (grandfather of W. Mason and chief at one of the villages) had about a dozen slaves who worked for him. He started for Neah Bay (Makah) to trade his sea otter skins for European goods, taking his slaves along to man the canoe. His brother was married to an Ozette woman but often quarreled with her and abused her. He had wanted to go along on the trip but dared not out of fear for his wife's kinsmen at Ozette. Nicagwats landed at Quilleute and there his relatives warned him, "You had better watch out when you get to Ozette because we have heard that your sister-in-law's relatives are very angry about the trouble between your brother and his wife."

Accompanying Nicagwats were three of his wives, a daughter (W. Mason's mother), a son, several Quinault men, and two Makah who were to act as interpreters. At Ozette the party was invited in for a small feast. Nicagwats warned his men to take their guns and to be prepared for

---

[45]War arrows were of the same types as hunting arrows.

trouble. The host's house was on a hill. As the party climbed the hill two men came outside and fired twice at Nicagwats. He returned the fire and killed both—even though they were his relatives. All except Nicagwats and one slave ran back to the beach. Nicagwats was about to shoot the Ozette chief but refrained for fear the Ozette (who were now rifling his canoe) would kill his womenfolk. They had already captured one of his wives and the daughter.

The party walked south, some stopping with kinsmen at Hoh, the others going on to relatives at Quilleute where Nicagwats related what had happened. All the Quilleute came into one house and discussed whether or not to go to war. Nicagwats advised them not to fight, saying he would be content if they could get back the two women. He offered to pay them well if they succeeded. Four or five Quilleute, including the tribal speaker, decided to undertake the mission. They first went to the Makah at Neah Bay where they had relatives through the Quilleute chief's daughter's daughter, who had married there. A number of the Makah were persuaded to accompany them to Ozette, because the captured woman was part Makah. At Ozette the men fired volleys, shooting over the houses, and none of the Ozette dared show themselves. Then two Makah who were kin of Nicagwats went to the house where the captives were held, chopped a hole in the roof, and rescued the two. On the beach the raiders painted in black (for war), held a war dance, and dared the Ozette to come out and fight, but they did not. The girl was taken to Neah Bay to visit relatives for a few days. The son brought the wife back to Quilleute where his father was waiting.

The next year the Quinault involved made a trip to settle the feud and to demand payment for the unwarranted killing of xàla'skàn's father. A potlatch was demanded for this death, but the Quinault finally settled for three canoes, a quantity of blankets, and some other goods.

The methods of warfare are illustrated by the following accounts.

Both the Quinault and some of the Puget Sound tribes used to hunt and gather berries along the summit of the Olympic range. Some Quinault of one of the upper villages (who were regarded as "outlaws") once came upon a Skokomish camp. The men were away hunting and four women were alone in camp. These were taken captive and carried to the home village. Along the way the women secretly tore off bits from their grass skirts and dropped them to enable their menfolk to follow the trail. Once back home the Quinault were fearful for what they had done and all the people of the village were warned not to venture on the upper lake. But as time went by without sign of attack they again started visiting the district. It so happened that one party of hunters heard the sound of a black duck (to'tels) which does not frequent the lake. They knew that enemies were about. They landed and succeeded in catching sight of several men. They immediately returned to the village and reported what they had seen. That night a watch was set.

At dusk a sentry saw what appeared to be a bunch of moss floating near the fish weir. But it behaved strangely. He signaled to several others and together they went down to investigate. Hiding among the canoes tied just above the weir was a warrior of huge stature. They took him into a house and tied him securely to a post. They then went in search of the rest of the party. The raiders were sound asleep under the trees and were located by the sound of their snoring. They had hung their weapons on some small trees near by. The Quinault seized these and then proceeded to attack. Many of the party were killed. The few who escaped were intercepted by canoe and all but one or two killed. Places were named from the fact that hands, feet, heads and entrails of the fugitives were hung on trees along the trail of flight. The victors returned home, cut off the heads of the slain and placed them on poles in front of the village. The captive ordinarily would have been kept as a slave, but because he was so powerful a man they were afraid to keep him, and he too was killed.

The headman of the village was a fierce old fellow, fond of war and fighting. When he died they cut open his body and found that his heart was covered with hair. (It was believed that this was true of nearly all hardboiled men or those with specially potent guardian spirits.) He used to relate that his spirit power was tcitxwàn nalànu'xʷ (the bear that lives in the air).

The chief of the village of taàxe'ls (now Westport) was one Tsili's by name. He was known as an unscrupulous fellow much given to making war. He had more than ten warriors (!) He had several fights with the Quilleute and the Tulalip but was never defeated. He once sent a messenger to Quinault with the message: "I want ten slaves. If you do not send them, I will come and kill everyone in the village." The Quinault chiefs met and decided to send the slaves. One man was sent along with them. But when they arrived Tsili's only laughed and said, "I didn't mean what I said. I only wanted to see if the Quinault were afraid of me." Then he sent back the slaves.

It is said that about 1800 some of the villages of Grays Harbor united in war on the Queets. The fight was carried to Queets territory. The Chehalis succeeded in burning all the Queets villages and killing a great many Queets. The survivors fled to the woods and lived in temporary shelters.

The people of Oyhut were enemies of the people of Westport and frequently raided back and forth. Usually the Oyhut were the victors. Two Westport young men were on a vision quest but only one, Tsili's by name, succeeded in getting a vision. The old people were drying fish. The two went hunting and Tsili's' power aided him. When they returned he built a huge fire, hoping the Oyhut people would come to raid. The next day they saw a canoe-load of Oyhut men approaching. Tsili's ordered all except his friend to hide. As the Oyhut warriors were carrying stolen food to their canoe, Tsili's shot all except the chief, whom he spared to carry the word back to the village. In a few days several canoe-loads of Oyhut warriors came and tried to surround the village. But Tsili's and his friend killed all but two, who were spared to carry back the message. A third and larger party was also defeated. Then Tsili's and his friend raided Oyhut and succeeded in killing nearly everyone in the village. The houses were burned and the infants thrown into the flames. Tsili's came to be a great chief and a fierce warrior. He had slaves and wives from many tribes. In the end one of his wives got her kinsmen to ambush him as he lay asleep in his canoe. His time to die had come so nothing he could do availed.

SECRET SOCIETIES

The Quinault themselves state that they were at the southern limit of the secret societies found distributed among the tribes north of them, but it seems that a few groups of Lower Chehalis, perhaps even the Chinook, had vestiges of the same organizations. The secret societies among the Quinault died out many years ago and no member of the tribe now living was ever a member. (Pope had seen the performances, but he lived at the lake, whereas "chapters" of the societies were limited to some of the lower villages.) As a consequence my information on the societies is very fragmentary and much of it contradictory. I offer it largely for comparative purposes.

The two societies were known as the tsa'djăk and the klo'kwalle. The latter is usually referred to as the "Black Tomanawus."[46] The names themselves offer the clearest evidence of the northern provenience of the societies. The Quinault are quite definite in their statements that they acquired them through intermarriages with the Quilleute and Makah. The people of these tribes were much more given to the practices of the secret societies than were the Quinault; in fact, it is said that the klokwalle was known only at the villages of kwi'naił (4), djagakå'lmix^w (10), no'skałån (8), pini'lks (12), t'o'nans (15), and nokedja'kt (16).

The klokwalle was considered a special kind of spirit: "His name is klokwalle and one gets him in the same way as the sna'xos type. He lives beyond the ocean in the west, and comes (to this world) all alone in a canoe. He is black all over and wears a black blanket. He may not be used in curing, only for dancing and songs.

---

[46]The Quinault use the jargon word tomanawus as meaning guardian spirit, or even "power" in a sense almost equivalent to mana or impersonal, unpersonified power.

(There was no idea of bringing back the spirits of recently deceased relatives—which was a motive among the Quilleute.) He has many tricks which he does in the dances. A slave named Kai used to sing a klokwalle song in her own language. It ran, nol̶-amen nol̶amen tsis e l̶okalli e."

A.J. frequently dreamed of the klokwalle spirit. In her dreams she saw a big canoe rounding Cape Elizabeth. The people in it could be heard faintly, singing klokwalle songs. The songs grew louder as the canoe approached. Another night she dreamed that the canoe landed and the people came into the house, crawling on their hands and knees. She heard them beating the drums (a tambourine and a square box [?] form). She heard the rattle of the bone skewers they used for thrusting through the flesh. Their faces and bellies were painted black. But she was afraid and told people what she had dreamed so the actual power never came to her.

There were no elaborate payments necessary to the acquisition of membership in the klokwalle. Friends and relatives of members were often taken in without any initiation fee. The dances were held only during the three months following the winter solstice. During this period the members frequently met at night in the village potlatch house which served as a sort of clubhouse. Here novices were instructed in the ritual, songs, and trickery of the organization. The novitiate usually lasted five days and nights. During this time the novices were kept in a dark room. Non-members heard continuous drumming and singing and believed that the spirit entered the candidates at that time. The members made no claim that the novices were dead and were to be brought to life. In the subsequent ceremonies open to the public there was no "death and resurrection" rite,[47] nor did "blood" appear on the mouth of the novice. But the klokwalle had the reputation of killing and eating people during their secret rites. If an outsider stumbled in on them he was sworn to secrecy, cut about the arms, shown how to thrust bones through the flesh of arms and lips, and forced to join the organization. The leaders of the society (rich men) usually wore masks representing not the klokwalle spirit but their own individual guardian spirits (wolf, bear, birds, etc.). The Quinault used masks in no other rite. Only in the klokwalle and tsa'djàk dances was a carved rattle used. It was said to have been in the form of a duck with pebbles inside. The ordinary members wore no masks, as the mask was a signal that the wearer would shortly give a potlatch. In such a potlatch the secret society performances were a major feature.[48] All the dancers wore headdresses of twisted cedar bark dyed red in which were placed un-dyed eagle and sea-gull feathers.

The public was usually invited to witness the rehearsed dances of the society. While the audience waited the members retired to the secret room, or behind a screen, or to another house and made the necessary preparations: painting, dressing in costume, etc. It was said that most of them came out with numbers of bone skewers thrust through the flesh of arms and lips. During the songs and dances the spectators maintained a strict silence. If one of them smiled or laughed two members would seize him while a third inserted his fingers in the victim's mouth and stretched

---

[47] See Loeb, E. M., *Tribal Initiations and Secret Societies* (U.C.-P.A.A.E., 25:249-288, 1929).

[48] There was no identification of the klokwalle with the wolves. No cutting of the tongue formed part of the initiation.

his lips in a painful fashion. Or he might gash the arms or put skewers through them. The culprit's face would then be painted black and he would be dragged around the fire by the hair of the head and later be forced to join the society. It was said that in a performance at Skokomish a girl was killed because she entered the secret room while the members were preparing for a dance. Non-members were rather afraid of the organization, and often feared to attend their dances.

During the dance the members worked themselves into a frenzy and frequently gashed themselves with knives or thrust bone skewers in their flesh or performed prodigious feats of strength. Many of the dancers imitated the actions of the animals they claimed as guardian spirits. New members usually acquired songs from the klokwalle spirit which they sang during the dances. A Makah member whose spirit was bear dressed in the skin of a bear. One man used to thrust arrows through the flesh of the cheeks and dance with them hanging from his mouth. Another mutilation involved thrusting a knife or arrow through the flesh of the abdomen. One man used to eat live coals. One informant claimed to have seen a dancer seize a dog, tear him limb from limb, and devour the quivering, dripping flesh.

I am not definite about how much of this self-torture was make-believe and how much was genuine. A Quilleute who had been a member showed me numerous scars on his arms reaching from elbow to wrist. He said they were the result of his gashing himself with a knife during a dance. Some claimed that the skewers were removed during the dance; that the leader sucked and rubbed the parts involved, causing the wounds to disappear.

The public dances were said to last two days, beginning about noon and lasting until midnight. When the dancers were ready they marched out from the secret room or from behind the screen and ranged round the fire. They faced the fire and constantly moved in a clockwise (?) direction. During the first part of the dance the upper arms were held horizontally, the lower arms vertically, the hands were moved slightly, keeping time to the songs and instruments. The second part of the dance usually involved the wearing of masks by the leaders. In this dance the arms were folded with the hands concealed.

The tsa'djàk (careful?) was quite as definitely a secret society as the klokwalle, but was not regarded as evil. It was regarded as a curing society. "The tsa'djàk spirit lives among the driftwood of the beach and travels along the ocean near the shore. The sound of surf (with its màm+ màm+ and whispered ha+ ha+) is the singing of this spirit. The spirit travels with the wind, going to the north when the weather is fair, to the south in times of storm. He has the form of a man and he paints his entire body red. He 'owns' the clouds."

The members of the society painted their faces in red and wore cedar bark headbands with feathers in them. They practiced their songs, dances, and tricks in secret. It is said that the members were mostly women. The performances consisted of singing over the sick and the public performances given for show. The songs induced a sort of hypnotic sleep in the listeners. In the public dances the members ranged themselves along the sides of the house. Those on one side beat time with sticks on a long plank which rested on the knees. Those on the opposite side seated themselves and accompanied the singing by holding the arms with elbows bent and hands open to one side of the body, moving the arms in unison. At a given signal all reversed the arms to the other side of the body. This change referred to the tsa'djăk spirit who "turns" from north to south. Halfway through the dance those not drumming stood up and went through the same motions with the arms, and stamped the left foot in the cadence of the song. At a signal the arms were dropped and the dancers turned their faces to the wall, keeping time with the left foot.

When the dance was finished a dish of whale oil was brought in and all members washed their faces with this. Non-members who might try to do likewise would be almost blinded, but to the members the oil was as mild as water! Then pulverized salmon was brought in for both spectators and dancers. When they had finished eating the dance leader would stand up and say, "We are going to have a little fun now. Everyone watch what we are going to do." Members then took some of the salmon and rolled it in their hands for a time. Then several novices who were aspiring to membership would be lined up against the wall. (These novices were kept in a special house the several [5] days of their novitiate and were not allowed to see non-members.) The members would then "shoot" the balls of fish into them, causing them to fall down as if dead. Within a few minutes the fish was taken out of them and they arose none the worse for this experience. The novices were similarly treated every night during the several days of the dances. It is said that public performances were held only when there were several candidates for membership.

There were no societies or dances which restricted membership on the basis of age or sex. The bullroarer was not a part of the paraphernalia, though it was known as a toy. The attenuated form of the Quinault societies is probably best explained as due to the peripheral position of the tribe relative to the highly elaborated societies of the Kwakiutl and neighboring groups.

POTLATCHES

The potlatch institutions of the tribes of the North Pacific coast vary from the simple wealth displays of the Klamath river tribes to the highly formalized and elaborate affairs of the Kwakuitl. The former probably represent peripheral simple forms, the latter fairly recent elaborations of earlier and less complex types. Midway between these two extremes stand the potlatches of the Quinault. Like those of the northern tribes, Quinault potlatches are not necessarily associated with other ceremonies, while those of the south can be called potlatches only by a liberal stretching of the term, since ordinarily no property changes hands and the display of wealth is merely an incident in a larger ceremony. Probably the most fundamental element in the potlatch is the prestige which is acquired by displaying, giving away, or destroying property. Property, accordingly, has little value in itself and is not desired for its own sake but rather for the social and material benefits which automatically accrue to the person who has, or once had, property. To a certain extent a rich man's prestige is diffused so that his kinsmen, his village, and even his subtribe share in the benefits derived. A commonly stated reason for giving a potlatch is that "it helps one's family."

We know next to nothing concerning the prototypes of the modern potlatch, but it seems reasonable to assume that such features as interest rates and actual destruction of property are late additions. Perhaps older forms of the potlatch among such groups as the Kwakiutl, Tsimshian, Haida, and Tlingit were more or less like the modern potlatch of the Quinault.

The Quinault state that anciently potlatches were not known to them. The following tradition is related concerning the first potlatch among the Quinault—perhaps about 1800:

Xle'kmałcu gave a big pótlatch at the village of kwi'nail. He invited tribes from far down the Oregon coast and from Vancouver island: the Kla'akał and the Tsa'sti (who live south of the Tillamook), the Tillamook, the Kla'kemał, the Clatsop, and the Chinook came. And the Chehalis tribes and all the people of Shoalwater bay and the people of Oyhut came, the Queets, Hoh, Quil-¹eute, Makah, and Clayoquats. All these were there. Xle'kmałcu had built a special potlatch house for the event. It was 150 fathoms long and 25 fathoms wide. The first day they had a dancing contest. The Clayoquat, the Tsa'sti, and the Kla'kemał were the best dancers. So many people were here that not all of them could get into the house. All around the walls they cut holes so that they could see. Still there were some who could not see. Some climbed on the roof and moved the boards. The people inside shouted to them "Get down from there or the house will fall!" But they wouldn't come down. Finally the roof fell in. A great many people were hurt but no one was killed. It looked like there was going to be a fight because of the people who were injured. Johnson Wakinas' grandmother hid him in the woods because it seemed certain there would be a fight. But finally the quarrels were settled. Then they rebuilt the house and went ahead with the dance. They say that the Tsa'sti and the Kla'kemał won from the Clayoquats.

Another informant gave the following account:

Tsamama'ttsitca'n ("parallel roof beams"), who was Tàxo'là's great-great-great-grandfather on Me'tsugutsalàn's side, was the first Quinault to give a potlatch. He started the potlatch in this tribe. He had the "wealth" guardian spirit. There were so many people on the roof looking in that the roof collapsed on the dancers, but no one was killed. Since that time people have not been allowed to climb on the roof to watch. Ever since that time the Quinault have given potlaches.

Potlatches were held either in the large houses occupied by the chiefs or in houses specially built for the purpose. Traditionally only chiefs gave potlatches. A man of ordinary means might, if he chose, give a minor feast to kinsmen and friends of his own and near-by villages, and small gifts might be distributed to the guests. But pretentious affairs were always given by the rich and well-born. Theirs was not only the right but the obligation to honor themselves and their families by means of the potlatch.

Among most of the tribes of the Northwest coast the period of the winter solstice is the "sacred season," the time of ceremonial, and most potlatches were given at this time. But the funeral of a near kinsman, or the first or second anniversary of the death were also occasions of potlatching. In native theory an ordinary potlatch was in a way suggested by a man's guardian spirit. If a man had the "wealth spirit" the spirit would tell him, "You had better throw (away) our money now. I (*i.e.*, the spirit) would like to see the people enjoy themselves and to hear all the shamans sing their songs. So you invite so-and-so and such-and-such tribes so I can hear them sing." In this way would a man's guardian power talk to him.

When a man decided to give a potlatch he counted up his assets: the number of fathoms of dentalium,[48a] the number of blankets, the number of canoes, etc. He then decided how much of this wealth he would give away. He must determine which villages or tribes were to be invited and the amount which was to be given to each "chief" and commoner. To keep accounts straight a tallyman (su·kxwȧ' nȧma·ł, "he who counts") was called in and the two prepared a number of sticks some two inches long of pencil size. These were the tally sticks and each one represented the head of a family. As the prospective guests were named a tally stick was set aside together with the money or other goods which he was to receive. In case amount of property fell short of what he needed, he might call on his kinsmen to help.

When the property to be distributed had been carefully reckoned, and the list of guests made ready, the chief called together all the people of the village and announced his plans. In the days or weeks that followed the entire village was a hive of activity. The chief task was the collection of the enormous quantity of food which would be consumed during the three days of feasting. Some men hunted, others fished, still others gathered firewood. The women busied themselves in the preparation of food. The chief himself was the busiest of all, going from one group to another directing, advising, seeing that everything would be in readiness on the appointed day.

Formality surrounded the inviting of the guests who belonged to other tribes. The potlatch-giver called the man who acted as his "speaker" and told him what villages and tribes were to be invited. The speaker chose four to eight men to accompany him and started his rounds about two weeks before the potlatch. If the village could be approached by canoe the following procedure was adhered to: the messengers were met by two men who escorted them to the village and informed them of the names of the leading men of the village and their rank. The canoe was halted perhaps fifty yards from the house of the chief. The speaker then stood up and shouted as loudly as possible: "Wu+ kiłma·ti·tsi'h kwi·'naił!" ("We invite you to Quinault village"). The chief would not accept at once but pretended to consider whether it would be possible for him to attend. The man second in rank was then invited in a like manner, then the third in rank, and so on. Twenty or more of the leading men would be invited by name and then the remaining members of the village were given a collective invitation.

The speaker's party then landed and was escorted to the chief's house. The people of the village were invited in and the chief formally accepted the invitation. The speaker then named the giver of the potlatch and the day it was to begin. The chief then gave the speaker a sizeable gift and smaller amounts to each of his party. The following morning the messengers went on to another village.

In case it was not possible to approach a village by canoe the party landed some distance away. At the house of the chief the speaker stepped inside the door and, jumping up and down, shouted with all his might, "So and so, you and your family and also your dog are invited. So and so is to give a potlatch at such and such a village on such and such a day!" When he had spoken the head of the house arose and

---

[48a]In recent years American money (usually silver) has taken the place of dentalium.

said, *e.g.*, "Here are ten dollars and a blanket for him who is giving the feast; and here are five dollars for you; and here is a dollar for each of your helpers." The speaker then thanked him and they made the rounds of the village, beginning at the house of the man next-highest in rank. The speaker would not jump up and down, however, while inviting commoners. Slaves were never invited by name, though they might attend the festival. The head of a village might give a greater amount when he was invited than he would receive at the potlatch.

When the speaker and his party had invited all the tribes or villages who were to be guests they returned to the home village. The speaker then presented the chief with the money and gifts which had been given to the chief by those invited.

Much the same procedure was now followed in issuing invitations to the families of the home village. Several men were delegated to go from house to house giving formal invitations, the head of each household being expected to make a gift to each of the party.

Perhaps a week remained before the festivities began. The chief saw to it that the "potlatch house" (which might be his dwelling) was in order, that all utensils were ready, that each person who was to assist him during the festival was familiar with his duties. Several women were delegated to supervise the preparation of the meals and usually one or two men were assigned the heavier tasks, such as cutting up the meat. The chief, the speaker, and the tallyman rehearsed the names of guests and the amount each was to receive. Each of these special helpers received "wages" from the host, probably on the theory that they were not wholly free to share in the general festivities.

On the appointed day everyone gathered on the beach in front of the village to await the arrival of the visitors. As the canoes of each village or tribe arrived, their chief led them in file along the opposite bank where they paddled up and down singing their songs. After a few songs the canoes were beached stern foremost and the visitors repaired to the houses of relatives or friends to feast and visit.[49] As the visitors landed the chiefs among them were given presents by the host.

In the afternoon there might be a shinny game between the tribes, perhaps wrestling matches and gambling games as well. Toward evening the guests separated by tribes to prepare for the dances. The people of the home village assembled in the potlatch house—they were to be the spectators on this occasion. When everyone had painted and donned his dancing costume the chief called them into line and they marched to the potlatch house in single file led by a drummer, and singing as they went. When they reached the door the drummer beat on the door, in a mock-threatening manner, keeping time to the song. After a time the leader pushed open the door and they marched in, the men followed in order by the boys, the women, and the girls. They marched round the fire singing and dancing. They then separated, the males dancing on one side, the women on the other. The visitors usually

---

[49] There was so much inter-tribal marriage in this region that every man had relatives among several tribes, perhaps dozens of villages. Some informants hold that the visitors repaired at once to the potlatch house.

staged a whole series of songs and dances. Some of these were by individuals, others by such groups as secret societies, etc. Usually the festivities continued until after midnight.

After the first day it was the duty of the host to feast everyone in the potlatch house. Tremendous quantities of meat, fish, clams, oil, and berries were consumed at every meal. Each guest must be amply fed, lest the host be counted stingy. The guests on the other hand were obligated to consume, in the course of the three days, every morsel of food which the host set before them. The second day was one of games of shinny, running, wrestling, jumping, and weight-throwing contests. Gambling games and further feasting filled in the time.

In the dances of the second night the visiting groups ranged themselves around the platforms of the potlatch house and were mere spectators. The people of the home tribe sang the songs, performed in the dances. To a certain extent the element of rivalry and competition entered these performances, but there were no awards of any sort. The incentive was merely the individual or tribal prestige which went to those who by common consent had staged the best "show."

The third day represented the climax of the ceremony. This was the day of real potlatch, the native term being smato's (lit., "give away"). Some time during the morning a large mat was spread on the floor at the door end of the potlatch house and on top of the mat a blanket was laid. On these were placed the blankets, shirts, shawls, money, etc., which were to be given away.

The host seated himself by the pile of goods with his tallyman (sukwa'nåmaɬ, he who counts) on his left side, his speaker on the right. All the guests were then called together and ranged themselves by tribes round the walls. Most major potlatches were given when an adolescent child was to receive a new name, but it is difficult to determine whether or not this constituted the *raison d'etre* of the festival. If the son of the chief were to receive a new name at this time the chief now took him by the hand and announced: "Here is the little chief who is giving this potlatch," or "I have here my son so and so, and now I give you gifts so that you may all know that that is his name."[50]

The gifts were then distributed by tribes and by rank within the tribe., *i.e.*, the head chief of a chosen tribe received the first gift, the man next in rank in the same tribe the second gift, and so on until all the guests of that tribe had received. It is said that in issuing invitations the tribe farthest north was invited first, and those to the south from them in order. The same order was followed in the giving of gifts. These gifts were likewise graduated in size, the man of highest rank receiving the most. The people of the home tribe were the last to receive. Each gift was disposed of as follows: the host gave the tallyman the name of the next recipient. The tallyman picked up a tally stick, sorted out the gift or gifts intended for this particular individual, and passed them to the host who handed them to the "speaker." The speaker arose and shouted: "Hey, so and so, such and such given you by this child! Come and receive it!" The recipient then came forward and as he took it repeated: "ans pana'x" (my gift).

---

[50]In the invitations the chief was always announced as the giver of the potlatch. In the return potlatch this child always received the first and largest gift.

If a man received a gift which he thought was beneath his rank, or which was perhaps of less value than his contribution at the time of the invitation, he then, instead of carrying the gift over his shoulder, dragged it along the ground. This was called ste'łpa·na·x (to drag the gift) and was the signal for someone to shout ,"He is not satisfied." He was, then, as a rule, called back and given more. Only a low commoner would "drag the gift" thereby injuring the host's pride. It may be mentioned in passing that men, women, and children received gifts; only slaves got nothing, though they shared in the feasts. High class women received more than commoners.

When the last gift had been distributed the speaker cried: "Has anyone been forgotten? Has anyone been forgotten?" If there was no reply the host folded up the blanket which was spread on the mat, stood up, and eyeing the members of visiting tribes, said: "he·n gwa·t tås tee· nsiniłin" (lit., "Right here who that wishes to take it"). This was a challenge to all comers to give a return potlatch, say a year later. The visitors would feel disgraced were the blanket to remain in the hands of the host, so usually one of the visiting chiefs was prepared to accept it, thereby obligating himself to give a potlatch in return. He would usually make every effort to give a greater potlatch than the one he attended as guest.

The host now arose and sang his "farewell to my wealth" song. This was in part a "farewell," in part a ritual song which would bring him more wealth. The visiting chiefs now made speeches praising the generosity of the host and so on. When these were ended everyone started for home, the potlatch was at an end.

The foregoing represents the only "real" potlatch of the Quinault, but directly similar festivals on a smaller scale occurred on other occasions. Thus, when Bob Pope's daughter was drowned all those who were present at the burial were invited to come to his house where each was given a present. He not only gave away money but all his potlatch equipment such as dishes, etc., thereby signifying that because of his grief (several of his children having died) he would give no more potlatches. Similar ceremonies might be held at the funeral of any near kinsman.

Present at the funeral of Pope's daughter were two Quilleutes. These received presents in the ordinary fashion. After all those present had been given gifts Pope called them aside and said,"And here is ten dollars Joe Pullen, and here is ten dollars Tommy Payne. Now you deliver a message to the people of Quilleute that I have lost my child." The money was to serve as "message carrier." On their arrival at Quilleute the two men added some money of their own and prepared a minor feast for the people of the village. Those present were told of Pope's generosity and of his sorrow. The leading men made speeches to indicate their sympathy and sorrow. They promised that next spring when sealing-time was over they would come down to kwi'nail. "Next year they will come and on a designated day will go to Pope's house where the chief will make a speech telling of their sorrow on learning of Pope's misfortune. The visiting chief will give a sum of money (perhaps ten dollars) saying, 'Take this to wipe the tears from your cheeks.' Each one present will likewise present Pope with a sum of money."

The mourning anniversary was usually initiated by the chief mourner (the foregoing ritual need not be a part of it). He would say on the first or second anniversary of the death: "I will rebury that dead person." Then he would invite a number of people from his own and other tribes. To these presents would be given and each in turn would give him a present. There is no feasting on such an occasion. These rituals attending funerals and mourning anniversaries obviously differ somewhat in nature from the elaborate potlatches. But in the native mind both types are regarded as potlatches and for this reason I have included them in the category.

I am not altogether certain just what other occasions are times of potlatch. But it is evident that the great potlatches always occurred during the winter "sacred season," and the greatest of these were those involving the giving of a new name to an adolescent. I was told that minor potlatches might even be given in May or June because travel conditions were especially favorable then and guests coming from a distance would be less inconvenienced.

The greatest potlatch which the Quinault remember was one given at Potlatch, Washington, by ten Skokomish chiefs who pooled their resources for the occasion. My informant estimated that $50,000 worth of property was given away at the time, but this is probably an exaggeration. It is said that twenty-two tribes were invited, including Quinault, Queets, Lower Chehalis, Upper Chehalis, Nisqualli, Puyallup, Muckelshoot, Tulalip, and Klallam. The feast lasted eight days. The potlatch house was more than fifty fathoms long and twenty-five wide. They held a footrace inside the house!

Quinault potlatches stand about midway in the scale between the simple wealth-displays of the south and the exaggerated and complicated ceremonials of the northern tribes. The actual giving of goods as opposed to mere display is probably due in part to a greater amount of wealth, in part to a question of social convention. In the potlatches of the Kwakiutl and neighboring tribes the features of bitter rivalry, high rates of interest, destruction of goods, fictitious values, and the "fighting with wealth" stand out as pathological social patterns. It is difficult to envisage these as natural or logical developments. They are more understandable in terms of a temporary mania induced by an attempt to remake a prosaic culture in the pattern of a foreign one—that of the Haida,, Tlingit, and Tsimshian. This interpretation might seem far-fetched were it not for the fact that other features of Kwakiutl culture fall into line—such as the lack of consistency in the matter of descent, and the illogical organization of their secret societies.

I mention these points for the reason that the potlatch of the Kwakiutl has long been regarded as typifying the whole potlatch system of the area. Actually it is an extreme type, an example of the lengths to which an institution may be carried. A potlatch more or less like that of the Quinault is far more likely to turn out to be the prototype. Its pattern remains fairly simple; no deeplaid plots, no egotistical mania surround its inception or execution. The fundamental elements are the desire to gain a moderate amount of social prestige—the element of rivalry scarcely enters. The giving of goods is almost as much a privilege or an obligation as the occasion of display of vanity. The feasting and games bulk large in the picture. It is a festival, a "good time" period, with the words of the guardian spirit best expressing its tone and the native conception of the institution: "You had better throw (away) our money now. I would like to see the people enjoy themselves and to hear all the shamans sing their songs."

DIVERSIONS

The Quinault were fond of all manner of games and most of those played by adults involved betting. Although it was recognized that some individuals were "lucky" and others clever at cheating, continued success was usually regarded as due to the good fortune of having control of an especially potent gambling spirit. Such a person, it was thought, was certain to win in any game of chance. Guardian spirits which conferred luck and skill upon their owners were much sought (see p. 150). Athletic contests and games played for amusement were not occasions of much betting. Heavy wagers were not often laid except when the opponents were of different villages or tribes, and this was usually during potlatches.

GAMBLING GAMES

The widespread slàha'l was played by four men, two on a side. There were two pairs of bones about two and one-half inches long, of a size which could be easily hidden in the hand. One of each pair was marked with a black band at the center. The players faced each other across a mat. At one side 20 or 40 marker sticks for each team were laid on a plank. To start the game one member of each team took the white or unmarked bone and concealed it. Both teams then guessed simultaneously. If both guessed correctly they exchanged bones and repeated the procedure. When one missed his guess the opponents took all four bones and now each of the two men on this team shuffled a pair of bones behind his back or under a blanket. Then both men placed their hands in front and the opposing two guessed, each at the same time and each directing his attention to the man opposite. A gesture to his own right (always with the right hand) indicated the left hand of the opponent, a gesture to the left, the right hand. The guess was for the white bone. If both guessers were wrong they lost one counter (or two); if both were correct they won one (or two) and the right to hide the bones; if only one was correct neither counters nor bones changed hands. Onlookers, who were usually partisan, backed their respective favorites and often bet among themselves. Bets were collected only when one side had won all the counters.

Another guessing game was called slàhàllam or sukuma'ł. Two men were the active participants but, as with most gambling games, onlookers frequently made bets, aiding in the singing of guardian spirit songs giving "gambling power." Each man had 12 yew wood discs about the size of poker chips but somewhat thicker. Ten of these were left their natural color, one was colored white, another black. The players faced each other across a mat, and a tightly rolled mat was fastened along its center. (In some cases each had a separate mat which was rolled up somewhat at the front to form a buffer.) Each man had two bundles of fluffed cedar bark. Twenty tally sticks for each were placed on a plank at one side. To start the game each man shuffled his discs somewhat like we shuffle dominoes and then placed them one by one in the bundles of bark. Great care was taken to prevent his opponent from observing in which bundle either of the marked discs were placed. The bundles were then shuffled very rapidly in the manner of the "shell game" shuffle. The bundles were then held one on each knee for the guessing. The first man to miss a guess had to guess first, and the game began with the other repeating the same performance in hiding, shuffling, etc. He studied his opponent's face trying to get a clue as to which bundle he was going to guess. The guesser used the same gestures in making a choice as were employed in the game of sláha'l, but indicated whether he was guessing for the black or white disc.[51] When a bundle had been chosen the hider took out the discs one by one and rolled them across the mat where they struck the barrier. If the guess was correct the guesser won the right to do the hiding. At each incorrect guess an onlooker passed a tally stick from one pile to the other. No bets were paid until one man had lost all twenty. He also lost his tally sticks, but not his discs. In a really big (intertribal) game each man (or there might be two players on a side) might have 40 tallies. It was believed that the man who lost the initial guess was certain to lose the game. When a man's luck was running heavily against him his guessing became bad and the singing of his side was weak.

Beaver teeth dice were used only by women in a game called smà'táom. Only the large upper incisors were used. A set consisted of four teeth. Two of these were marked on one side with zigzag lines and the other two with a series of dots. The former were called ka'djow (man) and the latter k̓lik̓uklik̓ᵘ (woman). The game was usually played with the opponents kneeling on either side of a mat. Onlookers might bet if they chose. It is said that some women were very clever with the throwing and were not above real cheating. Usually each woman started the game with 20 tally sticks. The following table summarizes the results for the thrower:[52]

"Men" up	"Women" up		Result
2	2	....	Wins 2. Throws again.
0	0	....	" 2. " "
2	0	....	" 1. " "
0	2	....	" 1. " "
2	1	....	Loses 1. Loses dice.
1	2	....	" 1. " "
1	1	....	" 1. " "
1	0	....	" 1. " "
0	1	....	" 1. " "

THE SHINNY GAME

Shinny was played with a ball of hard dry wood about two inches in diameter. The stick, of vine maple or young hemlock, reached from the middle of the chest to the tip of the middle finger, with a natural curve at the end. The striking end was flattened somewhat to give better control over the ball. Because of the wooded nature of the country the game was usually played on the beach, though it is said that a clear, level stretch of river bottom near ɬalciɬ was the site of a field. Lines were drawn on the sand about a mile apart. These formed the goals. At kwi'naiɬ one

---

[51]One informant stated that only one disc was marked, its rim painted black and a black dot placed in the center.

[52]I am not entirely certain that this listing is correct.

goal was just west of the village, the other at the south end of the beach. The playing field was the width of the beach. A spot guessed to be equidistant from each goal marked the place where play began. A team was composed of five to twenty men, with an equal number on the opposing team. The players were completely naked except for headbands of cedar bark, which were in the nature of uniforms. The Quinault always dyed theirs red, the Queets theirs black. There seem to have been no definite positions assigned to the various members, but the fastest runners usually stayed near their own goals, awaiting a chance to score. There was no goal keeper. To start the game the ball was buried a few inches deep at the center of the field. A man from each side was chosen and at a signal they dug with their sticks for the ball. As it was flicked out by one, the other seized it and the two wrestled to prevent each other from running with it. This was the only time during play that the ball could be taken in the hand. The ball was then placed on the sand and the players manoeuvered for it, each attempting to pass it to a man on his own side toward his own goal. A clever player dribbled the ball, attempted to dodge his opponents. It is said that now and then a man succeeded in carrying the ball from the center to the goal. When a score had been made the sides exchanged goals. The first to score two goals won the game.[53] If the losers were not satisfied with their showing they challenged, but a second game was never played the same afternoon. "Real" games were always between villages or tribes, but practice games between village mates were common. Although it was not usual to lay heavy wagers, rivalry was keen and dirty tactics and fights were a part of every game. Tripping the man carrying the ball, or stepping on his stick were favorite ruses. If there was bad blood between the opponents the side which had determined to fight continually seized the ball in their hands and ran with it. This forced the others to catch the culprit and throw him down. A general melee usually followed, with the spectators sometimes joining in. Bullies sometimes seized the smaller men or lads and tossed them in the surf. By common consent such bickerings were not continued after the game was over. At each goal were stationed two referees, one chosen by each side. I heard of one instance where a Quinault (Pope) played on the Queets side in a Queets-Quinault game, winning the game by a spectacular dash. The spirit of the game approximated that of our own athletic contests.

TUG-OF-WAR

Sides were chosen with eight or nine to a team. No rope was used, the two "centers" merely grasping the ends of a stout stick. The second man grasped the center around the waist, the third man the waist of the second, and so on. Heavy persons were put at the end of the line, but the strongest was chosen to hold the stick. A line was drawn just behind each anchor man. To win, the opponents' anchor man must be pulled across this line. But it was also counted a win if the opponents lost hold of the stick. Each side chose a man to act as judge. Contests were between villages or tribes. Women sometimes formed teams.

---

[53]Wakinas stated that a single goal ended the game. Others stated that the number of goals for the game was agreed upon beforehand.

WRESTLING

Like shinny, wrestling matches were usually held at potlatch time. A whole evening might be spent in the matches. The preliminaries were between boys of six or seven, with the better matches later, culminating in the bout between tribal champions. The wrestlers agreed beforehand on the type of hold to be used, as it was against the rules to change during a match. In the "hair hold" each grasped the other by the hair and attempted to swing the other off balance. Tripping, changing the position of the feet, or moving the feet was against the rules and referees watched for infractions. In "body hold" matches the contestants grasped each other around the body and by lifting, shoving, and pulling each attempted to throw the other down or over the shoulder. Since a man could not shift his feet, once he was off balance the match was lost since falling in any position was counted a "fall." The usual stance was with the feet wide apart, the left somewhat in advance. A third but uncommon type of wrestling was like the preceding except that the contestants rested on the knees. A single fall ended the match, but if the loser was dissatisfied he might ask for another. Boys were sometimes trained to become wrestlers. In the ritualistic bathing to acquire strength a wrestler used the hemlock boughs freely on the neck "exercising" it so that in the "hair hold" type his neck would not bend. Bets were seldom laid on the outcome of wrestling matches.

TESTS OF STRENGTH

One man would grasp the wrist of another with his left hand and the arm, just above the elbow, with the right and attempt to bend the arm at the elbow. A strong man could keep a straight arm. Men would pull fingers, pairing all four. It was said that these were the only tests of strength. Women did not engage in them, nor did they wrestle.

HORSE RACING

Probably few of the tribes to the north ever acquired horses, so the Quinault contested chiefly with the people of Grays Harbor, especially from Chenois creek and Humptulips. The horses were ridden bareback. The race was not to a point and return but merely a straightaway. Heavy bets were usually laid, with horses, blankets, shirts, and money the items mentioned as stakes.

CANOE RACES

These were invariably intertribal, except for test races to pick the crews. The distance was usually about a mile, and did not exceed two. The race was a straightaway, not to a point and return. The local course was the lower reaches of the river, the races being run at high tide. In most races there were eight paddlers and a steersman, but four-paddled races were also known. In the latter the man in the stern might switch from one side of the canoe to the other to alter the course. Sometimes crews were composed of women.

SWIMMING

Races were held now and then and usually there were many contestants. At kwi'naił the race usually started from the north bank of the river, with the south bank as the finish. The only stroke known was the "dog paddle" with the feet kicking up and down. In diving matches the usual point was to see who could remain under longest. Wading contests consisted of wading into water over the head, the winner being the one who waded farthest. It was said that most swimming contests were between men of the same village or tribe, few intertribal contests being known.

FOOT RACES

These were usually held at potlatch time. Each race was between two men of different villages or tribes. A starting and finishing line would be marked off on the beach, the distance usually being about one or two hundred yards. There were no relay or to-a-point-and-return races.

JUMPING

Contestants were of different villages or tribes. Two men, one from each, held a cord or pole between them, the contestants taking turns. The jumper faced the barrier and jumped from a standing start. There was also a running broad jump.

GIRLS' GAMES

Girls and young women played a game called ski'iḵutcanȧm ("hiding stick between fingers"). A group formed in two lines facing each other. Each side had a bone or stick about 2½ inches long. A long blanket from one end of the line to the other was held in front to conceal the hands while the bone was stealthily passed along the line until some girl retained it. When all ready, the blanket was dropped and each girl on that side held her clenched hands under her chin, rapping her knuckles together in rhythm to the song which had started. All the girls of that side smiled while singing to aid in the deception. A girl from the other side guessed who was in possession of the stick. Until a correct guess was made the same side repeated the hiding. In starting the game both sides hid a bone and both took a turn at guessing. The first to make a correct guess won the right to hide. There was a song for each side, one being a repetition of the phrase atmȧla he, the other of the phrase ala wi. My informant did not know the meaning of either. Old people and boys never played the game.

Girls and women played sxwate'xam ("person's head") on the beach. A group formed into sides and each proceeded to model of damp sand the head and shoulders of a woman. The eyes, eyebrows, teeth, etc., were indicated with white pebbles. When the figures were complete they were set up about thirty yards apart, and a stick about five feet long was stuck in the sand in front of each. Someone would then say to the other group, "You'd better come and get my stick." A girl would then start to walk to the stick, while her opponents attempted to make her smile or laugh by shouting, making faces, or telling jokes. The trick was for the girl to reach the stick without showing even a trace of a smile. Then she had to return.

When all of one side had failed the others got their turn. The side which gained possession of the sticks the greatest number of times won the game. Oeh the Cannibal Woman was said to have been fond of this game and gave it the name.

SWINGS

Swinging was enjoyed by both adults and children. To make a swing-frame long poles were each forked with two others and lashed near the tops. Another pole was placed in the forks, making a cross-bar. The rope was of braided willow bark. There was no seat. A person sat on the swing-rope and another "swung" him. There was a certain amount of rivalry "to see who could go highest." Singing formed a part of the sport, a favorite song being a part of the myth of the cannibal woman killed by the boy hero who used magic to cause her to fall out.

BALL AND PIN GAME

This game was played with the spongy root of a skunk-cabbage for a ball and a sharp stick four to six inches long. A string connecting ball and stick measured from finger tips to elbow. The ball was jerked into the air and an attempt made to impale it as it fell. A variant was played with a forked stick and two balls, but it was seldom that the two could be impaled. There was no idea of "shortening the winter" by playing the game.

HOOP AND POLE GAME

In the hoop game, sàdjala kukuum, men and (or) boys formed two "sides" and took positions facing about 50 feet apart, each side forming two lines separated about 20 feet. A strong man cast the hoop with an overhand throw. As it rolled between the opponents' lines they attempted to spear it. The following hits counted: if the dart passed through the hoop; if the dart entered so that the hoop remained impaled; if the hoop rolled close enough for a player to catch it on his dart and raise it above his head. In case of the last the opponent forfeited a dart—an ordinary stick about 10 feet long. The number of points which constituted a win was decided before the game. Now and then bets might be laid on the outcome of a game, never on a single throw.

BOW AND ARROW GAME

A fungus[54] about four inches in diameter was placed in position and shot at from a distance of about 50 feet. A hit counted as such regardless of nearness to the center, but the arrow must remain in the target. When one hit and the other missed the loser forfeited his arrow. Side bets were sometimes made both by players and onlookers. In a variant of the game a smaller fungus was used and the arrow closest to the target (or a hit) won. Another variant was played at night with a tightly-wrapped 4-inch bundle of grass as the target. This was placed against a rotten log with pitch-wood torches lighting it. The contestants were always four men or boys. The nearest arrow won, the other three being forfeited to the owner. Arrows were identified by the feathering. A game somewhat like these was played

---

[54]It was believed that all echoes came from fungi, "because they are shaped like ears and throw the sound back."

with spears of salmonberry or young hemlock. Two large fungi would be placed as far apart as a spear could be thrown. The players stood near one, threw their spears at the other, then walked to the other target and threw back. At potlatches a board with a hole in it an inch in diameter would be placed at one end of the house and men, women and children would take turns shooting. The first to shoot an arrow through won. In late years it became customary to pay such a one.

A curious contest or "game" consisted in swallowing pebbles. If a contestant could cause a pebble to travel so that it could be felt beneath the skin of his body or limbs the game ended and he was declared the winner! There was no game of shuttlecock and battledore, springing board contest, or scramble for a ball tossed in the air. (Cf. Gunther, *Klallam*, pp. 277, 278.)

TOYS

I did not inquire about many types of toys and the following probably represent only a small part of those known.

Tops were made of sections of skunk cabbage about two inches long thrust through with a spike of salmonberry which formed tip and handle. The tops were spun by holding the handle between the palms. Men and boys played a game as follows: Each would have ten or twenty tops and these were spun in pairs on a disc of hide stretched tightly over a hoop about thirty inches in diameter. The tops migrated to the center, met, and one would be "thrown." The owner of the "winner" gained the "defeated" top. When one had won all the tops he won the game. Small bets were sometimes made on the final outcome, not on single spins. The winner usually threw all the tops in the air and there was a scramble for them, and a new game could begin, or each could keep those he obtained. The chief toys of boys were bows and arrows.

Girls used to play with a small pink clam shell; these would be placed around in the sand.

Dolls were made of a bundle of cedar bark folded double and tightly wrapped just below the doubled portion to form head and neck. A stick thrust through formed the arms. Wrapping below this stick-crosspiece formed the waist. Added shreds constituted the skirt.

The common type of sling (ta'mt) was a simple strip of cedar bark about four feet long, but rawhide was also used. It was employed only as a toy. Another stone thrower (fig. 20) was made by taking a slightly curved stick about two feet long, splitting it down some distance, and lashing the tip and below the split. The split was whittled away somewhat at the center so as to more easily receive a flat pebble. The throwing motion was an overhand flick of the wrist, imparted so that at the proper point the pebble was thrown free. This was also merely a toy. The bullroarer was known but was likewise a toy.

PETS

Like many other peoples the world over, the Quinault seldom killed the young of animals but took them home and reared them. It is said they fed them well, and spent much time taming and training them. Usually the animals were kept until grown, then turned loose. Although they returned now and then, finally they went back to their kind. Animals kept as pets were never killed for food. Dogs were kept as much for pets as for aid in hunting or for the supply of wool which a special breed furnished. Girls were never allowed to play with dogs lest there occur again the incidents of the Dog Husband tale. Among wild animals mentioned as pets are pheasants, sawbill ducks, and all manner of birds; bear, beaver, cougar, elk, seal, sea otter, marmot, and deer. Even cougar and wolves were not muzzled. Pope stated that the only animal he had not heard of as a pet was land otter; they never happened to catch the young. He had never heard of albino animals (nor of albino humans).

Pope had many bear cubs as pets at one time and another. Once he was hunting near Quinault lake and heard what he took to be a young elk. He caught the animal, but it was a young cougar! It made no resistance but seemed to like him. It would follow him like a dog. Finally he gave it to Walter Major who took it to Queets. There it took to killing dogs so they finally despatched it. Pope and others had pet marmots, but people grew tired of their infernal and eternal "whistling" so let them go.

SMOKING

It is extremely doubtful that the Quinault knew the use of tobacco before contact with the fur traders.[55] At first the trade tobacco was mixed with salal and hemlock leaves. It was customary to inhale until one grew so dizzy as to fall over. Pipes were made of a kind of clay which hardened on contact with the air. The only one of native manufacture which I saw was of a pattern not very different from an Irish clay pipe. A lizard representing a guardian spirit was carved in low relief at the juncture of bowl and stem. At the present time few of the men smoke, it being prohibited by the code of the Shaker faith.

CAT'S CRADLES[56]

The tribes of western Washington were familiar with a great variety of string figures. I heard of individuals who were able to manipulate complex figures, employing both fingers and toes, and of two individuals performing in concert. None of my informants, however, knew of these and I learned only the following:

---

[55]One informant claimed that no tobacco was used in pre-European times, but that "winter berries" or "shot berries" were smoked in an elbow (or angled) pipe carved from the hard blue clay to be found near natural gas wells.

[56]Preliminary positions are those referred to in Haddon, Kathleen, *Artists in String.* (London, 1930.)

Two mountains:

   (a) Position I (Haddon, p. 155)
   (b) Opening A (*Ibid*, p. 156)
   (c) Slip loops off index and fourth fingers on to thumb in that order.
   (d) Grasp with all fingers into the main loop.
   (e) Extend index fingers so that upper double strand is on back of fingers.
   (f) Grasp upper single string with index fingers and turn downward and outward, releasing thumbs. This gives
   (g) "The two mountains" (tsamsma'nitcuh). See figure 32.

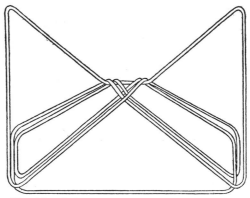

Fig. 32. Cat's cradle: "two mountains."

Two beaver (tàmà'h xlà'k̓klitc or sk̓lastàmmà'w xwt łàgwi'làmic, hunting beaver two men):

   (a) String around wrists at base of palms.
   (b) Fourth finger reaches under to engage thumbside strand.
   (c) Thumbs reach in like manner to engage lower string so that the strands cross on face of palms.
   (d) Index fingers take up under crosses on opposite palms.
   (e) Hold strings firmly by pressing all digits of each hand together and with teeth take loops from back of each hand and drop each in turn between hands and separate hands. Result is
   (f) "Two beaver." See figure 33.
   (g) Forefingers reach over and grasp the vertical strands at *x* in figure 33, dropping the strands at *y*. Tension is put on strands and
   (h) "Here are the two men (hunters). Now the beaver are going to run."
   (i) Forefingers release as this is said and the hands spread and again the two beaver appear. Hands seesaw, causing "beaver" to retreat. "Now they have run away." As this is spoken the loops are slipped off thumbs.

"Cut fingers" is performed exactly as in Ball's "Yam Theft."[57] This is called k̓wai'k̓làtcàsix̌ʷ (cut hands). Another figure of the same type is as follows: Left

[57]W. W. Rouse Ball, *An Introduction to String Figures*. (Cambridge, 1920.)

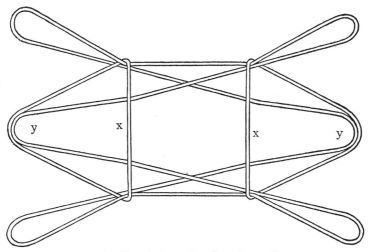

Fig. 33. Cat's cradle: "two beaver."

hand is held fingers up with back of hand toward operator. String is looped over little finger. Grasp both strings so that index finger is between the two, pointing downward. Twine strands in fingers of left hand so that ulnar strand passed to palmar
side of ring finger by a clockwise twist of right hand and so on, by alternating clockwise and counter-clockwise twists of right hand, the same string always remaining
on top. When thumb is reached the strings are not crossed but are run parallel
around thumb. Then a clockwise twist of the right hand passes them over the index
finger, a counter-clockwise over the middle finger, a clockwise over the ring finger,
and a counter-clockwise turn over the little finger. Release from thumb and pull
long ends.

Aside from the foregoing my informants knew of figures called two old ladies
with canes, bird, rabbit, person, elk, and canoe. The general name for cat's cradles
is màdje'enàm ("watch hands").

At night people used to manipulate their hands to cast silhouettes on the wall
which resembled various animals. This game was called màla'h (shadow).

MUSIC

The Quinault had only the drum and rattle for musical instruments. Accordingly they had no music beyond their songs. I obtained the notation of none of
these and recorded the words of only a few. Almost without exception their songs
involved at most a single repetition of the words, followed by almost endless repetition of the air accompanied by nonsense syllables, chiefly ho, o, and hai. Many songs
had no words. Dancing was in imitation of the animal or spirit being represented
or was merely a stamping of the feet (alternately) in time to the music. Songs were
composed on various occasions, as shown by the following.

Once upon a time a girl had a lover who often came to see her. He was only a
common fellow. Her friends learned of the affair and warned her, "You had better

tell him not to come so often. You had better act as if you were mad at him."
Whereupon she composed the following song:

> sinkaxwatc   xełih   madja′kåł   ȧnsȧgwa′nc
> Why angry   with him (who)   is the same as   my guardian spirit.

A woman once went with friends to Puget Sound. When she arrived she fell
fast asleep. Upon awakening she sang:

> snåxa′axȧs   ans   naxȧs   neȧsȧmeȧxȧn   nista′xwa′t′mix^w
> O I am sleepy   my   sleep   when my sight falls on   this strange place.

A young man's song was:
> tsa′qetcȧnȧ   le′es   tsa′ qetcȧnȧ   le′es   xweȧqwe′leeh
> They stood   up,   they stood   up   my friends.
> tci dja′xci au   k̇åccenȧ′a·lcit   łonagwa′lcit
> I picked out   which one   the best one.
> (*I.e.*: The girls were standing singing. I picked out the one I thought prettiest.)

Mothers often sang their children to sleep. One lullaby ran as follows:
> tsȧ′łal   au   hetsi′ho
> Sleep   now   little one.

The drum was usually of the tambourine type, though one informant mentioned
a skin-covered drum "shaped like a box." The drums were painted with crude representations of such subjects as eagle, owl, snake, sun, moon, or a man's face. The
drum stick was of the usual form, the knob covered with skin or cedar bark. The
usual rattle consisted of a bunch of deer hoofs tied to a stick. Singers sometimes
beat time with a stick on a plank held on the lap, or pounded the roof boards of the
house with a long pole.

RELIGION AND SHAMANISM

Aside from the beliefs and practices regarding guardian spirits, there were few concepts relating to the supernatural. There was no concept of a supreme being. Prayers were sometimes voiced but these were addressed to "the world," not to a personified entity. The world in this sense was regarded about as we regard "Nature." Words might be addressed to unusual animals but only because they might possess some "power." There was no worship of heavenly bodies or of the forces of nature. Above this world lay only the air, the clouds, and the sky, inhabited by special types of guardian spirits. The underworld was the abode of the dead. Supernatural animals and monsters of human and animal forms existed but were not objects of veneration or worship. Misp, the creator-transformer, was scarcely distinguished from Xwoni Xwoni, the lecherous trickster-buffoon. Ghosts were creatures to be dreaded. There were no offerings of thanks or propitiation. Quinault mythology reveals no beliefs regarding either deities or other types of superior beings.

Interest in the supernatural centered around the concept of the relation of individual and his spiritual helpers. Nothing bulked larger in Quinault life than the acquisition and control of supernatural power. Without the aid of guardian spirits even those of noble blood could not aspire to great things and were likely to lose their wealth and prestige. But even a man poor in the world's goods and of low caste might rise to a position of wealth and influence if he controlled or owned potent helpers from the other world. Such great store was set upon the control of supernatural power that all but a few sluggards made it a point to procure a guardian spirit. Only a few were said to be unable to get a vision. The "training" for the quest began at seven or eight years of age and continued for several years. Ordinarily a youth did not stop his search for power with the acquisition of one spirit but continued until he controlled a number. Spirits might continue coming to a man at intervals until middle age or later, but the earlier comers were the mainstays.

Girls did not search for supernatural powers as assiduously as boys, though they were supposed to go through a period of "training" in order to make them healthy (see puberty rites under Adolescence). But not many girls acquired supernatural power.

The average man controlled spirits which aided him in hunting. More fortunate seekers also acquired others. The spirit at the time of vision usually took the novice on a trip through the air or to a high mountain where he foretold the seeker's length of life, things which would befall him, taught him songs and dances, gave him certain paraphernalia (especially directions as to what type of wand or rattle to make), and told him what pursuit to follow. There were spirits which were wealth-giving, others which enabled the man to be successful at whaling, in war, or gambling. The "twice dead" spirits were employed in the search for lost souls; others cured illness by the sucking method.

The spirits which came from the land of the dead seem to have been the commonest type. Others might be powers of the air, monsters, or other creatures. With the possible exception of powers which came from submerged logs, from forked trees, or from the bones of the dead (see page 46), all spirits and powers were personified. They were ageless, usually sexless, and never died. As among many North American tribes the spirits partook of the nature of both men and animals. They came in the "form of animals, yet looked like men." After they came to a man they stayed fairly close to him throughout his life, often remaining in a corner of the house, or near their tangible symbols, the carved rattles. In any event they could be called back if they were away on whatever business or mischief they amused themselves with. The control exercised by the master over his supernatural helpers seems to have been pretty complete—he could in most cases compel them to do his bidding. A few might do things contrary to the wishes of their masters.

A man to a certain extent partook of the nature of his guardian spirit. An old fellow who lived above Quinault lake "could jump 20 feet, because his power was mountain lion." A curing spirit gave the power to see the body of a sick person with an X-ray eye and so determine whether a disease-object or soul loss was causing the illness. Except for the glimpse into the future at the time of the vision there was little prophesying in Quinault shamanism. A shaman could usually predict recovery or death for a patient, could name the party guilty of shooting spirits or objects into a person, but could tell little about the future. A shaman could recover stolen goods, but he seldom named the thief; instead, using the rattle and guided by the spirit he followed the thief's trail to where the goods were hidden. In cases of evil magic the shaman was helpless.

Shamans did not constitute a class apart. This was probably because every man was, so to speak, his own shaman. However, a man did not often try to cure himself but called in another. There was no idea that homosexuals, hermaphrodites, the insane, or other abnormal individuals were more likely to become shamans than were normal persons. A shaman was merely an ordinary individual who had been particularly fortunate in acquiring exceptionally potent guardian spirits of the type or types which enabled him to perform deeds ordinary mortals could not.

If the salmon run failed it was thought that the dead people were preventing them from coming to this world, for all salmon came originally from the land of the dead. A shaman was then called in to make the journey and attempt to steal a fish or two. This caused the salmon to run. If he (or the guardian spirit) failed it was only necessary for the latter to rub his feet in the fish slime where the dead had been cleaning them. Upon coming back the spirit then washed his feet in the river in this world, and the salmon would soon appear.

The shaman could cause illness or death by throwing or shooting objects, mere "power" or the spirit itself into a human or an animal. He could also cause small snakes, lizards, frogs, night owls, and other creatures to appear in his hand.

Shamans sometimes engaged in contests by "shooting" power into each other, usually at potlatch time when there was an audience. Shamans who were enemies might engage in bitter contests even when in different villages! This was accomplished by causing their guardian spirits to do battle. If one shaman and his spirit helper were searching for a wandering soul another shaman might send his guardian spirit to block the road, preventing their return. One informant claimed to have seen a shaman die as a result. The "guide" tried to go around the obstruction but lost his way. His master became insane and died within a few days. Guardian spirits were sometimes afraid to make the trip under such circumstances, and were always fearful of venturing where they did not know the way. Hoh said another shaman once blocked the path for him, but he was fortunate in having Mole for a spirit, who was of course able to burrow under any obstruction.

THE VISION QUEST

During the later years of a man's life guardian spirits might come to him and give him of their power without much effort on his part. There seems to have been the idea that possession of certain powers made the shaman attractive to other spirits. A man controlling a score of spirits need not go on a vision quest for each one. Some came to him after the death of relatives who had controlled them. Spirits might even come to a man against his will. Only men wishing to work magic sought malevolent spirits, yet a good shaman was likely to have several such. These he must carefully watch, lest they work harm without his knowledge. They might bewitch his tools or his arrows, which would then become "like poison to people."

The supernatural helpers which came to a man in his youth could be acquired only by means of prolonged ritual. From earliest childhood he was impressed with the necessity of obtaining shamanistic power. Over and over he would be told that distinction in hunting, in gambling, or in any other pursuit depended on it. When he reached the age of eight or ten the boy's father started him in his "training." Every morning at the break of day the father told him: "Wake up and go and bathe before the water wakes up. It is not as cold now as it will be after it wakes up." The lad then ran naked to the river and plunged in. Then he came out and scrubbed his body with braided hemlock bough or vine maple until his flesh burned, the blood came through the skin, and the water "felt hot." Usually he plunged in five times and then returned to the house. This ritual was repeated every morning throughout the year. H.S. told me that he remembers many occasions when icicles formed in the hair and the frosty stones on the bank stuck to his feet as he walked back to his house. During this preparatory period there were certain taboos observed. Foods which were greasy or which had a strong odor (such as dried salmon) were disliked by the spirits who would smell them and remain away. If the novice ate fish heads it was believed he might become insane. Salmon eggs which were fully formed made a noise when eaten and were taboo, for their crackling would be heard by the spirit who would cause the bather's head to ache. The skin of dried fish crackles when placed in the fire so the novice was forbidden this food for it was thought this noise would be inside him and would frighten the spirits. The seeker also avoided women, for the spirits would not come to a man who was constantly having affairs.

Usually a young man made it a point to acquire supernatural power before he married, lest he remain poor. Guardian spirits avoided a man who smelled of women. If a seeker ate at night the spirit might come to him in his sleep, smell his breath, and go away.

Sometimes a man sent his son to another village, or even to another tribe, to seek the power. There he was under the guardianship of a man (usually a chief) well versed in the art. The lads paid him by helping him in various work and hunt. Boys sent to the village at Westport were sent to a creek called Leme'me to bathe, and they were told to bail out the canoes anchored there when they had finished.

After several years of daily bathing the youth began to make long trips up the creeks and in the mountains in search of a place where the spirits would come to him. He might spend a year or more looking for a likely place. The place known as "Burned Hill" on the Quinault river, the falls on the Raft river, and a spot on the Queets river about 15 miles above the mouth were considered the most likely places. Certain classes of spirits were thought to travel on the ocean or along the beach and if the novice was anxious to acquire their kind of power he bathed in the surf and performed his vigils along the shore. During the time that the son was searching the father often "talked to the world" in the only prayer which the Quinault seem to have used. This was called tàme·'xa, stàkwe'tsix^w or nomixwantà'mix^w. The same prayer was used by the youth himself while bathing and on his searching trips. He would stand in the water, lift up his face and blow toward the sky, saying, "I want you to help me." There was no definite form and a person might ask for anything he wished. For example the father might say, "May you have mercy on my son and send thy spirit to him that he may become a shaman." A man might pray for luck while on a long or hazardous trip; but there were no prayers for the sick, nor did a woman pray in childbirth.

The vision-seeker might be gone several days at a time. Sometimes he dreamed that he should go to a certain place for his vigil. If he dreamed of the place five times he would certainly get his vision there. During this time he slept but little and ate very sparingly or not at all. At the spot chosen for the vigil the novice built a fire and stayed all night, bathing in the stream now and then, and praying. If after several days the spirits had not come, he returned home and resumed his bathing, keeping his mind constantly on the object of his search. It was believed that if one had followed the prescribed preparatory rituals the spirits were sure to come in the end. Perseverance assured success.

The vision itself was terrifying in nature, and the faint-hearted usually ran away. It was usually preceded by a roar of rushing wind. Huge trees and logs might come hurtling end over end through the air. These were signs that the spirits were coming. These manifestations might last an hour or more. The following account of a vision illustrates the type:

"I stayed two nights and a day at the place. In the middle of the second night there came a roaring as of wind, things came through the air and the ground swayed and rocked. Then I heard the scream of an eagle. He came near and I saw him in the guise of a man. He went round and round the fire and then went away. I was very much afraid and wanted to run away. Then I heard the sea monster (sta'noǩ) near by, and he, too, walked around me. I was afraid he was going to carry me off. Then there came a monster snake (o'lkàh) who made a noise like the land otter. Finally Turtle came and walked around me and went away. Each of them gave me power. They gave me (the power of) good eyesight which enables me to see the sickness inside people. Snake sucks the blood and poison out of people."

Usually the youth fell asleep after he had seen these things. As he lay sleeping the real guardian spirit came to him and carried him away to the abode of the spirit. There the spirit talked to him and told him that he had sent the vision. He was told "such and such will be your trade" or specialty. The spirit would give him special instructions regarding the rituals and methods to be used in hunting in the mountains or for sea mammals as the case might be; or for curing the sick, controlling the weather, or causing illness or death. The novice was instructed to make certain objects, especially figures representing the spirit.[58] The spirit also taught him the songs and dances he was to use in connection with the power. The Quinault did not buy or sell songs received in vision, though they knew that the Makah and Nootka did.

Sometimes the spirit came while the youth was asleep and, instead of taking him away, left a token of his visit, *e.g.*, a feather. The seeker would then get only a slight amount of power.

A youth who especially desired to get the ocean spirit walked along the beach during the months following the winter solstice. It was believed on the day of the lowest night tide (in December) the sun "jumped" quite a way to the south and the spirits came back to this earth with the sun. That night one was almost certain to meet ocean spirits, especially the one for hunting whale (who was known as slào'ĭtcà or the "Western" spirit). The seeker usually fell down at the edge of the surf and was cared for by the spirit. When he came to himself and knew that the power had come to him he walked home. Usually he was ill for several days because of the potency of the spirit. People were then called in to hear the songs he had received. This singing soon cured his power-illness. But nearly all his life the lad continued his ritualistic bathing.

Even rocks and other natural objects were thought to possess a mana-like power which humans might acquire and control. Forked trees were also potent and it was considered dangerous to have one near a village. At night lightning could be seen darting between the forks. Lightning was often seen emanating from cliffs, rocks, etc., and was a sure sign of power in the object itself, or that it was the place of residence of a spirit or the site of some power.

GUARDIAN SPIRITS

The following were claimed to be spirits which could be controlled, listed in the order of their type and potency:

1. sena'xo·s is a powerful spirit who lives in the air in the west. Only a few are fortunate enough to have this spirit, and a shaman who controls one is much in demand and is paid high fees for his cures. The supernatural power is useful for all manner of things but primarily for curing by the sucking method (removing bones stuck in the throat, etc.).

2. adjà'xos also lives in the air in the west. He specializes in the same things as 1 but is not quite so powerful.

---

[58]These were commonly made by a friend or relative according to instructions given them, but might be made by the person who had the vision. The "spirit catcher" of the northern tribes was unknown.

3.   kalixtalmix^w also lives in the air and is a curing spirit. But he is tricky and not to be depended on. His "owner" could send this spirit into a man's food or drink and cause him to choke. Even when his master desires him to do good he may work harm unless closely watched. Only this spirit has an invisible web or net and he is continually watching for a chance to catch a person's soul in it, causing illness or even death.

4.   Most of the spirits of the skà'djap class also live in the air in the west, but a few live to the east. His owner may either cure or harm and may milk his victim of nearly all his wealth before curing the disease he has effected.

The preceding are spirits which live in the air or upper world.

5.   sta'nok is the head, the oldest, of the family of snakes, and comes from the rivulets at the head of creeks. He has considerable power, which is used mainly in curing.

6.   The group of spirits known as tciła'kwikulc (he who comes from the dead place) are adept at finding souls who have started toward the land of the dead. When a shaman controlling one of these was called in he might say "Yes, your soul has gone. My tciła'kwikulc tells me so." The spirit led the shaman and his helper along the trail the soul had taken. (See Death and the Land of the Dead.)

7.   There was no sharp distinction between the "real skuku'ms," who were cannibal women named oɛ'h and those called skuku'm ma'łikulc or heca'itomixw (devil of the forest), who live in the high hills and mountains. One of the cannibal women was Xwoni Xwoni's aunt. Misp killed the last of these. But the second type still exists. Most old people had one spirit of this type. For some reason it was known as an elk spirit. Some of the skukums were in the form of men. Lizzie Copalis lived for a time at Copalis beach. Many times a skukum came to her and talked. He told her never to marry, for he was her husband. He wore a blanket of elk skin with the hoofs attached. She kept these visitations secret until just before she died. Some skukums were said to be "long, black and tall, with a human face." They disappear at the approach of humans.

About 50 years ago there lived at Westport a famous hunter who was the son of the chief. On one occasion he had killed several elk and was wondering how he could carry all the meat home. He lay down beside the fire built under the drying rack. When he awoke the fire had died down and on the other side of the fire he saw a woman sitting with her back toward him. Her two braids reached the ground. He suspected she was a skukum. He built up the fire the better to see her. He felt as if he were dreaming, yet knew he was awake. Soon he felt very sleepy and lay down to sleep again. She came into his bed. He thought, "I'll take you along with me. I'll not leave you." She knew what he was thinking. The next morning he got ready to go home and she helped him pack up the meat. Now he saw her face for the first time (for since he had lain with her he could see her face without harm), and was pleased that she was so good looking. Between them they carried the meat to his canoe.

When he arrived at his village all the people came out to see the woman he had brought. But he motioned them back, because now he knew that she was a skukum and that others would be harmed if they looked at her or she at them. She followed him with averted face. In the house she sat face to the wall. The young man's mother handed her a piece of dried salmon which she took without looking up. That night she slept in his bed but left the house before daylight, returning again after dark. After a few days the villagers became used to her and thought that perhaps she had changed to a real human. In due time she gave birth to a son. After that she acted like a human but still refrained from speaking to anyone except her husband. The baby grew far more rapidly than any human child. When he was three years old he went hunting with his father. The woman frequently went away for several days at a time, returning with a huge pack of cooked camas, which she gave to the people.

She warned her husband, "Don't take our son along when you go to hunt sea lions or you will both be drowned." But once while she was away the men organized a sea lion hunt. One of the three canoes was lacking two men and they persuaded the father and son to fill in. When far out a storm came up (because the woman was a skukum) and the third canoe was lost. The other women in the village heard the skukum woman cry, "Oh, I told you not to take our son! Now you are both drowned. I knew while I was still at the prairie." The bodies of all but the father and son were found. She stayed in the house for two days, then burned her own and her husband's belongings. She cut her hair in mourning. When she threw it in the fire the flames leaped up as if oil had been poured on the fire. Then she started back to the place she came from. She told her mother-in-law, "You will hear me mourning on the top of that hill." For several years they heard her. She used to leave wood outside the mother-in-law's door at night, but she never came in.

Several families were in the mountains hunting elk. They camped near tàmtoɬ (noise place). They heard roaring sounds intermittently from a near-by mountain but were afraid to investigate. However, there were two lads who determined to ocate the cause of the sounds. They climbed up to where there was snow. Issuing from a cavern in the ice was a roaring stream which every so often stopped flowing. One said, "I want to see what it looks like inside." He climbed to the opening and when the water stopped looked in five times. Then he threw back his head and laughed. "There is a whale in there," he said. Then he told how he had seen a live whale which stopped the flow by plugging the opening with its tail. The other said, "It must be a skukum. Let's go back. We may die from it. How could there be a real whale up here?" When they returned to camp the one who had looked into the cavern laughed and told the people what he had seen. He had hardly finished speaking when he fell over. Blood ran from his nose and mouth, and his eyes burst from their sockets. In a few minutes he was dead. The other lad fell ill but recovered. They covered the dead boy's body with stones, dirt, and rotten logs and then returned home lest they all die.

Another skukum spirit called tsa'álo was formerly a man but turned into a monster. His great toes had nails five feet long, which looked like icicles and stuck up like spikes when he was lying down. A favorite trick of his was to sneak up behind a hunter and kick him in the rear with one of his spiked toenails. He also carried a spear and sometimes killed humans with it. But finally humans succeeded in killing all such monsters. Their ghosts, however, are still seen in the form of fog rising from the waters of creeks.

It was dangerous for two men to see a skukum monster, or even an animal guardian spirit. The skukum would not kill a man alone but would shout at and kill a group of persons.

Some kinds of skukum monsters live in the woods or on the tops of cliffs, others in the water. If one camps near by he may hear their mournful cry of a·ta·ta·t-at (each in a higher pitch than the preceding). One woman skukum lived near Hoh village. A white man built a cabin near by. One night when he came home he saw her and wondered who she was. When he went to bed she climbed in beside him. He had intercourse with her, but at the moment of orgasm he fell dead. The skukum died too. People found them the next day.

Pope had six spirits which he classified in three groups without fitting them into the above classes. One was sligwilamice'los ("among the humans"), who travels about only in this world of the living. He was adept at finding the lost soul of a young person, but he could not travel toward the land of the dead. Two were called djilo'tsoomic ("along the beach") and were used in finding souls which had taken the beach trail to the land of the dead, or had even reached the lower village there. Three were called tcislakwikulc, and were familiar with the upper trail.

Pope also controlled other spirits which were not definitely categorized. Thunderbird (or Thunder) was one of his most dependable hunting spirits. For years he bathed in the ocean and in lakes and creeks, trying to get this power. Finally it came to him in a form like a huge eagle, yet like a man, dressed in a bearskin, and taught him how to hunt. The spirit had a huge knife which he told Pope to use in case he wanted to kill someone. Pope was told to carve an elbow pipe out of a hard clay with an eel in the angle. (In some way the eel was regarded as the spirit also.) This pipe could travel about, for somehow it partook of the nature of a spirit. The power of this spirit was such that many times Pope was able to kill elk without shooting them! One spirit carried a stone club and in his search for lost souls frequently fought with the dead, killing them with the club. In one such fight a dead person struck him in the mouth and thereafter his mouth was twisted. This spirit first came to Pope's mother's mother. When she died the spirit went to his mother, and at her death to Pope. Another of Pope's spirits was called màkwi'lsadjuc ("sun reflecting on his forehead") because it was always good weather whenever the spirit traveled. He was a wealth-giving spirit and therefore his master was never without money. Every spring when the geese fly north this spirit went with them, returning in the autumn. While he was away he left a partner spirit (or part of himself?) to guard Pope's house. At the time this spirit came he told Pope to make a water bucket. Once a year this is filled and the spirit drinks it in a single draught, then for a whole year he goes without drinking. He likewise told Pope to sweep out his smoke-house (i.e., give a potlatch) but once a year. At potlatch time Pope might give away all his money one day but the next day he would find his purse full.

In a dark corner of his house Pope kept an array of the carved figures representing his various spirits. These ranged in size from twelve inches to three feet in height. Most of them had deer hoofs attached so that they might serve as rattles during the shamanistic performances. Some were represented by painted planks (fig. 34 illustrates these shamans' rattles). From left to right they ranged as follows:

1. skà'djap, represented by a single painted plank about 30 inches wide. Pope controlled three spirits of this type. Each was believed to possess a canoe by means of which he traveled in the air. They were tall men, the color of Europeans, but always painted themselves with blue. The board itself was painted with horizontal stripes of black and red. Their canoe was a crude drawing near the top. The moon was painted as a red circle. During potlatches the plank was placed at one end of the house and served as a target, both men and women shooting at the moon from the other end of the house.

2. Four spirits of the sena'xos type represented by a single carving. A single ocean canoe sufficed for them because they always traveled together through the air. They talked a great deal as they voyaged. The symbol for them was a moon painted in red.

3. A carved figure 24 inches high represented łàgwilàmi·cce'los, a being like a man, who could travel only in the world of humans.

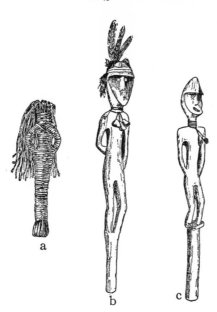

Fig. 34. Shaman's rattles. *a,* of cedar bark; *b,* "Grasshopper"; *c,* "Robin." Ht. of *c, ca.* 18″.

4.   A figure some 20 inches high with the lower part of the face and forehead painted red represented the spirit djilo′tsánomic. He was able to travel on the beach road to the land of the dead.

5.   A figure two feet high represented tciła′k ("down"), who traveled the downward road to the country of the dead. He was of human form but only half as tall as a man. He wore a skin shirt reaching to the thighs and carried a stone club for fighting with the dead.

6.   Xama′mux was said to be as tall as a man. He was adept at running on the beach and in searching for the souls of children in their village or land called olskuł.

7.   sȧgwili′sadju was thought of as a very strong man who went to the land of the dead.

8.   The brother of the preceding was named lata′tadju. The two always traveled together.

9.   An unpainted board sixty inches high and eight wide represented a female skuku′m named stx^wkoi. She traveled in this world and frequently built camp fires for elk hunters.

10.   A carved face at the top of a board four feet high represented the spirit xȧnȧsa′h. He was said to be an exact double of Pope himself. The forehead was painted red, a band of black across the eyes, and the lower face red. The hair was represented by shredded cedar bark.

11.   Two brother spirits were denoted by uncarved sticks nine inches long and one and one-half inches in diameter, painted red and black respectively. The two always traveled about in this world in an ocean canoe.

12   Three skà'djap type spirits were represented by three sticks like the preceding, except that small faces were carved on the sticks.

13.   Three plain sticks (2 red, 1 black) denoted three brothers of the sena'xos type of spirit. They traveled in the air, each in a large canoe.

14.   Two carved figures represented two brothers of the skà'djap type who were spirits but 30 inches high. They traveled in a European type skiff.

The northern spirit (ḳeleḳe'los) was something of a special type. One of W.M.'s ancestors had one which was from the Hoh country. He drifted down the Hoh river in the form of a sea bird called to'tils. On the ocean he became half moxo'h (ocean spirit) and finally landed on the beach at Point Grenville where his future master was on a vision quest. The songs he revealed were in the Hoh and Makah languages.

A person who had Raven (tocà'n or kwa'k') for a spirit could eat fire and hold live coals in his mouth "because raven eats blood" which is the same color as fire.

WEATHER SPIRITS

Only a few shamans had power to bring good weather. I heard of none who brought bad weather (which was sometimes accomplished through black magic, see page 165). The weather spirit was known as atàmà'ntàn (dangerous?) and had to be carefully handled lest he kill his human agent. The spirit was most powerful when controlled by a shaman of the tribe to which it had belonged when it lived in this world.

Old Tom Mouse had a Quinault weather spirit. After a storm of several days he would call the people together and say, "I'm getting tired of this weather. I am going to stop it." Then he would place a mat on the middle of the floor, sit down on it, and start his songs. The onlookers helped in the singing. His spirit would say, "The sun is shining on the middle of my (spirit) canoe. You will soon see the sun low over the horizon." After about an hour the shaman would send a man out to see if the sun were breaking through the clouds. If it was not they continued singing. But before the day was done the sun was sure to appear. Weather shamans could cause the rain to cease but had no control over snowfall.

GAMBLING-POWER SPIRITS

Certain spirits gave their owners or masters skill and luck at gambling. W.M. named five kinds: làa'opàt ("sit down"), who sat down; tsele'utnisam ("kneels"), who knelt; towłḳala'xuts ("collar bone"), who was headless; cḳwała'łopàt ("lie down"); and xwiḱla'lasuk ("stand up"), who stood up. The owners of the first two always assumed the pose of the spirit (sitting or kneeling) while gambling. The last was the type W.M.'s mother controlled. It came to her in the form of a salmonberry bird (skwit) in a canoe. She heard its song and its directions to turn around. Then she saw two marked beaver teeth dice lying in the canoe of the spirits. She always gambled with these and seldom lost, and during her lifetime became quite rich from her winnings. She once staged a gambling bout with the most famous woman gambler of Puget Sound. The game was played at Elma and onlookers bet large sums on the outcome. Each woman started with 100 tally sticks. A half day passed before the contest was over. W.M.'s mother would prepare for an important contest such as this by singing her spirit songs for two or three days.

The following accounts represent examples of the Quinault attitude toward the supernatural.

I had been fasting and bathing for a long time. I went up the river and went walking in the woods. I heard someone behind me talking. I looked around and saw three men, Mole, Robin, and Grasshopper. They said they had come to help me. Then Grasshopper took me (in a trance) and showed me all over the world. He showed me that the world is just like a range of mountains. A man dies if he crosses to the other side of the ridge. He said, "Just go along slowly and easily and watch where you are going. You will be all right. You have quite a way to go yet (in this life)." Once when I was very ill I dreamed of a beautiful valley full of flowers. I wanted to go down there, but Grasshopper warned me not to. If I had gone there I would have died. He showed me that after my death there would come a great storm which would wash away this village (Taholah) and there would be only gravelly beach here. My grandfather's guardian spirit told him that the village at Hoh would be washed away. Soon after he died it stormed and rained for five days and the village was washed away.

When Grasshopper was a dead person (*i.e.*, before he died the "second death") he was watching a girl dance. She wore bluejay feathers in her hair. He seized them, hid them behind his back, and ran away. Now he wears them in his hair, but he always carries his hand behind his back (fig. 34*b*). Grasshopper goes so swiftly (along the road to the land of the dead) that the man who is holding the rattle for me often becomes ill and vomits. Robin and Grasshopper frequently make their trips together. But in recent years they have stayed rather far away and it has become hard for me to call them. Mole, on the other hand, often comes before I have sung two songs. Robin lost an eye and got his crooked mouth (fig. 34*c*) while he was living among the dead. One day he saw a monster (skukum) which killed him. His face has been that way ever since. At his death he became a guardian spirit and came to me. (Sammy Hoh).

When I was a young girl my parents took me to the mountains. On the way we camped on a bar across from a hill where many huckleberries were growing. I wanted to pick some but they told me, "It's too late in the evening; there might be a skukum there." But I went anyway. It was already dark among the hemlocks. All of a sudden a warm wind came. Soon a second, warmer and stronger than the first. I was afraid, and ran back and told what had happened. That night a middle-aged woman stood beside my bed and said, "Why were you afraid of me? I've been watching you ever since you started. If you had not run away I would have shown you everything. I have a good home over there. I had five children, but they have been dropping, dropping into that bad place. Now I have but one son left, and he has gone away to the mountains. I came to you because I like you. You look like me. Your hair and your face are like mine. I watch the sun. I can tell when it is going to be a good day by looking over there. Then my son goes away." Then I looked and saw a beam of light pass between two trees and go down to her house. "If you had not been afraid I would have showed you all my good luck. Now I will just show you a little." Then she showed me where the cones were piled in little heaps under the drip of the hemlocks. This happened before I was married. The good luck she showed me I have kept in my mind and it has brought me luck. I never told anyone, because if I had my luck would not have lasted. This is the first time I have told it. (Like her) I have lost five children and only one son remains. I knew this would happen. (A.J.) [It is difficult to say to what extent this was regarded as a vision, to what extent A.J. regarded the supernatural woman and herself as the same person, or her other self.]

Once a young man went out in search of power. He found a forked tree, climbed it and stayed there that night. But no power came to him, although the tree moved and made a noise inside. The next day he went on up the creek until he came to a spot where two trees grew close together. "This is nice, I'll make my bed here," he said. He built a hammock-like bed by interlacing cedar boughs (this was used only by those questing for power) and slung it between the trees about 10 feet above the ground. Then he gathered a goodly supply of dry wood. He ate only a few morsels of food, then bathed. That night he lighted the fire and climbed to the bed, taking with him a hard spruce knot to bite upon when he saw the spirit he would accept. First there came to the fire a flock of small birds. He looked down and saw them but did nothing because he knew their power was of no importance. Then there came larger birds—eagle, raven, screech owl, and crow—but he didn't want them so they went away. Next came various snakes who went around the fire but he didn't want them either. Then there came a monster like an "alligator" (skukum) and later, land otters and other animals, but he let them alone and they went away.

At last he heard the sound of a rushing wind and he thought, "That is the one I've heard about." Then he saw the trees bending as if in a high wind. There came an animal called tcitcalai'-los (two-headed animal), which had a head at either end of its body and horns on each head. He controls (or *is*) the spirit stamále'h. The animal came and stood beside the fire. As he did so the mouth and nose of both heads started bleeding. The earth swayed so that he had to hold fast to the tree to keep from falling. He thought, "That's the one I want; they told me that this kind is a strong power." He placed the knot in his mouth and jumped down, then seized the creature around the neck. At this point he lost consciousness. When he came to he was lying beside the fire, which was almost out. His mouth and nose were bleeding and the ground was covered with blood from the animal and from himself. Then he went to the creek and bathed until the water no longer turned red from his bleeding.

He stayed there a month, bathing every day. Then he said to himself, "I am going to the mountains to find out how strong a power I have." He saw a deer, and as he looked at it the animal fell dead, burst open, and smoke arose from the spot. He had "poisoned" the deer with his look.[59] He went on and came to a large band of elk which fell dead as he looked and smoke arose where they lay. He ate none of the flesh, for he had poisoned them. He thought, "I'll wait a few months, then try again." But the same things happened again. Finally, after nearly a year, the power grew less and game no longer fell dead at his glance. His parents had given him up for dead. His wife was with child when he started his quest.

Finally he started the long journey home. He said to himself, "I'll go by that small village. If I don't kill the people there by my glance, then I'll not kill my own people either." He saw two men on the weir. He watched from the woods and was glad when they were not harmed. Then he went on to his own village, but watched from the edge of the forest. A child came out of his house and played in the sand without being harmed. He saw his mother go down to the river for a bucket of water. Her hair was cut short in mourning for him. His father came up the river with a canoe load of wood and the daughter-in-law came out to help him carry it in. As she walked away he shouted at her and motioned her to come. He told her to sit down a short way off. "We have a little boy now," she said. "There he is over there. We're still staying with your parents. I didn't want to leave because of the boy. We thought you were dead." "I'm glad to see you again, but I don't dare go in the house yet," he said. She wanted to bring the boy for him to see but he warned her against it. He told her to carefully clean the whole house; that he would return in a few days. She didn't tell the old folks, though they wondered why she was cleaning the house so thoroughly and why she was so happy. He came back carrying two huge packs of dried meat. His grandmother was so happy at seeing him that she fainted. The entire village was invited to a feast of rejoicing for his return. (A.J.)

Tak was an old Queets woman who lived at the village of na'ukalxʷ (big village) at the mouth of the Clearwater. Her guardian spirit was a dwarf. When it came to her it said, "I heard that you are a poor woman and that the people make fun of you because you have no property. I am going

---

[59]This was not the same concept as the "evil eye." It was merely the manifestation of the terrific power in him, power which would soon wane somewhat and become controllable. All shamanistic power is strongest when first acquired.

to help you." It gave her a carved rattle wrapped with cedar bark and with dentalia shells lashed to it. Her song ran heiiya, heiiya k̓átcaadjitán sk̓lo'inatcowco, making fun of me (because) I have no dentalium (*i.e.*, Some people used to make fun of me because I was poor). She had the power to foretell when visitors were coming. When the ducks flew past the village she could interpret their quackings. (Flying up and down the river they knew of all canoes on the way.) They would tell her who the people were, and how many.

Hers was a powerful spirit who could go far along the road to the land of the dead to find lost souls. Once a man was spearing salmon in the riffles. When he had speared several he noticed fog drifting toward him. He suspected it was a ghost so he paddled home. As soon as he was inside his house he fell in a faint and his legs twitched as if he were running. They sent for the old woman. She and her guardian took after the ghost, who had run far along the trail. The faster they traveled the faster the ghost ran, but at last her guardian spirit caught the ghost and took away from it the man's soul. On the way back the old woman saw that the elderberry bushes were loaded with berries. The spirit picked some. "There will be a big crop of elderberries next year, because it is bringing some back," she said.[60] She returned the soul to the sick man, who shortly recovered. He told of all that he had seen in the other world. He saw a beach on which strutted a flock of noisy gulls. The surf has a different sound from the surf of this world. It was a pretty place and he hoped that no one would come after his soul. The next year he really died, because he liked the land of the dead.

It was told that there was a man who had searched diligently but without success for a guardian spirit. At last there came to him the tcotsdja'ánikulc (up-river spirit). He saw men in ocean-going canoes coming down the river. They called to him to come along. His spirit went with them to the Duck people in the northwest. But when he came to himself he was still on the river bank. Then he went to Chow Chow prairie where he made a great number of grass figures of men and women and placed them at intervals along the edge of the prairie. He said to them, "I am all alone now and I am a poor man. When I shout I want you to answer." (This he did because all his kinsmen were dead.) Then he went a way off and sang his shaman's songs. Soon he heard the sound of people approaching. When they were close by he looked at them, but they fell dead and became spirits again. If he had not looked at them they would have become real people.

There was a young woman who wanted to become a curing shaman. She went to the mountains and fasted for ten days, spending her time collecting a great pile of wood. The tenth night she set fire to the wood and waited. As the flames rose high she heard a mournful howl, which seemed to issue from a near-by peak. As she looked the mountain swayed and seemed about to break asunder. The cry came closer and she moved away from the fire. There appeared an animal like a huge wildcat. He had a sharp nose and his face was so long it dragged on the ground. When he came to the fire he raised his head and howled. She was afraid. "I don't want that kind. I don't want you for a guardian spirit," she said. Then he went away. Soon she saw the water of the lake hissing and boiling up. Many kinds of animals came swimming toward her. Then she lost consciousness. They brought her five kinds of spirits to choose from. In her sleep she grabbed at one which could bring back lost souls. She called the spirit xoxwatc (a Quileute word). It gave her two white objects (quartz crystals?) to use in her curing. In her trances she always lay on a new mat placed across the width of the house and held a crystal in each hand.

A certain shaman came to a village on a visit and while there he captured the soul of a young man. Before leaving he wanted to return the soul to its owner but the young fellow scoffed at the idea. Some of the old men advised him to let the shaman put it back, but he refused. The shaman got into his canoe and started downriver. They saw him make a motion as if drawing something

[60]It is difficult to determine to what extent the shaman himself accompanied the guardian spirit, but it seems as if the soul or spirit of the shaman went along on these trips, as well as the spirit of the shaman's helper. Their bodies remained behind. Sometimes the guardian spirit spoke through the mouth of the shaman, at other times the shaman used his own words.

from his chest and throwing it into the water. They knew he had cast the soul away. The young fellow went into the sweat-house and came out after his bath and plunged into the river. But he never came up. His parents did nothing to the shaman because they knew it was the young man's own fault.

There was a poor young man who lived at Oyhut (called skudjano'l in Chehalis) who wanted to get the "Oyhut spirit" (skudjanolkulc). He told the villagers, "Watch me. When the geese fly north I am going with them in their air canoe." As the flocks flew overhead he would cry, "Not that one, not that one, nor that one." Finally there came a certain flock and he said, "That is my company." Then he waded out into the water up to his knees and disappeared. He stayed away until the geese flew south. After that he could find all manner of things on the beach. Sea otter, fur seal, porpoise, sturgeon, and even whales drifted in to him. Soon he had fur robes, blankets, slaves, and all manner of wealth. He became a sort of chief. Nearly every spring he went north with the geese, returning with them in the autumn. But finally he told the people he would never return. He was never seen again, but his wife was a rich woman now.

Old Lummi was a member of the klokwalle secret society and controlled other powers as well. One of his grandsons accidentally shot him just below the eye, the ball passing completely through his head and lodging under the skin at the back of the skull. He was brought to Quinault village, where a shaman treated him by sucking blood from his chest. Lummi told the watchers that if he were going to live they would soon see a black cloud in the west. Soon they saw the cloud coming, though it was a bright day in summer. Lummi then took water in his mouth and soon spat out the bullet.

A shaman named kapo'man was specially adept at shooting his power into people, causing illness or death. He usually wore a headband of cedar bark and painted his face and chest red. He had several long poles (used for beating time on the roof boards), which he would give people to hold. As he sang and they beat time the power would enter the poles so they shook and the people could not let go the sticks. He often extracted disease objects by sucking with a tube at the source of pain. He would suck out quantities of blood, being careful to get no blood in his mouth lest it burn him. At last he would suck out an object the size of a grain of wheat—this was the pain. During his treatment he sang and danced at intervals. If he became angry with a person he would "shoot" his power into him so that he usually died in a few days.[61] If a woman repulsed his advances he would threaten to kill her in the same way, so none dared refuse him. A number of attempts were made on his life. Sometimes a man's own relatives would kill him for such magic.

Hoh's grandfather achieved the ultimate in supernatural aid by acquiring the whale guardian spirit, which is called slào'ltcu (in the west). His brother had died and as the surviving brother he went every day to a rocky island to mourn, and to bathe in a small creek. One day he noticed something at sea moving toward him. As it approached he saw that it was a beautiful woman with flowing hair and feet shaped like the tail of a whale. He fell unconscious and was placed in a whale-shaped canoe by the woman. They traveled to the other side of the ocean, passed through a narrows to another ocean, and turned into a bay. They went into a house where the sena'xos and whale spirits lived. (They are brothers and the woman was their sister.) They showed him the lines, harpoons, floats, etc., to use in whaling, and gave him the lightning power which is used in whaling. (That is why there is thunder and lightning when a man harpoons a whale. The whaler calls for his helper, who gives him superhuman strength. Without such help no one could kill a whale.)

---

[61]None of my informants would state definitely whether the guardian spirit actually entered bewitched persons or whether it was merely mana (impersonal) power which entered them.

When he returned to his home he fell ill from an over-abundance of power. He lay at the point of death for two months. He could neither eat nor drink, and could not speak above a whisper. His relatives hired famous shamans to cure him but they could do nothing. Finally a woman shaman came. She told what he had seen in his vision and said that he was ill because his soul had remained at the spirit village. She got a man helper to hold her rattle, sprinkled eagle and seagull down about, and the two went to the spirit village. Within a day they had brought the soul back. In a few days he was able to take a little food. He drank only water from a special spring, as the spirit had ordered. Every day he sang the songs the spirits had given him. When his strength had returned he went out in his canoe to hunt. His power was so great that porpoises and other animals died before he could hurl his harpoon. Later he speared whale. He would talk to his guardian spirit and a fair wind would come which enabled them to raise the sail and tow the whale home. During his life he speared 77 whale. He cut the back fins from them and nailed them to the beams in his house. In potlatches he used to sing his paddling, harpooning, and fair wind songs. He used to drink gallons of whale oil at a single draught, then spew it on the fire, making the flames roar up to the smokehole. (S.H.)

There once lived a skeptical young fellow who said to a powerful shaman, "I don't see why people pay so much attention to that stick of wood (the shaman's carved rattle). It is only a stick. If I put it in the fire it would burn just like any other piece of wood." "All right, young man," said the shaman, "you shall see." That night the villagers came to the shaman's house. The shaman handed the young fellow the stick about 8 feet long (used for beating on the roofboards). The shaman began his songs. Soon the stick began to shake, and the young man couldn't release his hold. "Now let us see you put it in the fire," the shaman said. Soon the stick was taking the young fellow all over the house, and as time went on it caused him to jump madly about. Someone opened the door and the stick took him out and away so swiftly that none could follow him. He became a kind of a spirit himself. Ever since that time he has traveled about in the woods and in the air. One is apt to hear him near a prairie. The supernatural power still takes him. Those who have seen him say that he has become like a bear, with a body covered with hair. Pope has heard him twice. He is known as "He who did not believe." As he travels he continually shouts, hi hi hi ånsån tisaito'slån, I am he who did not believe. Those who doubt the power of the shaman are told this tale as a warning.

The following account was told by Billy Mason. It presents a fairly good picture of the acquisition of supernatural power, of the relation between a man and his guardian spirit, the attitude toward the unknown, and the manner of retaining a *rapport* with the beings of the other world during a man's lifetime. It also illustrates the blended beliefs of the old shamanism and the new Shaker cult.

When I was about seven years of age and old enough to bathe, my mother called me early every morning before daylight, telling me to bathe. When I was about ten years old my grandfather Nicagwats said to me, "Now when the new crescent moon comes you must go down to pomoså'djiltcu (cold place) and bathe for four nights. Then when you become a man you will be strong and a good hunter." Every new moon I went there for a number of years. Then he told me, "You are old enough and your skin is tough enough so that you can rub yourself with hemlock boughs." A few years later he told me, "From now on you must rub your skin with cobbles (the size of your fist) while bathing. Rub your left leg with one, then throw it into the river; then take another and rub the right leg in the same way; and then the left arm, the right arm, and last of all the trunk and head. Each time use five stones. This will make you tough and strong. When you are injured you will not feel it, because your skin has been rubbed off with the stones and thrown into the water." I used the rocks for about two years, each time rubbing my skin until it was sore and the icy water felt hot.

Another thing he told me was: "When a child or a grandchild is born to you take the water out of a devilfish and bathe the child in that to make him strong. Remember this as long as you live. Tell your children and grandchildren to tell their children and grandchildren of this, so that it will never be forgotten."

My father told me, "When the weather is stormy and cold I used to go down to Point Grenville, sometimes even as far as Damon's point. Now even though I am old and not fat, I can stand the cold. Whenever it blows hard from the south you must go at dusk along the beach and bathe in the surf, then run a little way and bathe again. When you get to Point Grenville stop and talk to the world. Then come back. You need not bathe on the way back." I used to do that every stormy day. In the winter when the rain turned to sleet my skin would burn like fire and the sleet felt like needles pricking me.

Later my father told me, "Bathe at night in the creeks and lakes where there are snags and old logs under the water." This I did every month from the time of the new crescent until the moon was full. I kept this up until I married. After I married I bathed only before going hunting. (During the dark of the moon, when one does not bathe, there is no harm in sleeping with a woman.) My father told me that some day I would catch a bullhead among the snags; then I would be a man. I used to crawl around with only my head above the water, feeling with my hands for a bullhead, but I never caught one. But a little power came to me from the logs and snags.

During the time I trained, many men, animals and strange creatures came to me and talked with me. They came to me in my dreams. I used to see a man come and stand beside me. He wore feathers in his hair, like the Yakima Indians. Other times I saw a crowd of people who were building a village out over the ocean. My father told me this was a sign that I would visit other places when I grew up. But now I never dream such things, because my training and bathing days are over. Sometimes I dream about the old days, how we used to make things, how we used to travel places in canoes, and so on. Not all my helpers come to me at one time. One of my helpers is of the sågwanc (underground) type. He knows the road to the land of the dead and is good at finding lost souls. He once lived among the dead but he died his second death there and came to be a (spirit) animal in the form of a man. It is hard to describe his appearance because I never saw him plainly but only dimly, as if through a fog. He is about 14 inches high. When he enters me I can no longer see him but he talks to me and through me. Once I saw two of them standing together in a dark corner, a black one and a red one. One said to me, "I come from the other world. I see that you need help. I was sorry for you when I saw you walking around alone. I have come to help you. You are going to be my master. I was in this world once before, but my master died. Since that time I have been going around looking for another." Then it seemed to me the house began to spin. He began singing and came over and entered me. He said, "I used to live (in the land of the dead) at a place just like Point Grenville. There was a creek there in which the water ran upstream on one side of the channel, downstream on the other." Since I became a Shaker I have seen almost the same. Sometimes when I prayed I would see a little man come down and go into me. He was an angel. Perhaps the old guardian spirits were angels too.

When I first started bathing among the snags the sa'xtikulc spirit (which lives on the clouds) came to me. He came to me in the form of a man, but larger than a man. He came up out of the water and I saw that he was Mountain Lion. I saw him at the same place each year for three years. The third time he put me in his small canoe and took me through the air toward the east and landed the canoe on his house. When I came to myself I was inside. He said, "Look now and see where I live. I live in the sun. See where I stand." Then I saw that he was standing on ice. Because he was a strong animal I, too, am strong and a single bullet could not kill me (because it takes more than one shot to kill a mountain lion).

Two other spirits of this same kind came to me in a dream. They were big men, dressed like the Yakima. One said, "I come from Baker's prairie. My house is there. This is my brother." One held a bow and arrow, the other a knife. One said, "You see my creek beside the hill at Baker's prairie. The water is blood. If you ever get hurt, come and bathe in this creek and it will cure you." He took me into his house and I saw that it was lined with tule mats. After I joined the Shakers I saw that those brothers were not really men, but were wolves. Their faces were like the face of a wolf, and they were hairy and had tails. My "shake"[62] power showed me that. I saw that the costume they wore was only the tail of a wolf. My Shaker spirit said, "You see, he (the wolf spirit) said he had a house on a prairie (meadow), but he really lives at the edge of a cliff. If you needed help he couldn't aid you—you would only fall over the edge of that cliff and go down."

When my son Percy was very ill there came to me the snosku'l (sun spirit). This kind lives in the land of the dead in the village of the dead children. He told me that Percy's soul had long since left him but that he would try to find it. He traveled rapidly and came to the Old-woman-of-the-halfway-place. He asked her but she said, "No, he has gone on. He came here but he only stayed a little while." He went on and came to a big house beside a hill. It sounded as if many people were inside. He inquired, but they told him Percy's soul had gone on. On the other side of the hill he came to a place where many boys (spirits of the dead) were playing. Near by was a huge house where they lived. He asked them, "Is Percy here?" "Yes, he is here. He just came. He is in the house." My guardian spirit went to look for him but as soon as he was inside all the boys became spirits and disappeared. Then he told me, "Well, I will have to give up. I can go no farther."[63] When he came back and I woke up Percy was dead.

Soon after I was married I went up the river and camped at the mouth of Cook creek (Chow Chow creek). Before I started I bathed every night and morning for a week, plunging in three or four times. (A young fellow takes five plunges each time.) I rubbed myself with the leaves of a plant called xwà'stap or mà'xstap, which my grandfather showed me. This is the plant one must use after he has slept with a woman. In a branch of Cook creek I saw thousands of small eels coming downstream. I ran away because a monster (skukum) often follows them. I set traps for beaver where there was a dam. The next day I went to inspect them. Suddenly I felt dizzy, and things grew dark and misty before my eyes. I leaned against a tree and thought, "What is the matter with me? Am I going to die, or am I getting crazy? My arms and legs feel strong, but things look strange to me." Then I thought of what old Andrew Martin had told me: "If you ever come near a lake or a pond and things suddenly turn dark, don't go near, because it is a sure sign that a monster is in the lake. Be careful of your steps when this happens, and don't look around, don't look at the water lest you see the skukum and kill your family. If you should see the monster you must not go home for ten or fifteen days, until the 'poison' is gone from your eyes. If your people are camping with you, you must go back and warn them. But keep your back to them, tell them what has happened, and tell them that they must go back home." The kind of monster which causes things to turn dark is called smàltco'tcàn (Thunder's rope).

One summer my wife and I went to Montesano, where we had relatives. My father had a small house there and quite a group of us used to go there, often staying nearly all summer. I went on a horse to Oakville and on the way back, at a little lake near Elma, I heard a noise in an alder tree. It sounded like an eagle and I got ready to shoot him. I looked at the water and saw it swirl. Then I saw the first skukum I had ever seen. It was in the middle of the day so I could see him plainly. He looked almost like a huge lizard but he was eight feet long and had a very wide head. This kind of monster is called sta'ànox.

Once my wife and I were fishing at Sandy island in the Chehalis river. It was night and my wife was lying down in the canoe nursing the baby while I managed the net. All at once we heard a sound overhead, hi hi hi, hu+ hu+ tisaito'slàn, in a high voice.[64]

Soon after I got one of my spirits my nephew came to me and said, "Well, uncle, I don't believe you have that spirit. But if he will shake me I will believe." I said to him, "All right, you come to my house this evening." He came, and I gave him the carved rattle to hold; soon he began to shake and went into a kind of trance. When he came to himself he told us, "A man appeared to me and said, 'Look up there to the north.' Then I closed my eyes and saw a canoe in the

---

[62]The power which comes to one through the Shaker cult is personified in the same way as the shamanistic spirits.

[63]It was thought to be impossible for a guardian spirit to go farther along the road than the place where he had lived before the "second death".

[64]Here was interpolated a variant of the common tale of "He who did not believe." See p. 155.

air. The bow was carved in the form of a snake's head with the mouth open. Then the spirit said, 'Now look over toward the west—that is where I travel. You can hear my song from afar when I am traveling.' " This was a sign that my nephew would not live long, because the spirit showed him so little and he saw the vision only dimly.

Once my son Harry and I were up the river. He wanted to use my shaman's rattle. The power came to him and shook him. He talked (in the trance), naming all the people of Taholah and how many were away. Then he said, "But one man is soon going to die at the mouth of the river." A few days later Andrew Martin came to our camp, and said he had heard about the message we received. He took the rattle and after his trance said, "Yes, that is true. A fellow will die there." But it was he, though he didn't know it. He was drowned there within two months.

Mrs. Mason had a skukum spirit. Perhaps that is why she didn't live long. She told me how she got it. The skukum appeared in the form of a woman and said, "I am coming to you because I like you. Your hair is just like mine, and your face is just like mine. I want you to own me. I have a sister but she lives across the river. Look at me, I am nearly alone now. Nearly all my children are dead. Once I had many children but stamali (a male skukum) killed most of them. I will show you where my dead children are." Then she took Mrs. Mason to her house in the woods. She pointed out her dead children laid out in a row along one side of the house. She said, "My husband is dead too. But I have three children left, two boys and one girl. The boys have gone hunting and the girl is picking berries." Now I [Mason] have left only two boys and one girl.

When Percy got the Shaker power he said, "I am not going to stay long in this world. My kinsmen do not believe in God. The power tells me I will soon die if you refuse to believe. I will soon be going to a place where I will have a nice house and no more worries. Nine years from now there will be a great war (the World War) and the United States will be in it. Soon after that war is over the world will change. After the wicked people have died then Christ will come."[65]

DISEASE CONCEPTS AND METHODS OF CURING

Illness was ordinarily regarded as due either to the loss of the soul or spirit (spes) or to the presence in the body of a disease object. There might be a preliminary event which might cause the soul to leave, as the sight of a ghost, a bad fright, a sneeze, or an ordinary accident. Pains in the body were caused by the disease objects. Some illnesses could be successfully treated (either by a shaman or a layman) by means of baths, herbs, and so on. It was believed that the life span of every person was somehow foreordained. "When a man's time came then he would die, even from a very slight injury." I did not hear of illness caused by breach of taboo.

When a person fell ill a shaman was usually called in to diagnose the malady. Not only could he ordinarily tell the nature of the illness but often knew whether a cure was possible. There was no penalty for failure to cure. If the first shaman failed to produce results another was called in. Certain men were regarded as "specialists" in curing certain diseases, though exceptional ability depended more upon the type and potency of his supernatural helper than upon the skill of the shaman himself. A shaman of exceptional reputation might be called in from another tribe. The fees of noted shamans were higher than those asked by men of mediocre talent. Fees varied from the payment of an object of slight value to things representing high values. In modern times a fee of two or three dollars was considered low, one of a hundred dollars very high. The average was perhaps five or ten

---

[65]This is a recent tenet of the Shaker cult. John Slocum, the founder, did not preach of the second advent or of the return of the dead.

dollars. Payment was made whether or not a cure was effected. If the illness were of the simple "pain" type a disease object was thought to cause it (the "intrusion" theory of disease). The cure was effected in one of two ways: (1) The shaman sucked out the object either by means of a sucking tube (a bone about eight inches long) or by applying the mouth directly. (2) By means of rubbing and other manual manipulations the object was located or caused to move to an accessible spot and was then pulled out through the skin or one of the bodily orifices. The object (a pebble, a quartz crystal, or an insect) was then produced and exhibited to the patient and onlookers. Some of the objects were reputedly small animals or insects "which looked like big lice" or like maggots. These were killed after being extracted. Usually a considerable amount of blood was sucked out along with the object. These objects were thought to travel in the air "on the wind" and to enter people without outside (shamanistic) aid.

There was a certain relation between the type of animal of the guardian spirit and the methods of the shaman. A man who controlled such spirits as mosquito, fly, or eel cured his patients by sucking, either directly or by means of a tube. A man who controlled the snake spirit also cured by the sucking method.

When illness was not the simple "pain" type, or when it was not due to an obvious physical injury it was considered as due to the loss of the soul. But it is difficult to say whether the wandering of the soul was considered the *cause* of the illness or whether the soul left the body with the onset of illness. The ghosts of the dead (especially of recently dead friends and relatives) were constantly about, ready to seize the souls of the living and start with them for the country of the dead. The speed with which the soul traveled varied. It might dally along the road, stopping here and there, or it might go swiftly. Two days were ordinarily necessary to reach the river. Once across the river no shaman could reach it and the person inevitably died.

The soul (spes) was of a form like the body but much smaller, being only a few inches high. "It looks like a tiny baby, yet looks like fog."[66] It might wander along the way for a year or more. In the land of the dead the soul became a person again, assuming the form of a human with flesh and blood, but without bones, "because the bones of a dead person stay in this world." The dead speak in a language that humans cannot understand. Their only words are ku ku ku ku, etc. Now and then a person goes all the way to the land of the dead, stays there a few days, and then returns to this life, usually because he "was not treated well there." The soul of a person killed instantly goes at once to the other world. The soul is able to choose the path it takes, going either along nago'lcgwał (big road) or along talsálaqwawk (along the beach).

Sometimes one's soul left suddenly. Then if it took the upper road to the land of the dead it could be seen flying through the air as a ball of fire (a meteor?), throwing off sparks and making a crackling sound like burning spruce twigs. The soul of a man appeared to be eight or ten inches in diameter, that for a woman smaller.

---

[66]One informant (S.H.) insisted there were two souls, the spes and the swàta'mtsih. The first left at the onset of illness, the second at the instant of death, when the first crossed the river. All other informants claimed there was but one soul. S.H.'s mother was a Hoh (who believed in multiple souls) and this no doubt explains the variation from other accounts.

Curing by means of recapture of the soul was more common and also more spectacular than other types of treatment. The shaman called in must have the proper type of guardian spirit or spirits—those who were from among the "twice dead" and who therefore knew the road to the land of the dead. He brought the rattle or wand associated with that spirit. (Usually a shaman had a carved or painted rattle for each of his supernatural helpers, though a single one might suffice for several of the same type, particularly if they were "brothers.") A man was chosen as "helper," who held the rattle and helped in the singing. Bystanders also joined in the singing, some keeping time by beating on a plank with sticks or pounding the roofboards with long poles. The shaman and helper lay down on a mat spread on the floor and the shaman started a song taught him by the guardian spirit at the time of his vision. The shaking of the rattle and the singing attracted the spirit who, usually after one or two songs, entered the body of the shaman who went into a trance. The guardian spirit entered the shaman's body either through the front of the torso or the back of the neck, causing a brief but sharp pain. From this moment shaman and guardian spirit were fused into one. The shaman spoke, yet it was the spirit speaking through him. There is not the slightest doubt that we are dealing with true "possessional" shamanism of the kind so typical of Siberia.

To a lesser degree the helper was also in a trance. Shaman, helper, and guardian spirit now began the trip along the trail taken by the soul. The spirit (between songs), speaking through the shaman, told of the localities they visited, of evidences of the soul having passed that way, and now and then encouraged his human aides or warned them against the perils they encountered. The spirit dared go only as far into the other world as the place where he had lived while there as one of the dead. If he ventured farther both he and the shaman died, or became lost and died without finding their way back. None could actually enter the villages of the dead, few could cross the river which ran just this side of the villages. The length of time during which the shaman remained in the trance depended on how far the soul had gone. The soul of a desperately ill person naturally traveled more rapidly than the soul of one only slightly ill. In case the shaman felt certain that recovery was impossible he reported failure—the soul had gone too far. The search might last two days and two nights. During the entire time both shaman and helper refrained from food and drink. If the soul was overtaken the words of the shaman indicated the fact and the return journey began. The guardian spirit might warn, "Now be careful! Mind what you are doing! Don't pay too much attention to what you see in this country lest your mind stay here and you fall ill." While in the trance the shaman was only half conscious of things about him. The voices of people sounded like meaningless babblings.

During the return trip the shaman held the captured soul in his cupped hands. Onlookers, seeing that the soul had been found, now became more vigorous and joyful in their singing. When the return journey was completed the shaman and helper came out of the trance and were usually so exhausted that the onlookers had to help them to seats on the bench. When the shaman's strength had somewhat returned he went over to the patient and made as if "pouring" the soul back into the patient through the top of the head. This was done repeatedly and each time the hands were passed down the patient's body without touching the body. This process was kept up until the soul was restored. It might be accompanied by gentle massage, warm water being sometimes employed. The shaman might continue to treat the patient, usually by means of massage, for several days after the soul had been restored.

There was also a type of curing which bordered on shamanism. When an exceptionally large eel (leech?) was caught he was not killed. Instead, people said, "Yes, we caught you. We hear you are a great doctor. I have a friend who is sick and I am going to take you to him. That must be why you came to meet me. I'll pay you with a young woman if you cure him." The eel was then wrapped in soft bark and taken to a person suffering with rheumatism. His mouth was placed over the affected part. When he had sucked his fill of blood he was placed on the floor where he vomited up quantities of slime (not blood).

An evilly-disposed guardian spirit might snatch a man's soul unbeknown to the shaman and bring it to his master's house.

> One time a man fell sick and called in Pope to doctor him. Pope came to me and said, "You have that man's soul." I said, "Perhaps my power has it." We went into a trance and I took the soul away from my guardian spirit and gave it to Pope. He returned it to the sick man, who soon recovered. The man didn't have to pay me because he had not called on me to cure him.

A spirit had the power to take one's sleep, appetite, sight, or hearing and keep it. The next day he might return it, or it might be necessary to hire a shaman to learn whose guardian spirit had stolen it. Shamans were often called in to cure illnesses caused by objects or "power" shot into the person by another shaman. A shaman was able to punish a thief or to harm an enemy by "putting a mark" on the person. The guardian spirit simply "stepped on his track," *i.e.*, placed a foot on the footprint of the victim, who shortly fell ill or became paralyzed. I was unable to learn more regarding this curious concept.

DEATH AND THE LAND OF THE DEAD

It is believed that when a person falls ill, or if he is suddenly frightened, or if he sees a ghost, his spirit leaves the body and starts on the path to the land of the dead. Usually only the shaman and his guardian spirit were able to follow the spirit and, if it had not gone too far, bring it back and restore it. But now and then the soul might return of its own accord, even after death. Persons who have returned after death are called slalatá'màn.

Alice Jackson's grandfather had been dead and buried five days. But he surprised and frightened his kinsmen by walking into the house. He had actually been to the land of the dead but the dead failed to take good care of him so he returned. His tales of what he had seen confirmed what others had told about the place. The country of the dead lay along a river much like Quinault river, in fact the whole country is almost a duplication of Quinault territory. There they have several villages. Near the mouth of the river on the south side is a village called nàgo'tsi (mouth of the river). A short distance up-river on the north side is a village called tcà'ɬakᵘ. About eight miles above the river mouth on the north side is a large village called naustała'tsix^w (big village), where there was a salmon weir. It was to this village that Bluejay went on his legendary visit. Farther up, nearly to the lake (situated like Quinault lake, but not so large) lies latataitámix^w (springing log village). The name comes from the springy alder log, which does not reach all the way across the stream and continually springs up and down. The guardian spirit must jump the eight or nine feet from shore to the log. Only the spirit named lata'tsomic of the type called tciła'kwikulc is strong enough to cross here. He lived near the place when he was one of the dead. The trails to these villages go nearly straight down from this world.

A person who dies young (before adolescence) goes to a village called gulesa'-itomix^w (dry sand blowing village), which is situated on the way to the river. The trail leading to it goes eastward toward the sunrise and then dips down to the land of the dead. But children become really alive in their world of the dead. When a child is born in our world he has come from that place—where there are no old people. Fruits and flowers grow in abundance there. "It is so good that it all reflects and is bright."

The soul of a person who is to die suddenly goes to a village called ḱapa'lskuł (from under the daylight), which lies toward the east where the sun rises. This village is not in the underworld.[67] Once a group of families was hunting in the mountains. One evening Pope and others saw a woman's soul rise out of her body and remain suspended in the air a short time. Then it went rapidly toward the east. It looked like the full moon. They had scarcely reached home a week later when she suddenly died. The soul of an ill person (as well as the shaman, his human helper, and the guardian spirit who are in search of the lost soul) starts along the road to the place of the dead. It is a long road and the trip takes at least two days. When it is day in this world it is night there. The first landmark along the trail is a small creek, called adja'álosmań, the water of which is reddish. Here the soul may stop to wash its face. In case it does so the face of the sick person can be seen to undergo a change for the worse, and he is sure to die. The shaman, when he reaches this place, can tell whether the soul has washed. If it has not he is confident of success.

The next landmark is a small house on the left of the trail beside a creek called mito'lcigwał (half way place). An old woman, who keeps a small woolly dog, lives there and is known as "the old woman of the halfway place." The trail leads past her door and she sits outside weaving blankets. All the wood burned in this world goes to her, the ashes turning back to wood again for her. When the shaman sees her he asks, "Have you seen so-and-so go by?" She tells him whether he has passed or not, or how long since.

The next landmark is a creek called gwile'saidámih (shining place) because the water is so clear that its gravel bottom can be seen. Then one comes to càxpa'lpac (no water), which is a dry stream bed. To this place go all the birds which die in this world, all other creatures going to the same country as humans. The birds are so tame that they hop on the shaman's shoulders. It is close to the river. The next

---

[67]Hoh claimed there is still another region in the other world, in the east, called ke'álskuł. One's spirit (soul) sees this place, may even visit it, while one is asleep. The aid of a guardian spirit is not necessary in going to this place. In dreams one sees this place because the soul is there.

place is called hadja'teɫmuh, from a dense growth of the berries of that name. Then one comes to a meadow ("prairie") called xagwa'ɫelmu' (jackpine land). Next is a large creek called xaxo'sniɫ (deer place). All the deer that die go to this place. But they look very strange because their necks are like those of cranes and much longer than the necks of living deer. Then one comes to a creek called pagwa'lsniɫ (candle-fish or smelt place). The water is full of candlefish and here the dead have weirs and traps for taking them. The shore is greasy from the oil. Near here the trail divides and paths lead to the various villages of the dead. Then one comes to the large river called tciɫa'k (death?). The villages are on the other side and the country is called no'skuɫ or he'álskuɫ (dead place). On this side of the river things are as in this world but the other side is dim and misty. If the soul of the sick person has not crossed the river he is not yet dead. But if the soul has crossed, it is useless to try to return the soul. Only Bluejay visited the land of the dead and returned. When the soul reaches the river one of the dead comes across in a canoe to ferry it over.

The dead live exactly as do people in this world. But they speak a language which not even a shaman can understand. Their only words are ku ku ku (and so on). The dead are called klodji'náxáp. They have no bones in their bodies because a person leaves his skeleton in this world. Their houses and villages are like those here. Some say that the same husbands and wives live together there, but the children live in a different village. They have dogs, tools, and so on, like the people of this world (because these are buried with them). They hunt and fish in the same way. Their canoes are the same except that bow and stern are not raised, and each has a hole in the bottom. On this side of the river they have gardens. Pope saw a fine crop of potatoes, but when his guardian spirit tried to take some of them they became dust. The dead dry their fish high in the peak of the roof so that the guardian spirits will not steal them for humans. In case the salmon fail to run on earth a shaman and his guardian spirit go to the land of the dead to steal some. It was only necessary for the spirit to rub his feet in fish slime to accomplish this. Then when they return to this world he washes his feet in the river and the fish come, or certainly there would be a good run the following year.

Near the village at the mouth of the river is a creek called lata'tsomic in which the water dries up suddenly, then comes down with a rush. Once Pope was nearly caught in the flood. But his guardian spirit seized him and his "helper" (the man holding the shaman's rattle) by the hand and shouted "Come on! There is no danger! I will take you across!" This creek empties into the ocean near a point like Point Grenville. There the dead go out to hunt sea lions. Pope saw them come in naked. They built a fire on some rocks. When the rocks were hot they placed the carcasses on them and covered them with grass.

The dead have children just as do people here. They also fight wars. There are trails between their villages, which show that they visit back and forth. They never travel singly but always go in bands. In time each dead person dies a second death. All of the dead attend the funeral. After the second death they are called tsama'msatámán (twice dead). They are now or may become sa'xtikulc (guardian spirits), the helpers of persons in this life. They then never die.

The world of the dead and this world are the only two. Above this one there is only air where certain kinds of guardian spirits live and travel.

GHOSTS

The Quinault ideas regarding ghosts were rather vague. In the land of the dead the departed followed the pattern of life of the living. Mates were reunited, but children lived in a village by themselves. The soul became a ghost, evidently at the instant of death. The other dead might not treat the new arrival well, or he might become lonesome for his living friends and relatives. In either case the ghost returned to this world and attempted to get companions for the other world. Ghosts were most likely to return shortly after death, and during the first weeks and months after a person died there was considerable fear of them. But the ghost of a person dead for years might also return. As might be surmised, ghosts were active only at night.

Ghosts had no definite form or identity. They usually appeared in the shape of drifting fog, yet in the form of a person. They most frequently haunted the vicinity of the graveyard. A ghost might speak in the language of the dead (kuku ku ku), or might make a sharp sound like that made by pursing the lips and drawing in air. Ghosts did not actually seize the soul of the living; rather, the person was so frightened that his soul escaped and wandered away. A ghost might come alongside a person (in the form of a person) and start doing the same task. One of them once appeared at the mouth of the river and drift-netted for salmon alongside of Alex Underwood. Frank Law once heard voices near the graveyard but could not understand what was being said. But soon he smelled an odor of mold and knew they were ghosts. Soon after W.M.'s wife died, her ghost returned and tried to come into his bed. He kicked at it and it went away. If a ghost was about and a person did not smell it he would soon die, but if he smelled something he would know it was a ghost and might live. One might drive the ghost away by saying "Go on your way and don't bother me." The Quinault still draw curtains over their windows at dark, lest a skuku'm or a ghost look in on them. No one dared whistle after dark lest he attract ghosts.

MAGIC

Shamanistic power and magical power were regarded as different in nature. The former worked through the medium of a supernatural being, the latter by means of a cause-effect relation. Shamans sometimes "shot" their "power" into persons or things, but this was regarded as differing from the practice of out-and-out magic. All genuine magic (skli'tcmał) was regarded as evil, and there was no mention of, nor concept of, beneficial magic. Magic seems to have been employed mainly to (1) stop the run of salmon, or (2) to bring stormy weather. Any person, shaman or not, could work magic.

If some person wished to stop the run of fish, either because of hatred or jealousy, or because his net or weir failed to catch a goodly number, he proceeded as follows: He took a pair of mussel or clam shells, laid a number of salmon hearts inside, and placed the shell in the hollow of a rotten piece of wood (preferably where a knot or limb had been). This was then buried in some secret place. Until these hearts are thrown back into the water the salmon in both ocean and river are "like asleep" and will not go upstream. Guardian spirit power is of no use in discovering the magician. In the old days a person found working magic was killed.

Weather magic was performed as follows: A section of hemlock several inches in diameter was split down the middle and one-half hollowed out. A kerf was cut at the middle and the piece bent so as to form a hollow cylinder closed at one end. Inside it were placed shells, pebbles, starfish, and other objects from the ocean. Then skulls of humans and animals were painted in a lifelike manner (?) and tied to the outside. Then the magician blackened his face and carried the prepared log to a pond somewhere in the woods and balanced it on the edge of the bank or across a pole. By raising and lowering one end the other was caused to splash in the water, the objects inside making a noise as they rolled about. Each time he allowed the log to hit the water he shouted, stȧła'k tȧlo'lks! tsadjȧ'kxʷ, South Wind! Heavy Wind! Come! He kept this up until a storm arose. Every day, as long as he continued to do this the weather would be stormy—he *made* it storm. Some people did this after a relative had died, because they didn't wish people to hunt, or trap, or catch sea mammals while they were in mourning. But a man caught at it would have been killed. No guardian spirit could aid in finding the culprit. Magic was seldom employed to bring harm to a person. Bits of hair or clothing, or other objects intimately associated with a person might be buried in or near the graveyard to produce illness or death. I did not hear of imitative magic used against persons.

MISCELLANEOUS BELIEFS

The rainbow was called kleḱko'lȧ gwiłen (arc or curve like a canoe). One must never point at it lest his finger become sore. The morning rainbow is a sign that it will soon storm. A rainbow in the afternoon is a sign of good weather. The rainbow is unlucky, but inevitable—"like the bad luck a man has if his wife has a baby while they are on the trail." If one points at the full moon it will bring on a storm, and his finger will become crooked or rot. If one points at the sun his nails will come out. There is no harm in pointing at the stars.

When a star is seen very near the moon it is an omen of trouble and sickness. Meteors are a sign that two stars are marrying. The aurora borealis (samla'tcȧngwas, lit., eloping, the same word being the name for a meteor) was also a sign of marrying stars. If a very large meteor is seen, it is the soul of some man going to the graveyard. The man himself will return the next day. If the meteor makes a hissing sound or if it strikes the earth, he will die within a month. If it dies out before it reaches the earth a very good shaman may be able to cure him. Ordinary small meteors are signs that somewhere two young people are eloping.

Once upon a time shadows (mala'h) were people who became real people at night, but visible only as shadows in the daytime. The village of the dead is sometimes spoken of as the mala'h village.

Echoes (t'owole) are caused by the sound striking the white fungi (t'owole) on trees which, being shaped like ears, send the sound back.

One should start a journey on the appointed day or bad luck will come. If one starts out and discovers that he has forgotten something he should go on, for it is bad luck to return. It is bad luck to see the moon over the left shoulder, but good luck to see it "with your right eye."

Lefthandedness is not regarded as bad. It is caused by the parent handing things to the child's left hand. Old people used to say, "Don't allow your child to take things with his left hand, or he will always be lefthanded." (One informant stated that lefthandedness was caused by the midwife touching the child first with her left hand.) Birth marks appear on a child because the pregnant mother saw something unusual or wonderful.

If one eats the livers of deer or elk, or the milt of salmon he would grow a beard (an undesirable adornment).

In the nests of humming birds will be found long hairs coiled up. These should be taken, carefully wrapped up, and carried home. The hair itself should be hidden in a hollow tree and the material in which the hair was wrapped placed in one's kit bag. So with other things found which might contain some potency—the wrapping material is kept, the object itself is hidden away. If one finds a butterfly with five holes in its wings it should be caught and rubbed on arrows, traps, etc., to bring luck.

If a crow alights near one's house and utters its cry it is a sign that there will soon be news of some sort. Its cry of dja dja dja means "news, news, news" (djà'-àdjàm). If one is hunting and a bluejay comes near and cries, sà sà sà, it is a sign of bad luck; but if it cries, tcip tcip, that means good luck and a safe return.

One must not handle frogs or snakes, for their urine is poison and will cause a sore which will grow in size until one dies from it. The big lizard (niɫtà'mux^w) is a real skuku'm and if its urine, which is white in color, should touch a person he will soon die. Skunks (poh, lit., "break wind") are not poisonous, but only stink (xoc).

If a land bird is seen in the water, or bathing, it is a sign of bad luck, or that a relative will die. When a crow takes a bath it will soon rain. If a squirrel or a wild-cat is seen swimming it is certain that bad luck will come. If one finds the tail of a flying-squirrel, he must carry it for luck. A snake seen hanging from a branch is a sign that one will or should return and start his journey anew. Bits of red fungus (?) called "cougar's dung" will bring good luck in gambling at slàhà'1. If a mole is found in the foam along the beach it is kept to bring luck in hunting all manner of sea mammals.

The old people believed many things about the pole'pole (gas well).

MYTHICAL ANIMALS

It was believed that for each species of animal there was one old male known as, *e.g.*, "the father of all the elk." This individual was larger than any others of his kind and was distinguished by some special mark. I give the following examples of these super-animals:

A man was hunting sea lions at Sea Lion rock one dark night. It was customary to creep among the sea lions and feel their flippers, in order to be certain of getting a fat one. On one he felt something like a third flipper. He crept back to the canoe and said to his fellows, "There is some strange animal there. I am going to spear it, so be ready to follow it." He speared it and it jumped into the water. At last they managed to kill it. They started towing it home and at daylight landed at Cape Elizabeth. They saw that the thing was a huge beaver with a tail more than three feet long. Spaced along the tail was a series of holes about two inches in diameter. They were afraid, but took it home. An old man came out to see it. He told them, "You did wrong. That is mismilka'usops (Big-beaver-with-holes-in-his-tail). He is the father of all the beaver. He has his house at ƚlapels [a branch of Raft river]." There were five inches of fat on that beaver. He was so huge that they made two robes of his skin.

Once upon a time a man was standing on the platform of the weir at kuku'mniƚ (skuku'm place). He saw something swimming and shouted, "Here comes a deer swimming! Come out to see! Come out to see!" People ran out; they saw that it was a water monster with a head like a deer, but a long body like a snake's, with feet near the head. In one house lived an old woman with her grandson. He started to run out, but she held him back, saying, "Don't go out. It might be a skuku'm." Soon a woman came in and told what they had seen. In a short while everyone in the village except the old woman and her grandson was dead. This kind of monster is called xexe'tàdjuh. It is said the Chinook used to paint its likeness on their canoes.

A man once killed a huge black elk. Its heart was covered with hair. It was the father of all the elk.

The salmon people have a home under the ocean. If the salmon are properly treated when caught, they return to the ocean to become salmon again (*q.v.*).

Creatures something like a cougar, but larger, called ƚàkxwatsgwa (water cougar), live in the streams and ocean and swim under water. Men fishing in the river often see them. Along the creature's tail are hooks like fishhooks. On these are often seen seal and porpoise caught in the ocean. A human is allowed to cast a spear at the last one, the one caught on the hook at the tip of the tail. If he strikes it the water cougar lets it go and the man may keep it. Water cougars never harm humans.

Until recent years people used to see a huge frog over thirty inches long. This is the frog which married the moon. On the frog's back there are five dentalium shells of various sizes. The person seeing the frog must take a stick, touch the smallest shell, and then turn his back on the frog. When he again turns around the frog will have gone, leaving the shell which was touched. This shell will multiply until a man becomes rich. It will bring him good fortune. One man made the mistake of touching the largest shell, which he put into a box. The shell multiplied until the box burst. But there came out a monster and killed everyone in the house. The frog was last seen about a century ago.

Sea serpents, huge creatures like snakes, were seen now and then. They were able to swim in the ocean or crawl along the ground. One lived in a small lake near Quinault lake. In the country of the Skokomish there were snakes with a head at either end of the body. They were able to travel with either head forward. Above Quinault lake there is a small lake inhabited by millions of snakes. If a person throws a stone into the water they all come to the surface.

Old Nicagwats once found a large mollusc something like a snail but shaped exactly like a whale. He put the strange thing away for medicine. Later he went with some other men on a sea lion hunt. They had not yet reached Sea Lion rock when the ocean took on a strange and dreadful appearance. A huge wave came and lifted the canoe high. As it struck the canoe their paddles were carried away and the bottom of the canoe fell away. They managed to tie the six sealskin buoys in pairs and cling to them and finally all reached shore. For a long time they were afraid to venture on the ocean again. The creature was some kind of an ocean power or skuku'm.

It was believed that (certain types of?) wolves are able to turn themselves into porpoises. On land they travel in large bands of forty or fifty, the largest ones always in the lead, the smallest bringing up the rear. When food becomes scarce they go out to the beach to hunt during the evening and night. At such times they will even devour persons. If they find no game or dead animals on the beach the leader starts running in a circle followed by the others. At last the bravest leads the way into the surf but the leader remains on shore. They swim out a way, then dive. When they come to the surface they have become porpoises. When they have killed as many sea creatures as they want they come back to where the leader is waiting to guide them. The moment they reach the shore they again become wolves. If one is killed out in the ocean his fellows bring the body back to shore. One man saw them tearing up a sea lion they had killed. As he watched, each took a section in its mouth, threw it across the shoulders and carried it away. Their home is in a cave far back in the mountains. The cave is half full of the bones of sea mammals which they have killed as porpoises and carried inland as wolves. People often see their tracks leading down the beach and into the surf.

Two boys were alone at Baker's prairie. They heard wolves howling, were afraid. One climbed a large tree, the other a small one. Soon there came hundreds of howling wolves following the tracks of the boys. At the smaller tree they dug and tore the roots until it fell. They ate the boy who had climbed it. Then they started to dig at the roots of the other tree. But the surviving boy remembered that he had been told to urinate on them, that they could not abide urine. He did so and they all ran away. He returned home and told what had happened.

The cåo'mcåo'm (the crying one) is an animal like a large wildcat but without hair. He can simulate the voice of a friend or relative. If a person hears the crying and recognizes the voice as that of a loved one it is certain that someone in the family is going to die.

One time my father was hunting near Raft river. He heard a voice which sounded like that of his brother's wife, saying over and over in the most mournful tones, "Oh, my children! Oh, my children!" The voice grew faint and then came nearer. He walked rapidly to overtake her. Finally he decided that the voice was not that of a person. He took a club and waited behind a tree to see what it was. Soon he saw a "headless," four-footed creature which seemed to have no head. When it came close he saw that it carried its head between the front legs and looked backward. It sat down like a person right near him. Then it raised its head, closed its eyes, and started to repeat its cry. The face was like that of a human being, which is why it is able to cry like a human being. He knew then that it was the cåo'mcåo'm. He raised his club and struck the creature over the head and ran a sharpened pole through its body, staking it to the ground. Then he got into his hunting canoe and paddled to the mouth of the river. Where the trail crosses he saw a man on horseback. When he came closer he saw that it was his eldest brother, who looked as if he had been crying. He said, "Both my boys fell ill, and both have died." Then my father knew why the animal's voice had sounded like that of his sister-in-law.

Thunderbird. Thunderbird (xà'nàsà) is a great creature with wings and feathers. Thunder (xàns) is caused by the flapping of his wings, lightning comes when he is angry. It issues from under his wings when he flaps them. His home is in the clouds and no human has ever seen him. Rain is his urine, hail is what he urinates when angry. He always urinates just before or after he flaps his wings. Most whale hunters get a part of their supernatural power from the thunderbird. The creature often caught whales in his talons and carried them back into the mountains where he ate them.

Some people were hunting elk far up in the mountains at the head of Center Fork. One night just after dark they heard a terrific roar of thunder and saw repeated flashes of lightning. They ran from camp and hid under trees and logs, believing the mountain was about to fall on them Rocks came tumbling down the cliffs. It seemed that Thunder was kicking the mountain, *i.e.,* causing it to shake. All night the thunder and lightning continued. In the morning the oldest man in the party said to some young fellows, "Go up toward that mountain and hunt. Elk are afraid of thunder and you might find them near camp." They set out and came to a flat place where they saw a huge black object that seemed to have a head and tail threshing about. They were certain it was a skuku'm (monster). They returned to camp and persuaded the others to come to see it. When the old man saw it he said, "That is not a skuku'm, it is a whale. Thunder was angry because he had caught it in the ocean and then lost it when he reached here." They approached closer and saw that it was a whale indeed. His dorsal fin was missing. The whale was threshing so that he had made a great hole. After several days he died and the people started cutting him up, storing the fat in the intestines. They remained there so long that the people in the home village, fearing they had met with some mishap, came to look for them. Before they had carried all the meat and fat to their canoes the snow came and they were forced to leave some behind. The bones of the whale can still be seen, but they are now covered with a growth of moss. This happened about a hundred years ago.

Four miles south of the village of nokedja'kt is a prairie. There is water at both ends of the prairie, but the middle is all grassy. In the old days rain and thunder came whenever the people went to this prairie.

Once I took my wife, my two boys, Percy and Bombo, and my aunt, Mrs. Chow Chow, to that place to gather basket grass. The boys went away by themselves. They found a hole in the ground lined with rocks. It was a little pool, and the water in it was blue like bluestone water. Bombo was going to dip some out with his hat to taste it, but Percy would not let him. Then they saw lightning shoot across the water in the pool. Then it began to thunder and soon it rained a little. Then the boys came back and told me what they had seen. And I asked them, "Did you see anything bad there?" They said, "No, only a little lightning." Then I told them, "Boys, you are foolish to stay around there. Maybe that is xànàsa's (Thunder's) basin. It is all right for one person to find it, but never for two to see it. Maybe something will happen to you now." Old Nicagwats used to tell me that sometimes people found Thunder's basin. Then it thundered all the time. The boys said that there were bubbles coming out of the water all the time.

And now both the boys are dead. Percy died first. The next year I went with Bombo to the prairie again. Bombo showed me a tree with crab apple brush growing around it. He said the basin was at the foot of the tree. On our way back we started to go there. But we had only gone a little way when it began to thunder and to rain very hard. Then we turned back. A little over a year afterward Bombo died. Every autumn I have planned to go back there but I never have yet. Before I go I must bathe and "train" hard for a month. This year I did not train enough to chance it. (W.M.)

GIANTS

In the mountains live many giants, called tsadja'tko or tsa'áloh, who look almost the same as humans. On their right big toe a long quartz spike grows up to six feet long. If a human is kicked with this he will likely die. They are great thieves. People avoid the creeks on which they live. Some still come around the village at night and borrow a harpoon or a drift net, but usually return it before morning. They are fond of playing tricks on humans, such as sneaking up and kicking them, tying them to trees with thongs lashed to the genitals, etc. Some even married humans, and even today there are people living who are half tsa'áloh. The giants can often be heard at night. Even if their whistling sounds far off it is certain that they are close.

A hunter saw a campfire on the mountainside. He approached, thinking he would find a companion or friend. He saw a man roasting meat, his back turned to him. He asked what he was doing. Instead of answering, the giant (for such he was) jumped over the fire and down a cliff, making a whizzing sound as he went. On the top of his head was a hornlike growth and at its tip a light. The hunter took over the camp and appropriated the meat.

At the village of tsimitc (?) lived five brothers. The eldest had a wife and a small daughter. One day he went up the river to fish but never returned. The next day the next-oldest went upstream and likewise disappeared. Each day another brother went up the river, until none remained. The widow took the child and went in search of them. Far up the river she came, one afternoon, to a small house. No one was inside so she went in and hid, waiting to see who lived there. At dusk she saw from her hiding a huge man come up the river. In one hand he carried a spear, in the other five salmon. She knew that he had done away with the brothers. He started roasting the fish. As soon as one side of a fish was cooked he peeled off the flesh and wolfed it at a single bite. Thus he ate all five salmon. The next morning he again went fishing. He soon returned with five salmon which he roasted and ate. Then he lay down to sleep. She made noises about the house but he only snored on. That evening he fished upriver, the next morning downriver. She looked under the sleeping-platform and saw the five brothers, dead. She hurried back to the village and related what she had seen. The men of all the villages along the river banded together and followed her to this place. They followed her directions and hid in the woods until the huge man returned and lay down to sleep. When he was sound asleep they took some of the planks from each side of the house. The upper class warriors were afraid to go in. But a commoner crawled in and struck the giant over the head with a heavy stone used for driving weir stakes. The others then rushed in, shooting arrows and thrusting spears into him. He had strength to beg them not to kill him. When he was dead they set fire to the house, burning his body and those of the brothers as well. When they returned home they decided to move their village downstream about two miles. The new town they called nonau'okał (big village) and in time it became one of the largest villages.

There were beings, about 18 inches tall, who were fond of playing practical jokes on men.

THE SHAKER CULT[68]

At the time of my stay with the Quinault only old Bob Pope and a few village rowdies were not members of the Shaker church. It was said that Billy Mason and Johnson Wakinas made a trip to Puget Sound about 1885 or 1890 and were con-

---

[68]I made no attempt to secure complete material on the Shakers. The notes which follow present only an outline of the religion.

verted. When they returned they succeeded in converting nearly everyone in the village except Bob Pope. Later the Quinault went among the Queets, Quilleute, and Lower Chehalis making converts.

The Quinault give the following account of the origin of the cult: A man named tcanslo'kàm (John Slocum), who lived at Mud Bay near Olympia, became very ill. His soul wandered to heaven but God would not let him in. He was told to return to earth and to dance and sing, using the cross, the bells, the candles, the white robes and so on, which figure in the cult. After five days he came back to earth, related what he had seen, and started converting people to the new faith.

While the cult was new the members followed certain customs no longer practiced. Before a meal a "blessing" was asked by the ringing of bells and singing. Sometimes this ritual lasted some time, until the food was cold. Nowadays a short prayer constitutes the saying of grace. Formerly no non-member was allowed to be present during the curing rites. No scoffing shaman was ever allowed to attend a meeting.

Religious activity is greatest around Christmas, following the old pattern of the solstice ceremonies. During this time "shakes" may be held every night for weeks. During the remainder of the year services are ordinarily held only on Sunday morning, Sunday night, and when a member falls ill. If a person dies the members dance around the surviving relatives to prevent their being carried off by the same disease.

Conversions follow a definite pattern. An onlooker at a meeting suddenly starts to shake (even against his will) and then usually joins. This has happened to several whites who were merely curious observers. One white woman married to a native started shaking in her own house. More commonly a person expresses a desire to join. He is told to abstain from liquor and tobacco and refrain from gambling, these practices being taboo to all good Shakers. At the next meeting the novice (or novices) stands in the middle of the floor with his feet together, his eyes closed, and his hands raised above his head. The members then start dancing around him, usually in a counter-clockwise direction, keeping step throughout. Several men hold bells in their hands, the other men and women go through various motions. The hands are most often held at the level of the face and usually tremble ("shake") as long as the person is dancing.

At the beginning one member starts his own song and the others join in. This song is sung ten or twenty times, then dies away and someone else starts another. As the members warm to their task the dancing becomes more violent, the bell-ringing more vigorous. Lighted candles are passed around the body of the novice, evil things are "pulled" out of him with the hands, or motions with the face indicate the sucking out method. The theory is that good things and spirits are to surround him and be put into him, the evil taken out. When the novice becomes weary and his arms sag, a dancer raises them up. If his hands show signs of trembling the dancers go on with redoubled vigor. After some hours the older or fatter dancers become weary and drop out. Not for an instant does the dancing and bell-ringing cease. The performance usually begins before 9 o'clock in the evening and ends around 3 o'clock in the morning. But if the novice shows signs of getting the power, it may continue all night. The winter rituals ordinarily last nearly all night.

The Quinault members of the cult follow the old tribal pattern and dance by stamping the feet alternately. I have seen members of tribes from Puget Sound and the Yakima bring down both feet in unison. None of the dancers wear rubber heels, yet they stamp solidly with the heels. Since there are usually ten or twenty dancers the floor of the hall, which is not well braced, springs up and down a distance of several inches with each beat. Some of the dancers keep step in a rather perfunctory fashion, but others, more suggestible persons, dance frenziedly. These last often raise the foot twelve inches or more with each step. Those genuinely under the spell (and I feel certain that there are such) dance in a completely reflex fashion with hands, and even the head, jerking convulsively. The male dancers doff their outside shirts before beginning and tie their suspenders together across the chest to prevent them slipping over the shoulders. So violent is the dancing that perspiration streams down the faces of the dancers and their clothing is soon saturated. "I've given up dancing," said one member, "because my underwear rots on me within a month, from the sweat." When the power comes into a person it is evidenced first by a trembling in the hands. The tremors may spread to other parts of the body. The power sometimes comes as a breath of warm, almost hot, air, perceptible both to the novice and the dancers. This constitutes the equivalent of the old pagan "getting of power." The novice usually receives a vision and is "given" one or several songs. Among the Quinault these songs are ordinarily only tunes without words (the singing phrase being variations of hai and ho). Some of the local members of other tribes sang songs with words. Ordinarily there are no further revelations, visions, or songs received.

The members chant a litany repeatedly at the Sunday morning service and now and then employ it in the conversion rites. Its "words" run: kwoks (or kwa·s) nas mansti ta nas santusple'klo ma sis ta. No one knows the meaning of the words, which are said to be from Nisqualli or another language. I was told that klo means "high," santusple is merely the "santo esprit" of the Christian ritual. I relate the following incidents which I observed, as illustrations of ritual and belief.

Mrs. H. C. "got the shake" for the first time and in turning around fell to the floor. She was raised to her feet and, still shaking, turned and pointed toward the cemetery. It was believed that this portended illness and possible death for her unless she acquired further shake power.

J. C. was accidentally shot in the foot. The wound got infected and he became very ill. He took a knife and threw it at the farthest wall of the room, saying, "If this knife sticks in the wall I'll get well; if not, I'll surely die." The knife remained in the wood. He then tried to cure himself by the old pagan means but his recovery was slow. His wife told him he would never get well unless he joined the Shakers. In a few months a song came to him and, soon after, the shake.

A young Indian from Oregon visited the reservation and asked the local members to shake over him. He had had tuberculosis and white physicians had given him up. But now, a year later, through the Shaker faith, he had nearly recovered. He told his story at a meeting. He stood with his right hand raised and said, "Jesus wants us. Jesus wants us. But some of us he can't get." Then he cried.

Mrs. T. S. was a backslider but decided to rejoin. One night during the dance the power came to her. She bent over until her fingers nearly reached the floor and in this posture started turning round and round counter-clockwise. She spun more and more rapidly and finally fell heavily to the floor and lay motionless. Some of the dancers were alarmed and wanted to carry her to the bench but were restrained by others. After some time she arose and walked over to the bench and sat down.

Mrs. J. C. stated that her helper (*i.e.*, the shake power) often tells her of things that are going to happen, such as visitors on the way, or the sickness or death about to come to someone.

The following accounts of personal experiences were related to me:

Quite a few years ago I went to the church and stood up to "join." For two or three nights nothing happened. On the next night, after several hours, J. C. and another man started to "shake me." They are strong for giving the shake. They shook around me and finally began to work on my arms. Soon I began to feel my arms, then my hands, get warm. Then my hands began to shake. Soon I felt that warmth in my breast. Then my arms began to tremble all over, and my shoulders, too. But I didn't feel the shake in my feet. They took me by one arm and turned me around. Then one of my heels began to tap the floor. Soon I began to stamp with both feet. The shake came strong in me. Soon I was shaking all over and jumping high with every step. Some say they see things (a vision) when the shake comes to them, but I saw nothing. Only the shake came to me so that I couldn't help shaking. (F.P.)

The C's were involved in a lawsuit over an estate. J. M. testified against them. Mrs. C. afterward said to him, "You lied at the trial; you know you lied. But you will soon see the day that you will be sorry. Trouble and sorrow will soon come to you." A year later his mother died. He must have thought about it then. J.M. often joins the Shakers but frequently backslides. Mrs. C. never stands near him when he is trying to regain the power. (A.J.)

All last year I felt sad. Every time I prayed I cried, and often I cried between times. My helper seemed to tell me that something was going to happen, but I didn't know what. Then two weeks before O. S. was drowned my crying stopped. My heart no longer cried. When he died I knew why I had been sorrowful, because his mother and I are cousins. (A.J.)

Three years ago Mrs. T. S. had an operation. She grew steadily weaker and finally was taken home, nearly dead. She could not even speak. That night the Shakers shook over her until morning. The next night they did likewise, and she began to improve. The third night Mrs. C. S. found her soul in the road in front of H.S.'s house. It had fallen out on the way to the hospital when the truck went over a bump. The Shakers put the soul back and every night kept up the shaking. She mended rapidly and in a year was entirely well. (A.J.)

Three years ago H. M. and H. C. got the shake power the same night. They took bells in their hands and went outside, ringing them as they went. The people followed them. The two went to the river, got into a boat, and rowed across the river (with closed eyes) to the cemetery. They walked into the cemetery and the bells soon "pointed" to a particular place. The onlookers dug there and produced a woman's shoes, dress, and a lock of hair. Someone was trying to bewitch her. The people threw the things in the river and saved her life. (B.M.)

My daughter C. (an adopted white girl) used to love to dance at parties. Some other girls were jealous because the boys liked her so much and they placed poison in her food. She was sent to the hospital in Aberdeen. She vomited blood continually and the doctors finally gave her up. One night she felt something shake the bed. Three nights this happened. The fourth night she saw a man standing by her bed. He had long hair, a face like a woman's, and was dressed in a long white robe with a yellow band across his chest. He looked at her and said, "I am Jesus from heaven. Your time to leave this world has not yet come. You will live to see the girl who poisoned you suffer more than you have. You must send a man to Quinault lake to get water from a creek which never runs dry. There he is to get water from a quiet pool. Do not get the water in the riffles, for there it is full of worms. That water is my blood. When you drink, it will become good blood in you. Now I am leaving this gown and its band for you to wear. It is to be your helper, and you will get a song." J.C. and a white man got the water as directed. C. drank a half glass. What remained in the glass soon turned red. The doctors (white) marvelled at it. A Catholic priest pronounced it the blood of Jesus. In a year C. was well. She never went to (social) dances afterward, for in her vision she saw that dance floors were three inches deep with blood. On Sundays she wears the gown and ribbon band to church and sings the song which came to her. (Mrs. J.C.)

My shake power is not as strong as my guardian spirit power used to be. God may be all right for white people, but for Indians the old kind is best. In the old days the shamans could cure anything; but the Shakers can only cure slight pains. Sometimes my guardian spirit comes near to me, looks at me from the corner of his eye, and says, "Why do you bother with this 'shake' business? The 'shake' can cure only little things. That power is only the light from the candles and in the bells. If you take away the candles and then shake, you will die." My old power doesn't stay in me now that I am a Shaker, but sometimes it comes close and watches me. (S.H.)

KNOWLEDGE

NATURE

The earth was regarded as flat, but the Quinault never speculated about its size. The earth was thought to be indefinitely alive, yet it was not personified. Prayers were sometimes addressed to the world or "to the air." The sun and moon traveled around the earth, going underneath it at night. Earthquakes (sdjopdjo'pam, moving earth) were caused by movements of the living earth.

To the west, far across the ocean, was a land inhabited by supernatural beings. Between it and the Quinault coast were islands. There was no elaborate cosmogony in the Quinault scheme of things. The "upper world" was only the air and clouds where dwelt a few beings who might become guardian spirits. The land of the dead was a place much like this world. Even animals had a spirit existence there, though it could hardly be said that it was believed that animals had souls in the sense that humans did. The legends refer to a Sky World and Sky People, but belief in these was so vague that informants disclaimed such a region until reminded of the legend.

Most natural phenomena were explained in terms of the body of mythology, were ignored, or explained in a matter-of-fact fashion. "We look at the stars and know they will always be there." There was no explanation of tidal phenomena. Nor were there special beliefs concerning the aurora borealis.

Eclipses were called cik̆tistáxan taánem (eating the moon, or sun). At the time of the war with the Sky People a large animal called sťáxwe tciłat (Upper Fisher) remained behind. Now and then he seizes the sun or moon and starts to devour it. People would then become frightened and would attempt to frighten him away by shouting and making all possible noises, and, if it were an eclipse of the moon, they would make torches of pitchwood to cause him to go away. But the Frog Woman really helps the sun or moon the most and always succeeds in rescuing them.

CALENDAR

The Quinault recognized no exact number of months in the year, but they kept a fairly careful count which began in the autumn "when the geese flew south" (September-October). In addition to the numbered moons or months there were descriptive designations of time periods of indefinite length. Neither these nor the lunar months were grouped into seasons. The following list is that of the numbered months:

1. łámkse'mał, a term said to have no meaning.
2. kwala'kàik, "big moon."
3. nostca'ła, "on the third (moon)."
4. no'smos, "on the fourth."
5. nostsila'ks, "on the fifth."
6. nostsita'tcà, "on the sixth."

7. nostso'ks, "on the seventh."
8. nostsámo's, "on the eighth."
9. nostágwi'xw, "on the ninth."
10. nospaána'ks, "on the tenth."

Here the count ended (about July or August) and there followed a period of indefinite length (two to three lunations), which was not kept track of but was called xaisáme'n (lost or waste time). Beginning with the first of these, count was kept by tying a knot in a cord at the time the new crescent appeared. In case of disputes about the number of the month (and it was said quarrels sometimes arose in this manner) the matter was settled in the spring by the coming of the robins, which proved it was now the seventh month. Pope did not know the number of days in a lunar month, much less the number of days in the year.

There was recognition of the time relation between lunations and the female menstrual cycle, but no causal relation was inferred.[69] It was also believed that epileptic fits (skuku'm) recurred at the same phase of the moon, usually during the dark of the moon.

Another system of time reckoning ran as follows:

paánka'áptsam, "time (of) winter."
kwamí'lámixw, "getting warmer" (about March).
paánskle'tstap, "time greens coming up."
paáni'lsták, "time of sprouts."
paánkulá'k, "time of salmonberries."
paánkallo'm, "time of elderberries."
paánamola'k, "time of summer" (about July).
silpa'álos, "in the autumn."
na'osilpa·'álos, "big autumn."
páánxaá'las, "time hear geese (come by)."

This last is more like the familiar Northwest method of describing the months than is the first system of month counting.

In a region where the winter season is one of almost continuous rain and storm one scarcely expects to encounter the reckoning of the winter solstice, yet the Quinault kept definite track of both solstices. At several of the villages were "seats" (a stump or stone) where the old men watched both sunrise and sunset. Usually they sighted from the seat to a pole placed in the ground, or to a designated tree.[70] If the sun traveled farther north than in ordinary years (!) it was considered a sign that a good year with a heavy run of salmon would follow. If the solstice occurred during a waning moon it moved but little each day, indicating that it was heavily loaded (with food) for the year to follow. But after a solstice which occurred during a waxing moon the sun traveled far each day and indicated a lean year to follow,

---

[69]One informant (A.J.) stated that women kept track of the days of the menstrual cycle by tying knots in a cord. She also claimed that knotted cords were used to check the months between a marriage and the elapsed time before the birth of the first child.

[70]A.J. stated that the sighting was done by marking on a stick placed horizontally the spot where the shadow of a certain tree fell at the moment of sunrise. One such mark indicated 15 days until the solstice.

with sickness and famine certain to come. The winter solstice was called xá'ɫtaȧnem (comes back, the sun). There was no name for the summer solstice but it was observed in the same fashion. It was believed that at the summer solstice the sun set four or five times at exactly the same place.

Whale hunters watched carefully for the winter solstice, for this season with its exceptional tides[71] was the time when the guardian spirit connected with whaling was to be met with.

I give the following list of terms for time of day and some other designations for reckoning time:

saȧyu'xwȧtc or me'tskuɫ, "light time," *i.e.*, day.

tuhqo'i, or pȧ'ttsȧȧt, night.

ci'alkahetȧ, before daybreak.

ɫa'ȧxoɫ, just before sunrise.

pe'sȧnatc, "sun coming from behind" (sunrise).

mȧipitsȧxan taȧne'm, "just raise, that light ball."[72]

potskuɫ, "middle of the day."

ewȧnuh, afternoon.

ḵȧ'ɫsȧnatc, "disappears in the water (the sun)."

tȧlȧ'psȧnatc, "sinks, the sun" (sunset).

e'wȧnoh, twilight.

po'tas, midnight.

mepȧtaxan taȧnem, just stuck up, the moon (new moon).

tcas taȧnem, "new, that moon."

su·kwȧxan taȧnem, "half, that moon."

ɫela'litcan, "full (the moon)."

kudjȧmmȧxan taȧnem, "no more, that moon" (dark of the moon).

taȧnem, "moon," *i.e.*, month.

CONSTELLATIONS

Only Bob Pope among my informants knew the names of more than one or two constellations, and his eyes were too dim to enable him to point them out. He gave, however, the following names and rough descriptions:

tcatkuxoi, "star which is the head or tender of the other stars" (the evening star).

tcatdjȧ'xutc, "star of daylight" (the morning star).

These two were the greatest of the stars, the heads or chiefs.

ɫi'kutcutan, "dipping dipper," the Pleiades.

It was believed that if a person could count but four or five of these he would always remain poor, but if he could see nine (!) of them he would become a rich man and a chief.

---

[71]An ebbing tide was called sḵaḵ, an incoming tide sxa'p'tce. High water was ta'sɫnal (heavy water) and low water neɫexa'p'tci (low out water). The relation of moon and tide was clearly recognized.

[72]This is "broken" Quinault, probably regarded so because moon (taȧne'm) is used instead of sun. Yet it is commonly used to express sunrise. Some claim taȧnem is the correct term for sun, that pȧ'tsȧȧt'taȧne'm ("night sun") is the correct term for the moon.

djàgàge'h, skate or ray (?). Orion (?).
ƙwa'naχ, "hide." The bowl of the Great Dipper (?).
tca'łà, "three." The handle of the Great Dipper (?).
pawh, the pole star (?).

The three which precede pawh are three hunters; pawh is their dog.

ƙulmi'nàm, "camping." A circle of stars somewhat to the east of the zenith.
tsala'p'oh, "spin a top." A small star to the north of the preceding.
gwa'cops, "long tail" (land otter). An irregular row of 6 stars in the S.E.
sƙe'le, dip net. A somewhat triangular arrangement of stars in the S.E.
qał, "water." Two rows of stars that run east to west. "They go with the dip
net."

DIRECTIONS

Six (possibly seven) directional points were recognized:

1. ołsƙeleƙ, north (lit., "people without sense"?).
   łàgwa'łmił, north (lit., a man).
   łàa'lsƙeleƙ, also given for north.
   ƙeleƙetuh, also given for north (lit., "coming from the clouds").
2. ciolskuł, "to the sunrise."
   slaałtcoxutc, "where daylight comes."
   eƙlo'łetuh, "far back clouds" or upriver.
3. tàło'lks, south.
   toola'k, "from over there." Southwest. Possibly a special direction. Clouds
   coming from the southwest were a sign of coming storm.
4. ciołtcu, "ocean side" or "far out."
   tcai'tcu, "far out to the ocean."
   ciołssalaƙkwa, "to the ocean beach." Also west, but no farther than the
   beach.
5. tcił, up or zenith.
6. tàƙe'ls, down or nadir, implying down to the land of the dead.

The winds were named from the directions. The sun was the chief means of
knowing the direction, e.g., when traveling. At sea the ocean swells were watched,
as they always came from the west.

MEASURES

There were but few terms for measures of distance, though undoubtedly more
were known than are given in the following list:

łil, the width of a finger. Multiples of this unit were indicated to four.
mauàtsu, the span, measured from tip of thumb to tip of middle finger when the
fingers are extended.
nostsàlkàts, from the inside of the elbow to the tip of the middle finger.
tagwa'xa, from armpit to tip of middle finger, an arm-length.

potexwȧts, from the depression at the base of the throat to the tip of the middle finger with the arm extended.

natcauc, the reach or fathom, the distance fingertip to fingertip of the out-stretched arms.

tsamauc, two fathoms.

tcanauc, three fathoms.

mosowexw, four fathoms.

Numbered fathoms were used for distances up to about 200 feet. Asked how he would measure a distance of a half-mile or so, Pope replied he would use a line long enough, then count its fathoms. Beyond "far" and "near" there seem to have been no designations of distances involving several miles or more.

NUMERATION

A modified decimal system was used in counting. I obtained the following set of numbers:

1, pa'uh or powh	17, ta'ltso'ps
2, sa'lih	18, ta'ltsamos
3, tca'ȧłȧ	19, ta'ltȧgwixu
4, mo.'s	20, tsȧmto'mic
5, tse'laks	21, tsȧmto'mic tcin pauh
6, se'tatcȧ	29, tsȧmto'mic tcin tȧ'gwixu
7, tso'ps	30, tca'nactomic
8, tsa'mos	40, mo'sałtomic
9, tȧ'gwixu	50, tselaktatomic
10, pa'naks	60, setatcȧnatomic
11, ta'lpow	70, tso'pstałtomic
12, ta'lsale	80, tsamostałtomic
13, ta'ltcatlȧ	90, tȧgwixwatomic
14, ta'lȧmos	100, panakstałtomic
15, ta'ltsi'laks	101, panakstałtomic tcin pauh
16, ta'lsitatcȧ	1000, panakspanakstałtomic

MEDICINES AND CURES

Although shamanistic curing formed a very important part of Quinault medi-cine, commonsense treatments, the use of herbs, etc., were extensively used. To a very limited extent the sweat-lodge was employed in curing.[73] Certain medicines, especially herbs and roots, were individual or family secrets and their nature and use were not divulged without a compensation. This and the fact that my visits were made in winter or early spring prevented my securing a complete list of rem-edies, much less a collection of the plants used. The following is therefore a very inadequate account of the medical lore.

The milk teeth of children were pulled, when loose, with a sinew cord. The parents then threw the tooth in the fire and the child blew on the coals until the

---

[73]See p. 65.

tooth was consumed. The child was then told to look for a squirrel and ask him for new teeth. This is why people seldom had poor teeth. The decayed teeth of adults were extracted in the same manner.

If a man was hurt while away from his village his companions made a litter of two long poles and two short cross poles. Thongs or cedar withes were lashed across to provide support for the body. Broken limbs were cared for by lashing boards on either side, as splints, until the injury mended. The aged or infirm used a cane as an aid in walking. Crutches were unknown.

Sore eyes were treated by bathing them with an infusion of snake head roots and stems. An infusion of crab apple bark served the same purpose. A third remedy for the eyes was a mixture of woman's milk and the juice pressed from snake head roots. The root of a plant called ƙwaih was also used.

Emetics were used when a person could hold nothing on his stomach or if he suspected he had been poisoned. An infusion of elderberry root (ƙwe'łap̓) produced the desired effect. Also used was an infusion of the bark of a plant called lo'pnił, said to resemble the salmonberry.

A very painful "cure" for rheumatism was effected as follows: A generous tuft of dry shredded cedar bark was wrapped around a short piece of the stem of a plant called tce'nåen (a lily-like plant which grows in the alpine meadows) and the bark lighted. When the bark was glowing well it was pressed against the afflicted part and held there. Hoh's arms about the elbows were covered with scars produced in this way. There were several variants of this method of curing. The root and stem of the same plant were boiled as a cure for tuberculosis. It was said that but two drops could be taken at a time.

Poison to be placed in an enemy's food was made from a lizard (niłtåmu'h, water dog ?). The animal was held over a small blaze and the juices allowed to collect in a shell. If placed in a man's food he would waste away and die within three months. To this might be added the juices from a small snake called o'lkah. To such a mixture could be added juices similarly derived from a lizard (?) called klaka'-łåk.

In addition to the foregoing medicines I learned of the following:

Spruce gum (kwa'åleł) was applied directly to cuts and wounds. The gum of cottonwood burls was also employed.

The root of the waterlily was heated and applied to the seat of a pain, especially rheumatic pains.

Salmonberry bark was boiled in sea water and the brew used by pregnant women to lessen the pains of childbirth. It was also used to cure infected wounds.

Nettles were placed in boiling water and applied as a hot poultice. An infusion made from the bark of nettles was considered a cure for headache or nose-bleed.

A clover-like plant called ƙaie'lokstont was heated on the coals and used as a poultice on sore or weak legs. An infusion made from the same could be taken internally or used to bathe afflicted parts.

An abortive was made by brewing the plant of a thistle (tsopo'ak) and taking the infusion as a tea.

The stem of the wild rose was reduced to ashes, mixed with skunk oil, and applied to syphilis sores.

An infusion made from the stem and leaves of a plant called xadji′djilniɬ was a cure for afflictions of the kidneys, stomach, or intestines.

Licorice root (tsumȧna′ȧmats) was eaten raw, or baked on the coals a bit, as a cough medicine.

The bark of the cascara tree (xwixwi′niɬ) was brewed and the infusion taken as a purgative. The same use applied to an infusion of cherry bark. A liquor brewed from the root of the Oregon grape was taken for coughs and stomach disorders.

The bark of white pine (tȧ′tskȧniɬ) was boiled and the infusion taken for disorders of the stomach and blood. The pitch in the blisters on the bark of the larch (balsam pine) was eaten for the same troubles.

An infusion from cedȧr leaves and the bark on the twigs was used for the kidneys. An infusion from cottonwood bark taken at the surface of the ground relieved tuberculosis.

An infusion made from a type of fireweed (xwȧdja′tsťont) was taken internally. The plant was also used as a blistering agent.

The shell of the fresh-water mussel (a′ḳalctȧn) was burned and the resulting powder applied to boils to "draw" and cause them to break.

The spinal cord of the sturgeon was eaten raw to prevent conception.

Skunk oil was applied to smallpox sores in the mouth.

THE AUTOBIOGRAPHY OF BOB POPE

The place where I first came to myself[74] was at the village of nokedja'kt. There were three houses there at that time. In one lived the village chief sa'utonux; the second was owned by tci'tȧmin; and in the third lived my father. These men were heads of their houses, but there were several families in each.

In those days people wore only robes for clothes. It was customary to bathe each morning the year round. Almost every night there was singing and dancing in one of the houses. Usually the only food was salmon, salmon eggs, and potatoes.

From that village the people of all three houses moved downriver to t'o'nans. Soon afterward there came an epidemic (smallpox?) and most of the people of the village died, and only a few of their descendants are alive today. We used to come frequently to the village of kwi'naiɬ to gamble at slȧha'l. Here we would meet people from Queets and Grays harbor. Sometimes a game would last for several days. Gilbert Sodomic's father once lost everything he owned—even his dried salmon, even to the last kettle of salmon that was cooking at the time, and the kettle as well. When the Queets and Chehalis had lost all they had they would send back to their relatives for more. The women would also gamble with beaver teeth dice. Doc Hays Otuk's mother usually won at this.

The war between the Queets and Quinault was before my time; they were living in peace ever since I can remember.

When I first started to hunt I was just old enough to handle a gun. At first I hunted only ducks with a flintlock. Later on I killed a deer; then a bear. The first big game I killed was two elk. After that I often went to the mountains with other hunters and we killed all kinds of game. I also trapped for furs. At that time there was a trading post at Wynooche and we went there to trade furs and hides for whatever we needed. We would come down the river by canoe, then go by horse down the coast to Oyhut, then by canoe to Wynooche.

In those days the old people of my village were able to get a young man a wife when he was about fifteen. They bought me a wife and soon I moved downriver to no'skaɬan. There I lived for a long time, hunting and fishing for a living. When I had collected enough property I began to think, about giving a big potlatch. This was the beginning of my potlatching. But the idea was not from my own mind, but my "property guardian spirit" told me to give it. To my first potlatch I invited the Queets tribe.

About that time many of the Quinault were invited to a potlatch given by the djoɬodjoɬ (a Nootka tribe). The Queets, Hoh, and Quilleute were also invited. On the way we passed one village where there were only women and children. All the men had been drowned while hunting seal. At the potlatch only blankets were given away. The white trader had a large store full of blankets. He had been there so long he could speak the Nootka language. Most of us were given nothing, even after coming so far. Chiefs were given two or three blankets each. We were fed only rice, with dried halibut and herring eggs. The next year eight of us went to the same place again to invite them to a potlatch that Chief Tȧxo'lȧ was giving at kwi'naiɬ. It took us two and a half days. The first day we got as far as Neah bay. There was a southwest wind and we used a sail. Near that village is a dangerous place. One can go between the island and the mainland only at high tide. Outside the island is a great monster that sinks all canoes and ships. I have heard that the whites have tried every means of killing it but never can. [This is Devil's pass?]

Across the strait from Neah bay we stopped at a village where a potlatch was being held. Ten tribes (villages) had been invited. When they danced they used two houses, for not everyone could get into the one. A middle-aged man was the host, but he did not give many presents. It was mainly a feast. He had a whole house filled with pilot bread. Chief Tȧxo'lȧ's younger brother (who was married to a Makah woman) was given nothing, and his wife received only a tin pan.

At Neah bay there was a canoe of xosit (another Nootka group) who had come from the north to invite the Makah to a potlatch. But as the Makah were at this other potlatch they were waiting for them. The xosit appeared to us to be real savages. They wore only fur robes and their

---

[74]*I.e.*, when I began to remember things. This is considered to occur at about seven or eight years.

bodies were covered with grease. Taxolà's brother asked us if he should give them some food. Finally he gave each of them a blanket. We were wearing red shirts and we took these off and gave them as presents. They looked clean then, for the time being. Then they stood up and danced for us. Their spokesman made a speech, saying they had never before met such good people.

The potlatch which Tàxo'là gave was the greatest ever given. They built a roof over the space between two big houses and thus made a single house so large one could hardly see from one end to the other (perhaps 200 feet). All the Hoh, Quilleute, Makah, and Queets were there. At that time I saw a Quilleute man with a strange guardian spirit. He came dancing into the house, a curious bird resting on his hand. When he extended his arm it would disappear. When he closed his hand it disappeared into his hand. It was the most real thing of its kind I have ever seen. He was a short man and was naked except for a belt of cedar bark. He led the Quilleute dancers into the house. It was one of the few times that I have seen a really great medicine man—most supposedly-good ones never did much.

At the same potlatch I saw two shamans challenge each other to a contest. One was a Queets, named Xwàtà'm, the other a man from Grays harbor. We liked to see such contests. They went down to the river and dove in. When they came up each had a piece of ice several feet long on his shoulder. They started ashore with it. But the Grays harbor shaman was beaten, for his ice melted before he got ashore. Xwatam carried his ashore and up the bank. Then he threw it down and it turned to water and ran into the river. It was not hard ice but was soft and quivered like jelly. Then the Grays harbor man planned to kill Xwatam with his power, in revenge for the beating. Xwatam was lying across an ocean canoe in the river. The Grays harbor man shot his power at him but missed because Xwatam's power warded it off. But I heard it hit the canoe, and it was so strong it split the canoe from end to end. Xwatam jumped up and said, "He missed me!" Later Xwatam told his friends, "Now I will try to get even with him for that." Soon he got a chance and shot the other from behind with his power. The Grays harbor man told his friends that the other had "got" him. He no sooner reached home than he was taken ill and soon died. (When Xwatam first got his power it was in him so strong that he could walk up to a green tree, seize a limb and tear it out, together with the knot to the heart of the tree.)

It was customary in those days to carry a nearly dead person out of the house and lay him near the grave. Once they had taken out a dying woman. I went over to her to test my spirit power. I saw that there was nothing really wrong with her except a "pain" (disease object). I told her she must not tell anyone if I cured her.

She said, "I am sure not to tell if you do me a favor and cure me." I told her she would not die if I took that "pain" out. Then I took it out and showed it to her and said, "This is the only thing wrong with you; now you will be all right." I asked her to give me a little camas root when she was well. She walked back to the village, bathed, and went into her house.

(That is the secret of some medicine men—they never tell that they have power until they have had a chance to test it. If they find that they can really cure people then they tell what spirit it is they have. But they do not talk about it except when they are curing. If a man talked frequently about his spirit power he would not live long.)

That was the beginning of my career as a medicine man. I knew then that I had power to cure people. It was one of the most real things in my life. Most shamanism is mere playing and contesting at potlatch time.

During my life I never traveled a great deal, only when I was invited to go somewhere to a potlatch.

When it was rumored that some new shaman had a powerful helper, then I used to like to see if he had the real thing. In my time not many men had great power. I know this because I went to see many. Perhaps long before my time there may have been many great shamans. That is all.

NOTES

Features of culture on which I secured little or no data beyond their presence are the following:

A purse for dentalium money.

The bullroarer (used only as a toy).

A heavy bone dagger, about 8 inches long.

A blunt "bird" arrow.

Snowshoes.

Swings.

The nature and types of dreams. There was no objection to the telling of dreams other than those experienced in the vision quest.

A game or test of strength by pulling fingers.

Sexual intercourse was customarily in the "normal," male superior, position.

The following traits were claimed to be wholly absent in the culture:

The harpoon arrow, the atlatl, the bola, gill nets.

The musical bow, the flute.

Hemlock bark as food, acorns as food, use of salt, use of seaweed as food, use of lime, use of herring eggs.

Animals not eaten: Eels, skates.

Hunting and warfare: impounding of game, bear ritual (traces of, however), shield.

Religion: breach of taboo as cause of illness, pictographs, petroglyphs.

Poetry, tongue twisters, tales or jokes relating to misunderstood directions, tales of dwarfs.

Cremation (except for monstrous infants).

Elevated house, elevated storehouse, wooden stool, wooden pillow.

The eye shade, snow goggles.

Use of copper or other metals.

Names for the separate fires of the house.

Property marks.

Climbing rings and other special devices for climbing.

Yarn or thread from feathers.

Use of pitch or gum to waterproof baskets.

The long-handled adze.

Mirrors of polished materials.

Kissing, hugging (as signs of affection).

BIBLIOGRAPHY

Cobb, John N. 1921. Pacific Salmon Fisheries. Bur. of Fisheries Rept. for 1921, Appendix 1, (Washington).

Curtis, Edward S. 1907-30. The North American Indian, vol. 9. Cambridge: The University Press.

Farrand, Livingston. 1902. Traditions of the Quinault Indians. Amer. Mus. Nat. Hist., Memoirs, vol. 4, part 3, pp. 77-132.

Gibbs, George. 1877. Tribes of Western Washington and Northwestern Oregon. Contributions to North American Ethnology, vol. 1, pp. 157-241.

Goddard, Pliny Earle. 1924. Indians of the Northwest Coast. Amer. Mus. Nat. Hist., Handbook Ser. 10.

Gunther, Erna. 1928. A Further Analysis of the First Salmon Ceremony. Univ. of Wash. Publ. in Anthr., vol. 2, no. 2, pp. 129-173.

Lewis, Albert Buell. 1906. Tribes of the Columbia Valley and the Coast of Washington and Oregon. Amer. Anthr. Assoc., Memoirs, vol. 1, part 2, pp. 147-209.

Olson, Ronald L. 1927. Adze, Canoe, and House Types of the Northwest Coast. Univ. Wash. Publ. in Anthr., vol. 2, no. 1, pp. 1-38.

    1929. The Possible Middle American Origin of Northwest Coast Weaving. Amer. Anthr., n.s., 31:114-121.

Ray, Verne F. 1933. The Sanpoil and Nespelem: Salishan Peoples of Northeastern Washington. Univ. of Wash. Publ. in Anthr., vol. 5.

Swan, James G. 1857. The Northwest Coast; or Three Years' Residence in Washington Territory. New York.

Waterman, T. T. 1920. The Whaling Equipment of the Makah Indians. Univ. Wash. Publ. in Anthr., vol. 1, no. 1, pp. 1-67.

Waterman, T. T., and Coffin, Geraldine. 1920. Types of Canoes on Puget Sound. Mus. Amer. Indian, Heye Foundation, Indian Notes and Monographs.

Waterman, T. T., and collaborators. 1921. Native Houses of Western North America. Mus. Amer. Indian, Heye Foundation, Indian Notes and Monographs.

Willoughby, C. 1889. Indians of the Quinault Agency, Washington Territory. In Ann. Rept. of Smithsonian Inst. for 1886, part 1:267-282. Washington.

(185)

EXPLANATION OF PLATES

PLATE 1. The village of kwi'nait, about 1850. (After Swan.)

PLATE 2.   Bob Pope, a Quinault.   Mrs. Pope, a Hoh.   The coast at the mouth of Quinault river, with Cape Elizabeth in the distance.

PLATE 3. *a*. Ordinary burden basket; warp of split cedar limbs; one weft element (rigid) of split cedar limbs, the other (active) of split spruce root. *b*. Large storage basket of cedar bark; decoration in overlay of bear grass. *c*. Small carrying basket of split vine maple in twilling technique. *d*. Storage basket of split spruce root with diagonal crossed warps. *e*. Watertight twined basket of spruce root; decoration in overlay. *f*. Kit bag of cedar bark in checker weave. *g*. Coiled waterproof basket; coil clockwise as seen from bottom; stitches split in sewing; imbricated decoration. *h*. Man's kit bag of grass; twined, with weft running vertically; woven as two flat pieces.

PLATE 4. *a*. Unfinished coiled basket of spruce root. *b*. Mat of cedar bark in twilling. *c*. Hand adze. *d*. Unfinished waterproof twined basket. *e*. Ordinary burden basket of spruce root. *f*. Water-proof hat of spruce root; painted decoration representing a frog. (Courtesy of Santa Barbara Museum.)

PLATE 1. KWI'NAIL, ABOUT 1850

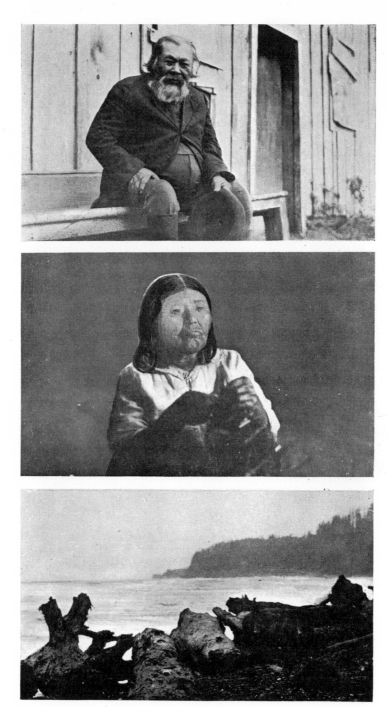

PLATE 2. BOB POPE; MRS. POPE; COAST AT MOUTH OF QUINAULT RIVER

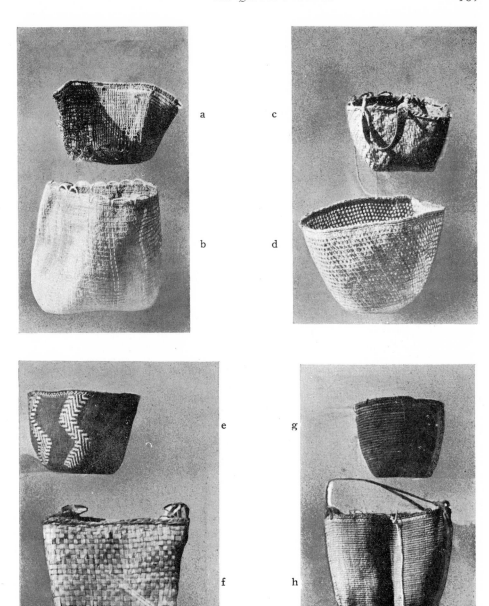

PLATE 3. BASKETRY

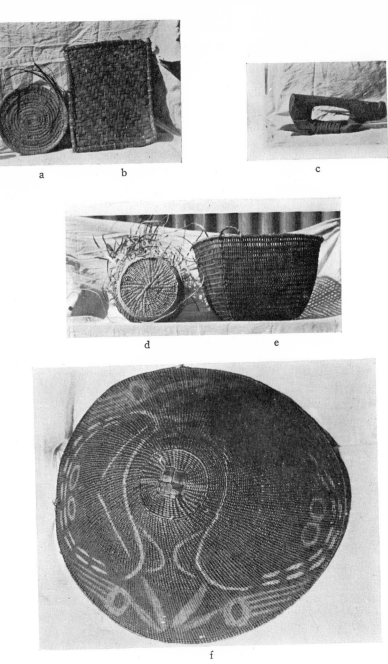

a   b   c

d   e

f

PLATE 4. BASKETRY; ADZE

INDEX

ADZE, CANOE, AND HOUSE TYPES OF THE NORTHWEST COAST

by

RONALD L. OLSON

UNIVERSITY OF WASHINGTON PRESS

Seattle and London

CONTENTS

PLATES

PLATE 1—Adze Types

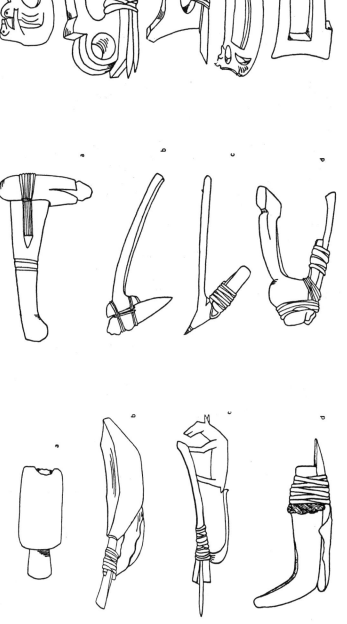

I Straight Adzes

a. Lower Fraser (after Smith).
b. Ozette (Wn. State Museum, 7155).
c. Puget Sound (Wn. State Mus., 5382).
d. Yurok (after Kroeber).

II Elbow Adzes

a. Eskimo (after Emmons).
b. Tsimshian (Provincial Museum, 518).
c. Makah (after Swan).
d. Skokomish (Wn. State Museum, 18).

III D Adzes

a. Kwakiutl (after Boas).
b. Nootka (after Boas).
c. Southern British Columbia (Provincial Museum, 1185).
d. Puget Sound (Wn. State Museum, 4588).
e. Quinault.

IDENTITY OF TRIBES IN THE DISTRIBUTION MAPS

1. Dog Rib.
2. Slavey.
3. Eskimo.
4. Aleut.
5. Yukon River tribes.
6. Copper River tribes (Ahtena).
7. Tlingit.
8. Tsimshian.
9. Haida.
10. Kwakiutl.
11. Bella Coola.
12. Nootka.
13. Vancouver Island Salish.
14. Lower Fraser Salish.
15. Lillooet.
16. Thompson.
17. Shuswap.
18. Chilcotin.
19. Carrier.
20. Kutenai.
21. Klallam.
22. Puget Sound tribes.
23. Nisqualli.
24. Makah.
25. Ozette.
26. Quilleute.
27. Quinault.

28. Lower Chehalis.
29. Chinook.
30. Cowlitz.
31. Wishram.
32. Walla Walla.
33. Yakima.
34. Nez Percé.
35. Spokan.
36. Fort Colville.
38. Kalispel.
39. Okanagan.
40. Tillamook.
41. Coos.
42. Tolowa.
43. Yurok.
44. Hupa.
45. Karok.
46. Klamath.
47. Modoc.
48. Atsugewi.
49. Achomawi.
50. Shasta.
51. Wiyot.
52. Maidu.
53. Yokuts.
54. Chumash.
55. Gabrielino.

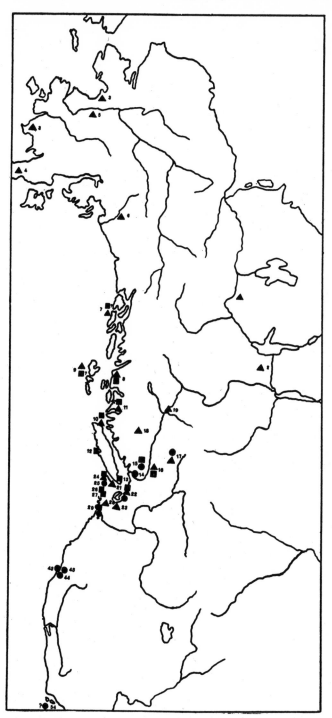

PLATE 2—Distribution of Adze Types

● Straight adze   ■ D adze   ▲ Elbow adze

8

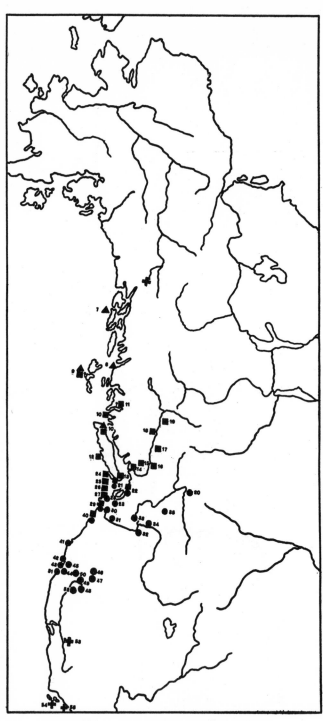

PLATE 3—Distribution of Canoe Types

● Shovel-nose canoe ▲ Northern canoe
■ Nootka canoe ✚ Form unknown

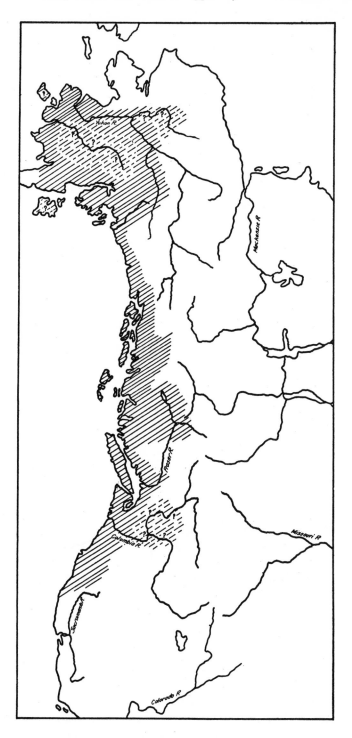

PLATE 4—Distribution of Rectangular Plank and Log Houses

ADZE, CANOE, AND HOUSE TYPES OF THE NORTHWEST COAST

I

INTRODUCTION

It is the thesis of this paper that the variations that occur in any cultural feature, noted for any one people or group of peoples, represent the cultural processes at work; and that psychologically and historically the combination and re-combination of elements, the appearance of new details, and the development of new concepts relating to a trait are quite as important in the development of culture as the original invention of an entirely new trait and its spread over a given area. Without such processes at work the culture-trait loaf must ever remain unleavened bread, never rising above the form it presented at its reception by a people.

To illustrate such developments and to analyze the processes at work I have chosen three traits of material culture (adze, canoe, and plank house) found in the Northwest Coast culture area. These have been analyzed in some detail and the areas of their distribution traced. Certain features of form and special usages connected with them have formed the basis for classification into general types. More specific features of form and usage for each type have been analyzed in an attempt to isolate originating points and to gain an insight into the process of diffusion. The parts played by cultural environment, external geographical environment, and motor factors as determinants of form and as stimuli to development have been noted where there seemed to be definite evidence of their influence.

The results seem to justify the general thesis. While it can not be doubted that all the examples of any one trait in the area are historically related, the wide variety of forms that are found argues for a considerable working of variational and developmental processes. Without these differences a trait would assume a drab sameness everywhere in the range of its occurrence. On the other hand the complex of forms, techniques of construction, and usages connected with a trait retain much the same flavor over much of the area but tend to disappear outside. It is this peculiar quality which gives the culture of an area its individuality and which marks it off from surrounding areas quite as much as actual substitution of traits.

A number of inferences are suggested by the data examined. All three traits seem to reach their highest development in the relatively restricted area between the Straits of Juan de Fuca and Southern Alaska. Within this area Nootka, Kwakiutl, and Haida seem to play a larger part than the other tribes in the elaboration of what is essentially a common culture. But outside this focal area appear features which show that the action of culture-processes is not restricted to the culture center.

(11)

For the traits analyzed in this paper the whole area seems to divide into areas of lesser extent. The northern canoe, the elbow adze, and the northern types of gabled house tend to disappear outside the cultural center formed by Tlingit, Tsimshian, Haida, and perhaps Kwakiutl. The Nootka canoe, the shed-roofed house, and the D adze seldom occur except between the Columbia in the south and Queen Charlotte Sound in the north. The straight adze, the southern types of gabled house, and the shovel-nose canoe are found only south of the Straits of Juan de Fuca. Within these areas of lesser extent a certain amount of specialization has gone on. This cautions one against giving the typical tribes of the area too great a share of the credit for innovations. Inability or unwillingness to see the importance of local developments is largely responsible for the inadequacy of the mechanistic view of the culture process.

Environmental factors seem to play a relatively minor part in determining forms. The presence of large trees whose wood might easily be worked was particularly favorable to the development of highly specialized canoes and of elaborate houses, but could hardly have determined the particular forms which such traits took. Plank houses and dug-out canoes could certainly have been constructed outside of the area where they occur, but the rarity of suitable material seems to restrict their spread. Lack of emphasis on elaborateness and workmanship in wood-working is a factor of social environment which undoubtedly inhibits the diffusion of forms of tools specially adapted to such purposes.

What seems to be a motor factor influencing form is seen in the thumb rest found in both the D adze and in the straight adze of Northwestern California. The prevalent habit of using all cutting tools with a stroke toward the body is undoubtedly historically determined.

The problem of the relation of the culture of the Northwest Coast to that of Asia has been given some consideration.[1] The traits discussed here have analogues in Asia but definite proof of historical relationship is difficult to establish.

The findings bear out certain theoretical considerations, such as the prevalence of diffusion and the comparative rarity of independent invention and parallel development, the passive part played by environmental factors, the relative unimportance of motor elements, and the major rôle played by the tribes at the culture center in development of the culture of an area.

I am indebted to Mr. Francis Kermode, of the Provincial Museum, Victoria, B. C., and to Mr. Frank S. Hall, of the Washington State Museum, University of Washington, Seattle, for their kindness in allowing me to examine storage material.

---

[1] See Boas, *Jesup Expedition; Development of Culture of Northwest America; History of the American Race*; Jochelson, *Archaeological Investigations*; Kroeber, *American Culture and the Northwest Coast.*

II

ADZE FORMS

On the Northwest Coast adzes were the most important tools used in wood-working. Knives were employed in fashioning articles whose shape or small size made it difficult to use adzes. Wedges and chisels, used in conjunction with hand hammers or long-handled mauls, were employed for rough work, such as felling trees, splitting out planks and rough-shaping canoes. Yet in the shaping, smoothing and carving of objects of wood the adze was the one indispensable tool. The other tools mentioned have been almost wholly displaced by axes, knives and wood-chisels of European manufacture. The old adze forms, however, persist to the present time, though steel has of course replaced the blades used in aboriginal times.

Adze blades were of bone, shell, or stone throughout the area. In the north a stone blade weighing several pounds, and grooved for lashing, was a common form, though small blades set against a shoulder of the handle were also used. Aside from this heavy, grooved blade there seems to be no material or form sufficiently distinctive or localized to serve as a basis for classification of blades. Elsewhere a small blade of a variety of materials, lashed with the butt resting against a shoulder of the handle seems to be the only form known, with the exception of some archaeological specimens and the heavy type mentioned.

There are, however, several patterns of adze handles which seem to be sufficiently distinctive to justify a classification. A comparatively simple form is a straight or somewhat curved piece of wood, bone, or stone six inches to a foot or more long. On the under side a section is flattened for the reception of the blade. A broad flap of leather is commonly lashed to the bottom to protect the back of the hand. Another form consists usually of the limb of a tree with a small portion of the trunk left attached. The limb forms a handle while the trunk portion is shaped so that the blade can be lashed to it. Blade and handle form an acute angle. The length of handle depends on whether the tool is designed for use with one or both hands. A third type, often called the D adze, is a rough parallellogram of wood, bone, or horn much resembling the handle of a carpenter's saw. The blade is lashed to the bottom, usually resting against a shoulder to prevent its slipping out of place. Regardless of pattern, adzes were everywhere used with a back-hand stroke.[2]

The straight adze (see Plates 1 (I), and 2) occurs along with other forms among the Shuswap, Lillooet, and Lower Fraser Salish of British Columbia.[3] It is found in the Puget Sound region and among the Ozette of Cape Flattery,

---

[2] Lewis and Clark, *Journals*, IV, 32; Mackenzie, *Voyages*, II, 98; Sproat, *Scenes and Studies*, 86; Swan, *Cape Flattery*, 34; *Northwest Coast*, 81; Boas, *Kwakiutl*, 344-369.
[3] Provincial Museum, catalog nos. 587, 1140; Teit, *Lillooet*, 204; Smith, *Lower Fraser*, 164; Newcombe, *Museum Guide*, 58.

but again is not the exclusive type.[4] What is evidently an adze of this form is mentioned by Lewis and Clark as occurring in the Lower Columbia region where it seems to have been the only pattern known. Curtis has the indefinite statement that "horn pointed adzes" were used by the Spokan and "Western Salish."[5] In Northwestern California adzes of this type are reported for Yurok, Hupa, and Karok. Here the handle is of stone, often curving upward near the tip and having a groove on the upper side evidently intended to serve as a place for the thumb to rest.[6] Data are lacking for eastern Washington, all of Oregon except the immediate valley of the Columbia, and for all but the extreme northwestern section of California.

From the valleys of the Columbia and Fraser are some few archaeological specimens which are quite different from those used in historic times. Those from the Columbia are pestle-shaped stones with handle and cutting edge in one piece. A specimen from the Lower Fraser is a celt socketed in a bone handle.[7] Adze blades hafted in this manner seem not to have been found elsewhere in the area though they are common among the Eskimo. These several specimens, though not closely related to any of the historic straight adze forms, belong, because of their simplicity and general pattern, in the category of straight adzes rather than with either of the other types.

Elbow adzes are rare in the southern part of the area (see Plates 1 (II), and 2). With one exception, they first appear among the Makah of Cape Flattery.[8] Among the Klallam, Skokomish, Swinomish, and Nisqually of the region about Puget Sound and among the Lower Chehalis, a modified type of elbow adze was used. The handle was short, designed for use with one hand. The blade was parallel to the handle, or nearly so.[9] The long handled form again occurs among the Bella Coola, Kwakiutl, Haida, Tsimshian, and Tlingit.[10] Data for the Nootka and for the Coast Salish of British Columbia are lacking.

Outside the Northwest Coast culture area the elbow adze occurs among the Shuswap, Chilcotin, and Thompson of the southern interior of British Columbia.[11] It seems to have been used throughout the area occupied by the Athabascan tribes of the north. It is reported for Carrier, Slavey, and Dog Rib in Canada, and for the Copper and Yukon River tribes in Alaska.[12] In the Eskimo-Aleut area of Alaska the elbow type occurs very generally and

---

[4] Washington State Museum, catalog nos. 5382, 7155.

[5] Lewis and Clark, *Journals*, IV, 32; Curtis, *American Indian*, VII, 72.

[6] Kroeber, *Handbook*, 83, 94, plate 19.

[7] Smith, *Yakima Valley*, 65; *Lower Columbia; Lower Fraser*, 164.

[8] Swan, *Cape Flattery*, 34. Since the above was written a single specimen has been noted for the Yurok (University of California Museum of Anthropology, catalog no. 1/11864).

[9] Niblack, *Coast Indians*, plate XXIII; Washington State Museum, catalog nos. 18, 7932; Haeberlin and Günther, *Indianerstämme*, 28. Lower Chehalis datum from personal observation.

[10] Mackenzie, *Voyages*, II, 311; Boas, *Kwakiutl*, 320, 344-369; Provincial Museum, catalog no. 2087; Niblack, *Coast Indians*, plate XXIII; Dall, *Alaska*, 414; Krause, *Tlingit*, 170-174.

[11] Teit, *Shuswap*, 474, 764; *Thompson*, 183.

[12] Morice, *Western Déné*, 46; Mackenzie, *Voyages*, I, 238, II, 98; Allen, *Expedition*, 133; Woldt, *Jacobsen's Reise*, 211.

seems to be the only form known. The chief difference from the Northwest Coast form is that the lashings commonly pass through holes in the handle, the head resting against the squared end of a straight handle. A small blade is generally used and is often socketed in a head of bone or ivory. In southern Alaska, some specimens are practically identical with forms occurring in the northern part of the Northwest Coast area.[13]

In Eastern Siberia the elbow adze is found among Koryak, Chukchee, and Yukaghir. It probably has a wide distribution over eastern Asia. This form also occurs in Polynesia.[14]

In this connection should be mentioned the adze-like skin-dresser which occurs practically throughout the whole of the Plains area. Not only is the form of this tool very similar to that of the elbow adze, but the chopping stroke with which it is used strongly suggests a relation to the latter tool.[15] These, the peculiar skin-dressers used by the Eskimo of Alaska, and the S-shaped tool of the Plateau seem to be the only implements for that purpose which diverge widely from the more generally distributed beaming tool. The Eskimo type differs markedly from the adze in that it is used with a stroke away from the body.[16]

The third adze type of the area, the D form (see Plates 1 (III), and 2) occurs among Kwakiutl, Tsimshian, Nootka, and Salish of southern Vancouver Island in Canada.[17] In the State of Washington it is reported for Makah, Ozette, Quilleute, Quinault, and Shoalwater Bay Chinook on the west coast, and for Snohomish and Lummi in the Puget Sound region.[18] A specimen in the Washington State Museum (cat. no. 4588, see Plate 1 (III), d), localized indefinitely as "Coast Salish," is rather remarkable in that the handle is carved of a single piece of elk-horn. Data are lacking for much of the Puget Sound region as well as for the Salish of southern Vancouver Island and the tribes of the mainland opposite. Definite information is also wanting for Bella Coola, Haida, and Tlingit. Outside the area this form occurs among Lillooet and Lower Thompson, but not among the other branches of the latter tribe.[19]

From the above data several inferences may be made. A survey of the areas of distribution for the various types (see Plate 2) seems to justify the earlier classification into straight, elbow, and D forms. While they do not occupy mutually exclusive areas, the types are rather definitely localized. Thus, the elbow adze is seldom found south of the Puget Sound region, the straight

---

[13] Cook, *Voyages*, VII, 373; Jochelson, *Archaeological Investigations*, 120; Nelson, *Bering Strait*, plate XXXIX; Woldt, *Jacobsen's Reise*, 211; Murdoch, *Point Barrow*, 165-172.

[14] Jochelson, *Koryak*, 610, 618-619; Bogoras, *Chukchee*, 210; Laufer, *Jade*, plate XIII; Giglioli, *Collezione*, plate II.

[15] Wissler, *Blackfoot*, 67; Mason, *Skin Dressing*, plates XCI-XCIII.

[16] Emmons, *Jade*, 47, 48.

[17] Boas, *Kwakiutl*, 320, 321, 344-369; *Tsimshian Mythology*, 49; Sproat, *Scenes and Studies*, 86; Provincial Museum, no. 1185.

[18] Swan, *Cape Flattery*, 34; Washington State Museum, no. 7154; Olson, *Quilleute Ethnography*, (ms); *Quinault Ethnography*, (ms); Swan, *Northwest Coast*, 39, 81; Gunther, information.

[19] Teit, *Lillooet*, 203, 204; *Thompson*, 183.

type does not occur north of the Straits of Juan de Fuca, and the Columbia River on the south and the southern tip of Alaska seem to mark the respective limits of the D adze.

The virtual restriction of the elbow type only to the northern part of the area and its wide range outside the Northwest Coast suggests that this form had its origin somewhere outside the area, possibly in Asia.

The D adze is found outside the area only among Lillooet and Thompson. Its presence among all but Tlingit and Haida of the more typical tribes (it seems legitimate to infer occurrence for Bella Coola) makes it likely that it was developed within the area. The fact that only that division of the Thompson nearest the coast possessed this type argues that they received it from this direction.

Judging by the relative number of specimens, the D adze was seldom used by the mainland Kwakiutl, and perhaps not at all by Haida and Tlingit. On the other hand, the Kwakiutl of Vancouver Island and the Nootka probably used it almost exclusively. The Quilleute and Quinault knew no other form. It seems logical to suppose that it is a much older trait among tribes possessing no other type, or where other types are but little used. This makes probable its origin among the Vancouver Island Kwakiutl, Nootka, Quilleute, or Quinault.

It appears that the D adze represents an attempt to develop a wood-working tool which lacks the defects of the elbow type. The heavy head and blunt edge common in the latter form in this area lends itself but poorly to accurate control of blows and the giving of a fine finish. Where both this and the D adze were known the latter was used for the finishing work and the putting on of "tool marks."[20] The finely tooled finish was a point of great importance. Very old specimens of woodwork frequently have no other decoration than the pattern formed by the rows of adze marks. With this in mind, it seems reasonable to eliminate the Quilleute and Quinault as possible originators, for they placed but little emphasis on elaborateness and fineness of finish in objects of wood.

Elaborateness of decoration of the tool itself among Kwakiutl and Nootka indicates a longer period of development among those groups. The Quinault and Quilleute rarely have carved figures on the handles of their adzes. The form which has spread from the Kwakiutl-Nootka center seems to be an older, simpler pattern. These points suggest that the place of origin of the D type is somewhere in the Kwakiutl-Nootka area. With the present data it seems idle to attempt a further localization of the originating point.

Several features present in nearly all specimens evidence the affinity of all D adzes. The same conventional form is used by every tribe. Most specimens show a depression for the thumb. Decorations, when present, are on the front of the handle, or, when the whole handle is carved in the representation of a figure, that part of the handle forms the head. Tribal pattern

---

[20] Boas, *Kwakiutl,* 359-364.

in decoration is seen in the motifs used by various groups. The Kwakiutl had a variety of types; the Nootka and Quilleute used animal figures; while human representations occur among Makah and Quinault.

In the depression for the thumb we evidently have a motor factor influencing form. This probably gives a firmer grip, with a lessening of the tendency of the tool to turn in the hand. It may also give greater control of the angle of the blade. It is rather significant that a thumb-groove appears in the more elaborate specimens of straight adze from northwestern California.

The very scanty material available for the area where the straight adze is found makes a discussion of its forms rather presumptuous, but several points come to mind. About the mouth of the Columbia River the adze was grasped at the junction of the blade and handle with the right hand, the left holding the end of the handle. The blow was delivered backhand. The Ozette specimen (Plate 1 (I), b) was obviously used in this same manner. While no information is at hand on the manner of using them, the curved handle specimens of northwestern California may have been held in this way, the upward curve of the handle serving as a grip for the left hand. If this is true it raises a strong presumption in favor of the historic relationship of forms outwardly quite distinct.

The relation of elbow, straight, and D-adze to each other is rather puzzling. The typical specimens of each form show little affinity to other patterns, but modified forms give some hints of possible relationships. The short handled elbow adzes of Klallam, Skokomish, and Swinomish in reality resemble D adzes quite as much as they do the elbowed form (Plate 1 (II), d). The blade is quite parallel to the handle. The tendency of the hand to slip off the end of the handle is overcome by a widening at the end. In the D adze this disability is taken care of by the nearer side of the parallelogram. The form of the D specimen from southern Vancouver Island (Plate 1 (III), c) has certain suggestions of these short-handled elbow adzes. The virtual absence of the fourth side of the parallelogram and the resulting angle of top and bottom hints at a similarity to the elbow pattern.

On the other hand, the D adze could quite conceivably be a development out of the straight adze, the bottom of the handle taking the place of the protective flap. How slight a change would be involved is shown by a glance at the elk-horn specimens of Puget Sound (Plate 1 (I), c and (III), d). From the data presented here it is difficult to see a relation between the elbow and straight adze. Additional information, however, might show the possibility of affinity. If I am correct in suggesting that the elbow adze is an intrusive type, it and the straight adze probably have no immediate historical connection.

III

CANOE FORMS

Dug-out canoes occur over a wide area on the Pacific slope (see Plate 3). In the north they appear near the mouth of the Copper River, the meeting place of Tlingit and Eskimo cultures. Southward they have a continuous distribution along the coast to somewhere about Cape Mendocino. Beginning again at the north, the eastern boundary follows the Cascade Range nearly to the southern tip of Alaska.[21] Somewhere about this point the boundary strikes eastward to the valley of the Fraser so as to take in the terriory of Carrier, Chilcotin, Shuswap, Lillooet, Thompson, and Kutenai. Okanogan, Kalispel, Pend d' Oreille, and Colville seem to have used only pine bark canoes, but dug-outs reappear among Spokane, Nez Percé, and Walla Walla.[22] From the territory of the last tribe the boundary runs westward to the valley of the Willamette and then southward so as to exclude the territory of the Northern Shoshoni.[23] From the upper Willamette Valley the boundary again swings to the east to include Klamath and Modoc territory. In northern California the boundary runs southward near the eastern boundary of the state to the southern limit of Northern Maidu territory. It then runs westward so as to exclude Yana and Wintun country and meets the coastline near Cape Mendocino.

While this is the approximate area of continuous distribution, boats of wood occur in other parts of California. Plank and possibly true dug-out canoes were known on the coast and islands of the southern part of the state. True dug-outs have been reported for the San Joaquin Valley, though the balsa raft was probably used almost exclusively. So little definite information on the form of these boats exists, however, that it is difficult to make definite statements on their relation to the dug-outs of the Northwest Coast. The rather specific feature of burial in canoes in the Santa Barbara region suggests a connection with the Northwest Coast, where such a practice is very common. The Yokuts method of shaping first the outside and then the inside of the canoe by burning with pitch-wood and controlling the fire by means of wet clay is identical with the method followed in the north.[24]

A variety of forms and sizes of canoes have been described for the Northwest Coast and adjacent territory where the dug-out is the prevalent type. Several attempts have been made to classify these various types and, to a certain extent, to work out their distribution and to reconsruct the prob-

---

[21] The Athabascan Takheesh or Stick, occupying a district across the divide from Skagway, seem, however, to have possessed crude dug-outs instead of the bark canoes common in the region (Schwatka, *Report*, 82).
[22] Curtis, *American Indian*, VII, 71-72; Spinden, *Nez Percé*, 223; Lewis and Clark, *Journals*, III, 150-151, IV, 30-33.
[23] Lowie, *Northern Shoshone*, 190.
[24] Yarrow, *Researches*, 38, 44, (see also pp. 21, 26, 123, 124, 233 of same volume); Yaple, *Survivals;* Kroeber, *Handbook*, 558-559, 812-813.

able processes of development.[25]   None of these studies, however, deals with the data for the whole area, and the classifications adopted are based more on the feature of size than on that of fundamental type.   There seems to be no complete set of measurements available for all the canoes used by any one group.   My own observations lead me to believe that such data would show a practically continuous series of sizes from the smallest "one-man" canoes to the largest specimens employed.   If this is true, and the canoes have a similar form, it seems hardly justifiable to separate them into a number of types.

I believe that almost all the canoes of the area fall into three types sufficiently distinct to enable one to tell at a glance what class any particular specimen falls under.   The "shovel-nose" pattern is characterized by rounded prow and stern, sloping upward to a squared end, with a straight gunwale line from prow to stern, and the absence of separate bow and stern pieces. The Nootka or "Chinook" type is pointed at both ends, the prow projects upward and forward and, except on small canoes, is a separate piece.   The stern is vertical and raised above the level of the gunwales, the upper portion in all larger canoes being a separate piece.   The cross-section is angular, the bottom being almost flat.   The Northern canoe (also called the Queen Charlotte Island and the Tsimshian canoe) is characterized by raised and projecting bow and stern formed of separate pieces, by the vertical cut-water, and by the rounded cross-section.

A few specimens have been described which are rather distinct from these types.   The Lkuñgɛn possessed a canoe whose bow resembled that of the shovel-nose, while the stern was square, formed by inserting a plank in a groove of the body of the boat.   On the Columbia, Lewis and Clark observed canoes with sharp bows while the sterns were "merely rounding and gradually ascending."   On Puget Sound a rough knockabout pattern was known with bow and stern resembling the stern of the Nootka type.[26]   Minor differences from the type, such as sloping instead of vertical stern, modified prow form, and the amount of decoration, also occur but are hardly of such an order as to constitute radical divergences.

The three types have quite distinct ranges of occurrence.   While these areas are not mutually exclusive, each type seems to have a continuous distribution in a particular section (see Plate 3).

The shovel-nose type occurs only in the area south of the Straits of Juan de Fuca.   In western Washington it was known among Snohomish, Nisqualli, Twana, Cowlitz, and Lower Chehalis.   Vancouver mentions it for the people living at Port Orchard.   It was probably present throughout the Puget Sound region.[27]   On the lower Columbia it was known among Cathlamet, Wakiacum,

[25] Waterman and Coffin. *Types of Canoes;* Boas, *Second Report,* 565-566; *Kwakiutl,* 344 369, 444-445; Niblack, *Coast Indians,* 294-296; Lewis and Clark, *Journals,* IV, 31-35.

[26] Boas, *Second Report,* 565-566; Lewis and Clark, *Journals,* IV, 32; Waterman and Coffin, *Types of Canoes,* 22, plate 1.

[27] Haeberlin and Gunther, *Indianerstämme,* 29; Eells, *Twana,* 641; Swan, *Northwest Coast,* 80; Olson, *Quinault Ethnography* (ms); Vancouver, *Voyages,* II, 127; Waterman and Coffin, *Types of Canoes,* 11-12.

Chinook and Tillamook. Above the Dalles of the Columbia only the shovel-nose form was used. It was the only type among Wishram, Yakima, Nez Percé, and Walla Walla. The Spokan and Kutenai dug-outs were probably of this form.[28] Vancouver mentions canoes of this type at Cape Orford (Cape Blanco) on the Oregon Coast and at Trinidad Bay in California. Klamath and Modoc dug-outs are almost identical with the shovel-nose form to the north. Waterman has advanced strong arguments to show the affinity of the Yurok-Karok-Hupa boat and the shovel-nose. Descriptions of the forms used by the Valley Maidu, Atsugewi, Achomawi, Tolowa, Wiyot, and Shasta of northern California are very scanty, but it seems probable that they resembled the shovel-nose, since there is undoubted historical connection with the forms to the north and west.[29] Data are wanting for western Oregon except for the immediate region of the Columbia, but it seems probable that the shovel-nose form was known everywhere west of the Cascade range.

The Nootka canoe was known along the coast from a point somewhere between Cape Blanco and the country of the Tillamook to the northern end of Vancouver Island. North of Grays Harbor in Washington it was the only type used.[30] On the Columbia canoes of this type occur as far eastward as the Dalles. Canoes of Nootka pattern seem to occur throughout the Puget Sound region. On the Strait of Juan de Fuca and the eastern coast of Vancouver Island and the mainland opposite north to Cape Mudge this was the only form employed. North of this point to the end of Vancouver Island both Nootka and Northern types were used. Up the Fraser Valley the Nootka pattern seems prevalent as far as dug-outs were known. The tribes using the Nootka type are: Tillamook and the Chinookan groups on the Columbia below the Dalles; the people of Shoalwater Bay, the Quinault, Quilleute, and Makah of the west coast of Washington; the tribes of Puget Sound and the Strait of Juan de Fuca; the Salish of Vancouver Island and the mainland opposite; the southern divisions of the Kwakiutl; the Nootkan tribes; the Lillooet, Thompson and Shuswap, and probably the Carrier and Chilcotin of the Fraser Valley.[31]

---

[28] Lewis and Clark, *Journals*, IV, 31-32, III, 150-151; Spier, *Wishram Ethnography* (ms); Spinden, *Nez Percé*, 223; Curtis, *American Indian*, VII, 71-72, VIII, 46, (plate); Chamberlain, *Kutenai*, 566; Gibbs, *Tribes of Western Washington*, 215; Winthrop, *Canoe and Saddle*, 217.

[29] Vancouver, *Voyages*, II, 414; Barrett, *Klamath*, 247-249; Spier, *Klamath Ethnography* (ms); Kroeber, *Handbook*, 416-417, 82-83, 812-814, 291.

[30] Waterman's statement (*Types of Canoes*, 32) that shovel-nose canoes occur on the coast of Washington is based on the photographs of Curtis. While it is true that the Quinault (the tribe evidently referred to) possess canoes of this type, several of my informants stated that these have only come in since the residence of members of other tribes on the reservation and that only pointed forms were known previously.

[31] Lewis and Clark, *Journals*, IV, 31-32, 199; Franchère, *Narrative*, 327-328; Ross, *Oregon Settlers*, 111; Curtis, *American Indian*, IX, plates facing pp. 6, 8, 10, 16, 50, 52, 60, 98, 100, 102, 126; Olson, *Quinault Ethnography* (ms); Swan, *Northwest Coast*, 79; *Cape Flattery*, 31-38; Waterman, *Whaling Equipment; Types of Canoes*; Haeberlin and Gunther, *Indianerstämme*, 28-29; Vancouver, *Voyages*, II, 127, 234; Meany, *Vancouver's Discovery*, 156; Lewis, *Columbia Valley*, 163-165; Eells, *Twana*, 641; Gunther, *Klallam Ethnography*; Gibbs, *Report*, 430; Kane (prints of paintings in the author's possession); Sproat, *Scenes and Studies*, 82-88; Boas, *Kwakiutl*, 444, 445; *Second Report*, 565-566; Teit, *Lillooet*, 228-230; *Thompson*, 255-256; *Shuswap*, 531-532; Mackenzie, *Voyages*, II, 169-170; Farrand, *Chilcotin*, 647; Morice, *Western Déné*, 114-115.

North of the area occupied by these tribes the Northern canoe occurs. The Northern Kwakiutl of Vancouver Island used both this and the Nootka type, but the remaining groups of that people seem to have used only the former. Definite material on Bella Coola canoes is wanting, but it seems likely that they were acquainted only with the Northern type. Tsimshian, Tlingit, and Haida used only boats of this pattern. (Krause, however, has a sketch of a Tlingit "shovel-nose," though he states that only one type was known. Niblack holds that the Haida sometimes possessed canoes of the Nootka form.) The form used by the Athabascans across the divide from the present site of Skagway is not known.[32]

A type somewhat akin to both Nootka and Northern forms may have been used to some extent by Haida, Tsimshian, Kwakiutl, and the Coast Salish of southern British Columbia and the Strait of Juan de Fuca. This canoe had elevated and flaring, but not projecting, bow and stern. A few from the southern tribes, however, seem to have had a projecting prow nearly identical with that feature in Nootka canoes. This raised section of the gunwale was carried almost level for a considerable distance toward the center of the boat before dropping sharply to the lower level. This is the traditional form of war canoe for Haida, Tsimshian and Kwakiutl. Its use by Lkuñgɛn and other Salish of southern Vancouver Island and by Klallam seems probable, and makes more plausible the possibility of its having actually been used by the tribes of the north.[33]

Several evidences of developmental processes are suggested by the data at hand. The shovel-nose canoe seems to be found only in the area of less complex culture. Except for some Yurok, Hupa, and Karok specimens, it is everywhere undecorated. Its simplicity of design and lack of sea-worthiness suggest that it probably represents an old undifferentiated type antedating the more specialized forms of the north. The tribes who have both this and the Nootka type seem to depend almost wholly on the Nootka, and especially on the Nitinat and Clayoquat divisions of that people, for the larger and better specimens of canoes of the Nootka type. This raises a strong presumption in favor of the Nootka as the originators of the Nootka canoe.[34]

The Yurok, Hupa, and Karok exception to the simple design of shovel-nose canoes presents an interesting problem. The exceptional features are the peaks in the center of each end, and a stern seat, two foot braces, and a small knob toward the prow carved in the same piece as the body of the canoe. In addition, a rich man going on a journey might crown the prow with a carved yoke resembling an inverted "V." These distinctive features may be developments on the spot, but without definite knowledge of the canoe forms of the

[32] Boas, *Kwakiutl*, 344-369, 444-445; Niblack, *Coast Indians*, 294-296, plate XXXIII; Waterman and Coffin, *Types of Canoes*; Waterman, *Whaling Equipment*; Krause, *Tlingit*, 170-174; Schwatka, *Report*, 82.
[33] Collinson, *Wake of War Canoe*, 161; Catlin, *North American Indians*, 113, plate 210½; Boas, *Kwakiutl*, 444-445; *Second Report*, 555-556; Songish and Klallam data based on Kane's paintings (prints in the author's possession).
[34] See Waterman, *Whaling Equipment*, 9; Swan, *Cape Flattery*, 31-38; *Northwest Coast*, 79; Lewis, *Columbia Valley*, 163-165.

Oregon coast it is rather presumptuous to state it as a certainty. The feature of the yoke, and especially since it is linked with use only by persons of wealth, seems to be the direct result of northern influence. The yoke may represent the added prow piece of the northern canoes. Certain features of the typical culture of the Northwest Coast, such as secret societies, emphasis on wealth, a sense of caste, and specialization in wood working seem to have spread much farther down the open coast than they did along the eastern margin of the area. It has been shown before that canoes of Nootka manufacture were traded down to the Columbia, probably to the Tillamook, and perhaps beyond. The bow and stern pieces of a Nootka canoe were often carved into ornamental figures. Carvings of various sorts also adorned canoes of local manufacture around the mouth of the Columbia. It is but natural that the Yurok, situated on the coast, should feel this influence more than their inland neighbors. It may be something more than merely interesting to note that the Makah, Quilleute, Queets, and Quinault call the highest parts of the prow piece "ears," and that the Yurok call the yoke "ears"—though the latter could hardly be said to resemble those organs.[35]

Certain features common to both Nootka and Northern canoes suggest that they represent developments from a common type. The bow pieces have a quite similar form. In canoes of both types this part is grooved down the center in so peculiar a fashion that it seems impossible that it could have originated independently. While the groove may incidentally serve as a resting place for the point of the harpoon, it seems improbable that its origin or special form is to be explained by that use.

The practice of landing large canoes stern foremost which is the prevalent method everywhere north of the Columbia may give a clue to the relationship of Nootka and Northern canoes. This is evidently done to avoid being boarded by a following sea while the navigators wait for an exceptionally high wave to carry them far up the beach. The high, projecting stern of the Northern type makes the practice quite unnecessary, since it breaks the waves quite as well as the bow. The possible explanation is that this practice points back to a time when the Northern canoe lacked this feature of stern construction, and when a canoe somewhat akin to the Nootka type prevailed over the area where the Northern pattern now occurs. Curiously enough, this mode of landing seems to have been practiced far up the Fraser. Mackenzie noted it at the northern limit of the dug-out.[36] Its practice in that region seems certain evidence that the dug-out has spread there from the coast, since the usage could hardly arise except on the sea where a dangerous surf would lead to such an expedient.

It seems possible to eliminate certain tribes as significant contributors to the development of the highly specialized types. The tribes to the south of the Nootka depended almost wholly on that people for their larger and better

[35] Waterman, *Whaling Equipment*, 16; Kroeber, *Handbook*, 83; Olson, *Quinault Ethnography* (ms).

[36] Mackenzie, *Voyages*, II, 169-170.

canoes, and it is therefore unlikely that they played a major rôle in development. The Tsimshian and Tlingit in the north were dependent on Haida for most of their canoes, and for that reason probably did little to foster the art. The Kwakiutl seem to have made most of their own canoes. Tsimshian, Bella Coola, and other Coast Salish are undoubtedly recent intruders on the coast and in all probability did little in the way of originating new features.[37] The absence of suitable timber except in the southern part of Tlingit territory would hamper their activities along this line. This leaves Nootka, Haida, and Kwakiutl as the tribes probably contributing most to the development of the specialized forms. The divergence into two rather distinct types from what may have been an identical older pattern must have required a relatively long period of time. All three of these tribes are so situated that without ocean-going canoes many features of their cultures would be impossible.

Perhaps historically related to the canoes of the Northwest Coast are the dug-out boats of northeast Asia. These occur among Yukaghir, Kamchadal, and Maritime Koryak in the north. In the Amur region they are found among Daurians, Manyargs, Goldi, Orochi, the Oroke of Sakhalin, and the Ainu.[38] The evident shovel-nose form, the Yukaghir and Koryak practice of lashing two canoes together and placing a platform of planks across the two, and the use of the crutch paddle by Ainu remind us of comparable features on the Northwest Coast. But until much more detailed information is to be had on the Asiatic forms it will be difficult to establish a relationship. The remarkable similarity of certain of the bark canoes of the Amur region and the "sturgeon-nose" type of the southern interior of British Columbia has been pointed out by Mason. Jochelson evidently regards the dug-outs of the two areas as historically related. If the Tlingit possess a shovel-nose form and a connection be proved for the dug-outs of northeast Asia and northwest America it would go far toward establishing Waterman's thesis that the shovel-nose was the forerunner of all the forms of the Northwest Coast, and was once the universal type in the area.[39]

There has been some discussion of the relation of the Eskimo umiak (the open skin boat) to the boats of Asia and the Northwest Coast. Steensby, in a summary of the data, assumes that the umiak has been borrowed from the Pacific Asiatics, though he admits the possibility of the reverse.[40] The relation of the skin-boat, the dug-out, and the various types of bark canoe to each other may eventually be solved, but our present knowledge is far too scanty to permit an adequate analysis of such a relation.

[37] Krause, *Tlingit*, 170-174; Abercombie, *Expedition*, 396; Niblack, *Coast Indians*, 297; Boas, *Tsimshian Mythology*, 872; *Conclusions*, 387-390; Swanton, *Clan System*.
[38] Jochelson, *Koryak*, 540-541; Bogoras, *Chukchee*, 126; Ravenstein, *Russians on the Amur*, 363, 372, 373, 378, 396; Hitchcock, *Ainus*, 472, plates CX, CXI.
[39] Mason, *Pointed Canoes*; Jochelson, *Archaeological Investigations*, 2; Waterman and Coffin, *Types of Canoes*, 29-39.
[40] Steensby, *Eskimo Culture*, 153-155.

IV

DISTRIBUTION OF HOUSE FORMS

Several studies have been made of the house forms of northwestern America and northeastern Asia.[41] The problem is still far from solution, largely because of lack of adequate data on the types of dwellings occurring among marginal tribes. The existing materials are, however, much too extensive to permit an adequate summary in this paper. For this reason, it seems best to limit the discussion to citing some additional data bearing on the areas of distribution of various types and to pointing out certain errors in existing studies. I hope to be able to enlarge this data in a future paper summarizing the materials on the rectangular plank houses found in adjacent parts of, the two continents and discussing their relation to the types occurring in adjoining areas.

In the southern part of the area of their occurrence, rectangular plank houses fall almost wholly within the tentative boundary of the Northwest Coast culture area. Their range is not quite so extensive as that of dug-out canoes. In northern California dwellings of this type seem restricted to the Yurok, Karok, Hupa and their immediate neighbors. On the Columbia plank houses are rare above the Dalles, though they occur among Wishram and, sporadically, nearly to the eastern boundary of the State of Washington.[42] On the lower Fraser River the plank house occurs only below Thompson territory. Houses of Thompson, Lillooet, Shuswap, and Chilcotin are conical underground dwellings.[43] The Carrier of the upper Fraser had rectangular plank and log houses so closely resembling those of the coast that the historical connection is indubitable.[44] Mackenzie observed this type about as far south as the present site of Alexandria, and throughout the region of the Blackwater River westward to the coast. Material is lacking on the houses of the Babine.

The rectangular plank house is the type throughout the coastal region of British Columbia and Alaska to the mouth of the Copper River. An exception must be made for the Athabascan Tsetsaut of the head of Portland Canal who seem to have only the temporary brush and bark lodge.[45]

It seems to be a common misconception that the rectangular plank house disappears in the north with the Tlingit peoples. But houses certainly akin to that form occur very widely in Alaska. Seton-Karr has described rectangular

---

[41] Jochelson, *Subterranean Dwellings;* Sarfert, *Haus und Dorf;* Morgan, *Houses and House-Life;* Waterman and collaborators, *Native Houses.*

[42] Spier, *Wishram Ethnography* (ms) ; Lewis and Clark, *Journals,* III, 108, 109, 115, 117.

[43] Boas, *Interior Salish,* 220; Farrand, *Chilcotin,* 646-647.

[44] Mackenzie, *Voyages,* II, 138-139, 140, 142, 149, 155; Morice, *Western Déné,* 184-191. Waterman (*op. cit.,* 20, 47) quotes Wilkes (*Narrative,* IV, 451) as authority for Carrier underground houses. Yet no member of the Wilkes expedition visited the region of the upper Fraser. Their information was hearsay material secured from officials of the Hudson's Bay Company (*Narrative,* IV, 450). The Carrier described the people of the south to Mackenzie as "a very malignant race, who lived in large subterranean recesses" (*Voyages,* II, 149).

[45] Boas, *Fifth Report,* 561-562. Waterman (*op. cit.,* 19-20) states that this is not an underground dwelling, yet he classifies it as such in his tabulations (*op. cit.,* 46-47).

houses on Kayak Island built of rough planks and slabs. Gabled roofs are usual, though a sketch shows a house with the central section of the roof nearly flat. The planks are notched in at the corners in log cabin style. Short planks are placed vertically around the smoke-hole, evidently to serve as a windbreak, a feature which reminds one of a similar Koryak practice. Sleeping places are built as small rectangular additions on the outside of the house, reached from the interior by a circular aperture.[46]

The Athabascans of Cooks Inlet have houses described by Petroff as "permanent dwellings of logs. These logs are so fashioned that the under side, hollowed out, fits down tight, almost air-tight, upon the rounded surface of the timber next below. Some of their houses are from fifteen to twenty feet square, and have regular rafters, giving a pitch to the roof sufficient to shed rain and melting snow. The covering of the roof is the bark of spruce trees. The fireplace is in the center, with a smoke hole directly above it. The entrance to the house consists of a low, square aperture, scarcely large enough to admit an adult person. The floor consists of the natural earth trodden hard, and along the sides of the enclosure are rude platforms, erected a foot or two from the ground, covered with grass mats and skins, and serving as sleeping and lounging places in the evening. In the houses of the well-to-do hunters we find wings or box-like additions to the main building, tightly framed and put together, opening into the main room. These additions are furnished with the luxury of a rough plank floor, and in many instances with a small window covered with fish-gut. They are used in winter as sleeping apartments, and as reception rooms during visits of ceremony, and also as bathrooms, being heated during the winter with hot stones carried in from the fire outside, thus enabling the natives to dispense with clothing during the night, which they consider a great luxury."[47]

According to Steensby this type is used by the Indians of the Kenai Peninsula, and is the summer dwelling among the Eskimo in south Alaska wherever suitable timber is available. Plank houses were also noted in Prince William Sound by Portlock.[48]

On the Copper River, houses much like those on the coast were noted by Allen. He states that the winter house "is about eighteen feet square, is built of spruce poles and slabs in a loose style, and is covered with spruce bark. In some cases moss is used to make it close. The walls under the eaves are nearly four feet high; about three feet from the ground around the inside is built a shelf four or five feet wide, which serves the double purpose of a seat during the day and a bed at night, the space under this being boxed in with vertical slabs and used as a storeroom and sleeping apartment for women, children, and pups. The roof is provided with a large hole in the middle to permit the escape of smoke from the open fire on the floor. The entrance to the house is through a small 'storm shed' about two by three feet, pro-

[46] Seton-Karr, *Shores and Alps of Alaska*, 153-157; Abercombie, *Report*, 397.
[47] Petroff, *Alaska*, 261.
[48] Steensby, *Eskimo Culture*, 188; Portlock, *Voyage*, 153.

tected at the outer end by an undressed sheep or goat skin. Opposite this at the other end, near the floor, is a round hole about fifteen inches in diameter, which is the entrance to the sleeping room and bath-house. . . . On one of the upright pieces of the barrabarra, opposite the entrance (the usual place for interior decoration of a Midnoosky house) were hieroglyphics, representing men and their actions, which our friends interpreted and enjoyed very much."[49]

From the Tanana River (the large southern tributary of the Yukon) Allen describes the houses as "large, and constructed without the use of bark. The absence of the attached sweatroom and the 'box' arrangement of the interior caused a marked difference in their appearance when compared with the typical Copper River house." Houses of this pattern were also seen near the present site of Fairbanks and seem to be the type for the whole valley of the Tanana.[50]

Along the Yukon below the mouth of the Tanana and in the valley of the Koyukuk (the westernmost large tributary of the Yukon flowing in from the north) rectangular plank houses are also common. But as Eskimo territory is approached an earth-covered structure with a pit is used as a winter dwelling, and near the margin of the Athabascan area and among the Eskimo the above-ground plank house is used only as a summer dwelling. Dall describes these as "built of split spruce logs driven into the ground and roofed with spruce bark. The door is in the end facing the river and is an oval opening some three feet high. The houses are about twelve feet square and entirely above ground, as in summer the underground houses are full of water." At one of the inmost Eskimo settlements on the Yukon were "eight large summer houses in each of which a hundred people might have been comfortably accommodated. These houses were built of immense planks, hewn out of single logs with stone adzes. Many of these planks were four inches thick by twelve feet long. . . . The rafters were carved into rude imitations of animals, and still retained traces of the red earth with which they had been painted." In this last instance the influence of the culture of the Northwest Coast is obvious, and, as Nelson has shown, is present in a great many features of the culture of the Eskimo of this whole region.[51]

Data are lacking for the house forms of the upper Kuskokwim basin. The tribes of the Yukon valley east of the mouth of the Tanana seem to have used only temporary skin or brush lodges.[52]

Waterman has an interesting discussion of the possible relations of the conical pit-dwelling of the Plateau-Basin area to the rectangular plank house.[53] Briefly stated, his thesis is that all the pit structures of western North America are historically related; that all the plank houses of the coast possess a pit;

[49] Allen, *Expedition*, 130-131, 47, 48, 52.
[50] Allen, *Expedition*, 75-76, 85, 137.
[51] Dall, *Yukon Territory*, 26-27, 225, see also 223, 228, 211, 236; Nelson, *Bering Strait*, 285-309, 347-421; see also, Petroff, *Alaska*, 259; Schwatka, *Report*, 102.
[52] Dall, *Yukon Territory*, 54; Schmitter, *Upper Yukon*, 3.
[53] *Native Houses*, 30-34, 28.

that this feature and the fact that the area of plank houses is quite enclosed by the area where the conical pit-dwelling is the type, makes it plausible that the plank house has its origin in the conical pit-dwelling, becoming rectangular rather than circular by reason of the employment of planks.

I propose to deal here only with the last two aspects of the problem. While it is true that a pit is a common feature of the houses of the coast, it is equally true that houses without pits were common in many parts of the area. They have been noted among Heiltsuk (Kwakiutl), Bella Coola, Haida, Tsimshian, Makah, Quinault, on the Columbia River, and at Trinidad Bay in California.[54] Haida, Heiltsuk, and Bella Coola often built plank houses elevated a considerable distance above the ground. The rectangular plank and log structures of the northern interior of British Columbia seem to have been wholly above ground, and, as we have seen, this is true of the comparable types found over a large part of the southern half of Alaska. Complete data would probably reveal many more non-pit houses among the tribes of the Northwest Coast. A sufficient number of instances have been cited, however, to indicate that the plank house of the coast is not essentially a pit-dwelling. It is also open to question whether what are often described as pits are such in reality. The accumulation of refuse about the outside of the house raises the level of the surrounding surface and in time creates a considerable depression of the space occupied by the house.[55] Another element affecting house construction on the coast is the nature of the soil. As everyone familiar with the region is aware, the decayed vegetation often reaches a depth of several feet. This would be cleard away in order to secure a floor of solid earth. The shallow pits, a foot or two in depth, which are common enough in the area, may in some instances be merely the result of such clearing away of rubbish.

In Waterman's study, the point dealing with the relation of the areas of distribution of the conical earth-lodge and the rectangular plank house needs but little discussion. It has already been shown that the earth-lodge extends no farther north than the southern boundary of Carrier territory. The rectangular plank house instead of occurring only in southeastern Alaska is found practically everywhere throughout the southern half of Alaska except in the Aleutian peninsula and the Aleutian Islands. The area of the conical pit-dwelling therefore adjoins that of the rectangular plank house only on the southern half of the latter. The section of the Northwest Coast where the plank house is mostly highly developed could hardly be influenced to any great extent by tribes so far removed as those having the conical earth-lodge.

Just what bearing, if any, the extension of the area, as worked out in this paper, has on the problem of the relation of that structure to similar forms in Asia will be difficult to determine until a more adequate study is made. The proof of occurrence of houses of this type on both shores of Bering Sea,

[54] Boas, *First Report*, 818; Mackenzie, *Voyages*, II, 256-257; Poole, *Narrative*, 113-114; Emmons, *Kitselas*, 470; Swan, *Cape Flattery*, 4-7; Olson, *Quinault Ethnography*, (ms); Lewis and Clark, *Journals*, III, 208, IV, 215, 259, 269; Vancouver, *Voyages*, III, 405-406.
[55] Jochelson, *Archaeological Investigations*, 108.

eliminating much of the area of interrupted ditribution between northeast Asia and Tlingit territory, makes the supposition of historical identity much more plausible (see Plate 4).

In northeast Asia gable-roofed, rectangular plank or pole houses built either on the ground or elevated on posts, are widely distributed. They have been noted among Mangun, Goldi, Daurians, and Orochi in the Amur region. But certain features of these structures, such as the fireplace under the divan and the smoke pipe to carry the heat and smoke around the interior and finally outside, may be due to Chinese or Manchu influence. Orochi houses not only lack these features but the winter dwelling is the earth-coverd lodge. The Gilyak and the Ainu of Sakhalin also have houses of the rectangular plank type.[56]

In the region farther to the north are found structures less like the plank house of the Northwest Coast but possibly related to it. Jochelson states that some of the Koryak of northern Kamchatka "live in houses of the Yakut type, which have been introduced into Kamchatka by the Russians. This structure consists of a flat roof with four slanting walls, and reminds one of a truncated pyramid. The walls are coated with clay to keep in the heat. Instead of the Yakut fireplace in the right-hand corner of the house, with a chimney for the escape of smoke, we find a hearth in the middle of the house and a smoke-hole in the roof."[57]

Bogoras states that "a few Chukchee families of the middle Anadyr live in wooden huts somewhat similar to the Yakut 'yurta.' These were copied from the yurtas of the Anadyr Russians. . . . . In ancient times wooden huts of this type may have been in more common use in this territory. Remains of huts on the Bear Islands are more or less of this type. In the deserted villages of the Yukaghir situated in the middle Omolon . . . . I have seen huts of the same type." These lack the wooden chimney of the Yakut dwelling, an open fire and square smoke-hole taking its place.[58]

Structures closely resembling these are used as storehouses and as summer dwellings by the Kamchadal. They are described as four-sided pyramids raised six or more feet from the ground on posts and thatched with bramble and grass.[59]

A summary of the data with some added implications is given by Steensby: "The Northwest Indian plank-house, which at times occurs in the form of a log-house, is still found with the Chukchees as a winter dwelling, and it is also said to occur with the Kenai Indians. With the Eskimo in south Alaska we immediately, however, find an earth-covered house as a winter dwelling, while the plank-house occurs as a summer dwelling in the summer settlements, which are inhabited during the fishing season. Where the forest ceases the plank-house disappears, and the skin tent predominates as a summer dwelling.

[56] Ravenstein, *Russians on the Amur*, 347-348, 375-379, 390, 394-395, 399; Shirokogoroff, *Social Organization of the Manchus*, 93-99; Lopatin, *Orochee.*

[57] Jochelson, *Koryak*, 468.

[58] Bogoras, *Chukchee*, 180.

[59] Grieve, *Kamchatka*, 182.

While the Eskimo have got this plank house from the North-West Indians they have got the pile dwelling from North-East Asia. It is a well known fact that the Palaeasiatic people in North-East Asia, such as the Gilyaks and Kamchadales, use the pile dwelling as their summer residence. The origin of this pile-work form, however, points still further south across Japan and right to South-East Asia. In Alaska, the pile dwelling as a summer residence has already been mentioned from the islands in Bering Strait, and in this connection is especially known from Kings Island. But it also occurs on the coast of Alaska itself; not, however, as a dwelling, but as a storehouse. Thus Petroff (p. 128; cf. Nelson p. 244) says about the Kuskoquim district 'the storehouses of all the Eskimo tribes are set on posts at a height of eight to ten feet above the ground to protect them against foxes, wolves and dogs.' According to Murdoch the pile-work structure is found at Point Barrow in the form of stands for preserving and drying meat and such like, and similar stands are found again right toward the east, for instance in Baffin Land, and also in Greenland, where they are commonly employed."[60] As we have seen, the true pile dwelling is also found on the Northwest Coast among Kwakiutl, Haida, and Bella Coola.

There are, however, serious objections to identifying the pile dwelling with the elevated storehouse. While it is true that the Kamchadal use the storehouse as a summer dwelling, such usage is exceptional. The Athabascans of eastern Alaska had the elevated cache but lacked permanent dwellings. About Point Barrow, where the only permanent house is of the underground type, the elevated store-house also occurs. It is also known among Copper River Athabascans, whose only permanent dwelling is the super-terranean rectangular house. Among the Athabascans of the lower Yukon and the Eskimo of western Alaska, who know both the earth-hut and plank house, the elevated cache is used. This very wide range of occurrence (by no means fully indicated by the instances cited), and its appearance as a feature associated with a variety of types of dwelling, suggests that it has spread as a distinct trait not necessarily connected with the spread of a type of dwelling.

The occurrence of the pile-dwelling on the Northwest Coast rather argues against Steensby's contention that, while the Eskimo plank house is derived from the Northwest Coast, the Eskimo pile-dwelling is from northeast Asia. If on this basis we derive the pile-dwellings of the Northwest Coast from those of northeast Asia, we must also include all the plank houses of the west coast as derivatives of that structure, for few would deny the historical relationship of all the rectangular plank houses of western North America. If we link pile-dwelling and plank house we must ignore not only those features indicating a possible kinship with various pit structures, but the possibility of an independent origin of the plank house on the Northwest Coast.

Various views are held on the possibility of historic relationship of houses of northwest America and northeast Asia. Steensby thinks it probable that the plank house of America is of Asiatic origin. Jochelson argues for a connec-

---

[60] Steensby, *Eskimo Culture*, 188.

tion in the case of underground dwellings of the two continents. Waterman, classifying the rectangular plank house as essentially a pit structure, implies that ultimately it comes from the Asiatic underground dwelling through a re-birth in the conical pit structure of the Plateau.[61]

The problem would be somewhat simplified if the intrusion of the Eskimo in the region of Bering Strait, held by some authors, could be adequately demon-strated. Evidences of such a migration are not lacking. Such features as shamanism, folk-lore, bear ceremonialism, and dug-out boats among the Palae-asiatics and non-Eskimoid groups of northwestern America bear a closer re-semblance to each other than they do to comparable Eskimo traits.[62] Studies of such features as the use of mortuary columns, and the practices connected with the capture of whales might show further similarities and in some measure add evidence to the possibility of transmission of the rectangular super-ter-ranean house without calling in the earth-hut and the pile-dwelling as inter-mediaries.

SUMMARY

While data for the study of the three traits discussed in this paper are lacking for many tribes and detailed observations wanting for many others, it seems legitimate to draw certain inferences from the materials presented. More complete information may necessitate modifications in certain respects, but the probability is that it will serve rather to strengthen at least those find-ings which are concerned with the processes at work within the Northwest Coast culture area.

Certain historical considerations are suggested by the distribution of the traits examined. All three are universal throughout the Northwest Coast area. Outside that area the dugout canoe is found over much of northern Cali-fornia, on the southern coast, and possibly in the San Juaquin Valley. It occurs on the Columbia in eastern Washington, and on all but the upper reaches of the Fraser in British Columbia. In the north it is found only along the coast, except for the single instance of the Athabascans of extreme north-western British Columbia. The dugout is unknown outside of Tlingit terri-tory in Alaska. In northeast Asia it has a wide but sporadic distribution. Both the birch bark and the dugout canoe of Asia may be elements which have spread from America: their wide distribution points to a great anti-quity in the New World.

Adzes in themselves constitute a distinctive trait as opposed to the axe, which is used over the greater part of the Americas. The adze of the North-west Coast and Mackenzie areas, and the western part of Eskimo territory may be an Asiatic element. Its occurrence in Polynesia in a form almost

---

[61] Steensby, *Eskimo Culture*, 196, 188; Jochelson, *Koryak*, 452-466; *Subterranean Dwell-ings*; Waterman and collaborators, *Native Houses*, 14-16.
[62] See, for example, Jochelson, *Archaeological Investigations*, 2-10; Hallowell, *Bear Ceremonialism*.

identical with the elbow adze of America suggests a hoary age and extra-American origin.

The rectangular plank house is confined to the Northwest Coast area in the south. Along the eastern margin of the area it occurs on the upper Fraser and sporadically in eastern Washington. To the north, as we have seen, it is found along the coast of Alaska to the mouth of the Yukon (excepting the Aleution Peninsula), and in the valleys of the Copper, Tanana, and lower Yukon. Over an undetermined part of western Alaska it is used as a summer dwelling, the winter house being the earth-covered lodge. More or less comparable types occur sporadically among the Koryak, Chukchi, Yukaghir, and Kamchadal of northeast Asia. In the Amur region are found dwellings bearing an even closer resemblance to the forms of the Northwest Coast. These latter, however, may eventually prove to be derivatives of Chinese or Manchu houses. Dr. A. L. Kroeber, in a personal communication, suggests that the log houses of the upper Fraser, Cook's Inlet, and the Copper River may be historically unrelated to the plank house, possibly post-European structures. But it seems to me that their location relative to the area of plank houses and the absence of suitable timber for the manufacture of planks argues for historical identity with modifications in keeping with the difference in available materials.

The basic features of the three traits are probably not developments within the Northwest Coast area. Thus, the use of adzes seems to be very common north of Mexico; the art of navigation is known very generally in the two Americas; and permanent dwellings of various types occur in a number of areas. The history of these traits probably goes back of the development of those features which belong peculiarly to the Northwest Coast and which give the area its individuality. But the restriction of certain qualities to the area in question induces a strong presumption in favor of their being the contributions of tribes occupying the area. Just what tribe or group of tribes is responsible for the modifications in the several cases is not easy to decide. But we have noted that highly developed examples of any single trait seem to appear somewhere near the center of the area of occurrence. The probability favors a longer history within this center. On the other hand, distinct features of a very special kind which crop up among single tribes (e.g., the combination of "shovel-nose" and pointed ends in a Columbia River canoe, and the Lkuñgɛn instance of a square ended boat) must be taken as instances of very localized developments, probably originated by the tribes in question.

BIBLIOGRAPHY

ABERCOMBIE, W. R. Report of a Supplementary Expedition into the Copper River Valley, Alaska, 1884 (*In* Compilation of Narratives, 383-410).

ALLEN, HENRY T. Report of an Expedition to the Copper, Tanana, and Koyukuk Rivers, in the Territory of Alaska, in the year 1885, etc. (Washington, 1887).

BARRETT, S. A. The Material Culture of the Klamath Lake and Modoc Indians of Northeastern California and Southern Oregon (University of California Publications in American Archaeology and Ethnology, 5, 1910, no. 4).

BOAS, FRANZ. The Development of the Culture of Northwest America (Science, 12, 1888, 194-196).

First General Report on the Indians of British Columbia (Report, British Association for the Advancement of Science, 1889, 801-902).

Second General Report on the Indians of British Columbia (Report, British Association for the Advancement of Science, 1890, 562-715).

Fifth Report on the Indians of British Columbia (Report, British Association for the Advancement of Science, 1895, 522-592).

The Social Organization and Secret Societies of the Kwakiutl Indians (Report, U. S. National Museum, 1895, 311-738).

Sixth Report on the Indians of British Columbia (Report, British Association for the Advancement of Science, 1896, 569-591).

Chapter on Conclusions *in* Teit, The Thompson Indians of British Columbia (Memoirs, American Museum of Natural History, 2, 1900, 387-390).

The Mythology of the Bella Coola Indians (Memoirs, American Museum of Natural History, 2, 1900, part 2).

The Jesup North Pacific Expedition (Proceedings, International Congress of Americanists, 13th Session, New York, 1902, 91-100).

The Salish Tribes of the Interior of British Columbia (Annual Archaeological Report, 1905, being part of Appendix to the Report of the Minister of Education, Ontario, Toronto, 1906, 219-225).

Ethnological Problems in Canada (Congrés International des Américanistes, 15th Session, 2, Quebec, 1907, 151-160).

The Kwakiutl of Vancouver Island (Memoirs, American Museum of Natural History, 8, 1909, part 2).

The History of the American Race (Annals, New York Academy of Sciences, 21, 1912, 177-183).

Tsimshian Mythology (Thirty-first Annual Report, Bureau of American Ethnology, 1916, 29-1037).

BOGORAS, W. The Chukchee (Memoirs, American Museum of Natural History, 11, 1909).

CATLIN, GEORGE. The Manners, Customs, and Condition of the North American Indians (London, 1841, 2 vols.).

CHAMBERLAIN, A. F. Report on the Kootenay Indians of South-Eastern British Columbia (Report, British Association for the Advancement of Science, 1892, 549-615).

COLLISON, W. H. In the Wake of the War Canoe (New York, no date).

Compilation of Narratives of Explorations in Alaska (Washington, 1900).

COOK, CAPTAIN JAMES An Account of the Voyages Undertaken . . . by . . . . Captain Cook (John Hawkesworth, ed., London, 1773, 8 vols.).

CURTIS, EDWARD S. The North American Indian . . . being a series of volumes picturing and describing the Indians of the United States and Alaska (Cambridge, 1907-1924).

DALL, WILLIAM H. Alaska and Its Resources (Boston, 1870).
Travels on the Yukon and in the Yukon Territory (*In* Trimmer, Yukon Territory).

EELLS, MYRON The Twana, Chemakum, and Klallam Indians of Washington Territory (Annual Report, Smithsonian Institution, 1887, 605-681).

EMMONS, GEORGE T. Jade in British Columbia and Alaska and Its Use by the Natives (Indian Notes and Monographs 35, 1923).

The Kitselas of British Columbia (American Anthropologist, n.s., 14, 1912, 467-471).

FARRAND, LIVINGSTON The Chilcotin (Report, British Association for the Advancement of Science, 1898, 645-648).

FRANCHERE, GABRIEL Narrative of a Voyage to the Northwest Coast of America in 1811, 1812, 1813, and 1814, etc. (Early Western Travels, R. G. Thwaites, ed., 6, Cleveland, 1904, part 2).

GIBBS, GEORGE Report of Mr. George Gibbs to Captain McClellan, on the Indian Tribes of the Territory of Washington (Reports of Explorations and Surveys, to Ascertain the Most Practicable and Economical Route for a Railroad . . . . to the Pacific Ocean made in 1853-4, 1, Washington, 1855, 402-434).

Tribes of Western Washington and Northwestern Oregon (Contributions to North American Ethnology, 1, Washington, 1877, part .2).

GIGLIOLI, ENRICO HILLYER Appunti intorno ad una Collezione Ethnografica fatta Durante il Terzo Viaggio di Cook (Archivio per l'Antropologia e l'Etnologia, 23, Firenzé, 1893).

GRIEVE, JAMES The History of Kamtschatka, and the Kurilski Islands, with the countries adjacent, illustrated with maps and cuts. (Translated from the Russian) (Glocester, 1764).

GUNTHER, ERNA Klallam Ethnography (University of Washington Publications in Anthropology, 1, 1927, no. 5).

HAEBERLIN, HERMANN, and GUNTHER, ERNA Ethnographische Notizen über die Indianerstämme des Puget-Sundes (Zeitschrift fur Ethnologie, 1924, 1-74).

HALLOWELL, A. IRVING Bear Ceremonialism in the Northern Hemisphere (American Anthropologist, n.s., 28, 1926, 1-175).

HITCHCOCK, ROMYN The Ainos of Yezo, Japan (Report, U.S. National Museum, 1890, 429-502).

HORETZKY, CHARLES Canada on the Pacific, Being an Account of a Journey from Edmonton to the Pacific, etc. (Montreal, 1874).

JEWITT, JOHN The Adventures of John Jewitt, only Survivor of the Crew of the Ship Boston, etc. (Robert Brown, ed., London, 1896).

JOCHELSON, WALDEMAR Past and Present Subterranean Dwellings of the Tribes of North Eastern Asia and North Western America (Congrés International des Américanistes, 15th Session, 2, Quebec, 1907, 115-128).

The Koryak (Memoirs, American Museum of Natural History, 10, 1908).

Archaeological Investigations in the Aleutian Islands (Publication, Carnegie Institution of Washington, 367, Washington, 1925).

KANE, PAUL Wanderings of an Artist among the Indians of North America, from Canada to Vancouver's Island and Oregon, etc. (London, 1859).

KRAUSE, AUREL Die Tlinkit-Indianer (Jena, 1885).

KROEBER, A. L. American Culture and the Northwest Coast (American Anthropologist, n.s., 25, 1923, 1-20).

Handbook of the Indians of California (Bulletin, Bureau of American Ethnology, 78, 1925).

LAUFER, BERTHOLD Jade, A Study in Chinese Archaeology and Religion (Publication, Field Museum of Natural History, Anthropological series, 10, 1912).

LEWIS, ALBERT BUELL Tribes of the Columbia Valley and the Coast of Washington and Oregon (Memoirs, American Anthropological Association, 1, 1905-1907, 147-209).

LEWIS and CLARK Original Journals of the Lewis and Clark Expedition, 1804-1806 (R. G. Thwaites, ed., New York, 1908, 8 vols.).

LOPATIN, I. A. The Orochee Tribe—Congeners of the Manchus (Manchuria Research Society, Misc. Papers, Series A., Fasc. 6, Harbin, 1925).

LOWIE, ROBERT H. The Northern Shoshone (Anthropological Papers, American Museum of Natural History, 2, 1909, part 2).

MACKENZIE, ALEXANDER Voyages from Montreal through the Continent of North America to the Frozen and Pacific Oceans in 1789 and 1793, with an Account of the Rise and State of the Fur Trade. (Trail Makers of Canada Series, Toronto, 1911, 2 vols.).

MASON, OTIS T. Aboriginal Skin-Dressing—A Study based on Material in the U.S. National Museum (Report, U.S. National Museum, 1889, 533-590).

Pointed Bark Canoes of the Kutenai and Amur (Report, U.S. National Museum, 1899, 525-537).

MEANY, EDMOND S. Vancouver's Discovery of Puget Sound. Portraits and Biographies of the Men Honored in the Naming of Geographic Features of Northwestern America (New York, 1907).

MORGAN, LEWIS H. Houses and House-Life of the American Aborigines (Contributions to North American Ethnology, 4, 1881).

MORICE, A. G. Notes, Archaeological, Industrial and Sociological, on the Western Déné (Transactions of the Canadian Institute, 4, 1892-93, Toronto, 1895).

MURDOCH, JOHN Ethnological Results of the Point Barrow Expedition (Ninth Annual Report, Bureau of American Ethnology, 1892, 1-441).

NELSON, EDWARD WILLIAM The Eskimo about Bering Strait (Eighteenth Annual Report, Bureau of American Ethnology, 1899, part I, 1-518).

NEWCOMBE, CHARLES F. Guide to Anthropological Collection in the Provincial Museum (Victoria, 1909).

NIBLACK, ALBERT P. The Coast Indians of Southern Alaska and Northern British Columbia (Report, U.S. National Museum, 1888, 225-386).

OLSON, RONALD Quilleute Ethnography Ms.

Quinault Ethnography Ms.

PETROFF, IVAN Report of Ivan Petroff on the Population, Resources, etc., of

Alaska (from the United States census report of 1880) (*In* Compilation of Narratives, 55-284).

POOLE, FRANCIS Queen Charlotte Islands. A Narrative of Discovery and Adventure in the North Pacific (London, 1872).

PORTLOCK, NATHANIEL An Abridgement of Portlock and Dixon's Voyage Round the World Performed in 1785, 1786, 1787, and 1788 (London, 1789).

RAVENSTEIN, E. G. The Russians on the Amur; its Discovery, Conquest, and Colonization, etc. (London, 1861).

ROSS, ALEXANDER Adventures of the First Settlers on the Oregon or Columbia River, 1810-1813 (Early Western Travels, R. G. Thwaites, ed., 7, Cleveland, 1904).

SARFERT, ERNST Haus und Dorf bei den Eingeborenen Nordamerikas (Archiv für Anthropologie, n.f., 7, 1908, 119-215).

SCHMITTER, FERDINAND Upper Yukon Native Customs and Folk-lore (Smithsonian Miscellaneous Collections, 56, 1910, no. 4).

SCHWATKA, FREDERICK Report of a Military Reconaissance in Alaska, made in 1883 (Washington, 1885).

SETON-KARR, H. W. Shores and Alps of Alaska (London, 1887).

SHIROKOGOROFF, S. M. Social Organization of the Manchus. A Study of the Manchu Clan Organization. (Royal Asiatic Society, North China Branch, extra volume 3, Shanghai, 1924).

SMITH, HARLAN I. Noteworthy Archaeological Specimens from Lower Columbia Valley. (American Anthropologist, n.s., 8, 1906, 298-307).

Archaeology of the Gulf of Georgia and Puget Sound (Memoirs, American Museum of Natural History, 4, 1907, part 6).

Shell-Heaps of the Lower Fraser River (Memoirs, American Museum of Natural History, 4, 1909, part 4).

The Archaeology of the Yakima Valley (Anthropological Papers, American Museum of Natural History, 6, 1910, part 1).

SPIER, LESLIE Wishram Ethnography Ms.

SPINDEN, HERBERT JOSEPH The Nez Percé Indians (Memoirs, American Anthropological Association, 2, 1908, part 3).

SPROAT, GILBERT MALCOLM Scenes and Studies of Savage Life (London, 1868).

STEENSBY, H. P. An Anthropogeographical Study of the Origin of the Eskimo Culture (Meddelelser om Grönland, 53, 1917, 39-229).

SWAN, JAMES G. The Northwest Coast; or, Three Years' Residence in Washington Territory (New York, 1857).

The Indians of Cape Flattery at the Entrance to the Strait of Fuca, Washington Territory (Smithsonian Contributions to Knowledge, 16, 1870, article 8).

The Haida Indians of Queen Charlotte's Islands, British Columbia, etc. (Smithsonian Contributions to Knowledge, 21, 1876, article 5).

SWANTON, JOHN R. The Development of the Clan System and of Secret Societies among the Northwestern Tribes (American Anthropologist, n.s., 6, 1904, 477-485).

TEIT, JAMES The Thompson Indians of British Columbia (Memoirs, American Museum of Natural History, 2, 1900, part 4).

The Lillooet Indians (Memoirs, American Museum of Natural History, 4, 1909, part 5).

The Shuswap (Memoirs, American Museum of Natural History, 4, 1909, part 7).

TRIMMER, F. MORTIMER (editor) The Yukon Territory. (The narratives of W. H. Dall, George M. Dawson, and Wm. Ogilvie) (London, 1898).

VANCOUVER, CAPTAIN GEORGE A Voyage of Discovery to the North Pacific Ocean . . . . in the years 1790, 1791, 1792, 1793, 1794, and 1795, etc. (London, 1801, 6 vols.).

WATERMAN, T. T. The Whaling Equipment of the Makah Indians (University of Washington Publications in Anthropology, 1, 1920, no. 1).

WATERMAN, T. T. and COLLABORATORS Native Houses of Western North America (Indian Notes and Monographs, 1921).

WATERMAN, T.T. and COFFIN, GERALDINE Types of Canoes on Puget Sound (Indian Notes and Monographs, 1920).

WILKES, CHARLES Narrative of the United States Exploring Expedition during the years 1838, 1839, 1840, 1841, and 1842. (Philadelphia, 1845, 4 vols., atlas).

WINTHROP, THEODORE The Canoe and the Saddle, or Klallam and Klickitat. To which are now first added his Western letters and journals. (John H. Williams, ed., Tacoma, 1913).

WISSLER, CLARK Material Culture of the Blackfoot Indians (Anthropological Papers, American Museum of Natural History, 5, 1910, part 1).

WOLDT, A. Capitain Jacobsen's Reise an der Nordwestkuste Amerikas, 1881-1883 (Leipzig, 1884).

YAPLE, JOHN   Survivals of the Stone Age.   Use of the Stone Axe (The Antiquarian, 1, 1897, 323-324).

YARROW, H. C.   Report on the Operations of a Special Party for Making Ethnological Researches in the Vicinity of Santa Barbara, Cal., with a short historical account of the region explored. (United States Geographical Surveys West of the One Hundredth Meridian, 7, 1879, 32-47).